SONGS
From the Heart

SONGS
From the Heart
MEETING WITH GOD IN THE PSALMS

Dr. Tim Riordan

GreenTree Publishers
Newnan, Georgia

Songs from the Heart

Printed in the United States of America
ISBN-13: 978-0692213476 (Greentree Publishers)
ISBN-10: 0692213473

Follow Dr. Tim Riordan through the following media links:
    Website/blog: www.timriordan.me
    Twitter: @tim_riordan

Greentree Publishers
www.greentreepublishers.com

FREE GIFT

Thank you for purchasing *Songs from the Heart: Meeting with God in the Psalms*. Dr. Riordan is currently working on a study/devotional guide that will help your reading of the Psalms take on an even deeper meaning. We would like to offer this to you as a gift to say thank you for your purchase. This guide should be available by March of 2017. Visit our website at www.greentreepublishers.com and click on the "Free Psalms Gift' tab. We will need your e-mail address so we can contact you as soon as this resource is available. We'll send you information on how you can receive your free gift. We respect your privacy and will not share your information with anyone else. Thank you.

GreenTree Publishers

DEDICATION

This book is dedicated to my mother, Mary E. Riordan (Betty), who taught me to love the Word of God from an early age and challenged me to be faithful in the teaching and preaching of God's Holy Scripture. She helped me write my first sermon when I was fourteen years old and has prayed regularly for my ministry all these years. She has always challenged me to teach the truth of Scripture while making the gospel message of salvation through Jesus Christ clear and accessible. Thank you, Mom, for your investment in me, your love of Jesus Christ and His Word, and your heart for the world. God will reveal to you, one day, the impact you have had on the world for eternity. I love you.

Special Thanks...

Completing this book would have never been possible without the encouragement of my wife, Sandra, and my six, wonderful children. I am also blessed to pastor an amazing community of believers in Newnan, Georgia called SonRise Baptist Church, and my church family has provided support and prayer for me as I undertook this challenge.

Thanks to my assistant, June Black, for her work in helping me with this project and to everyone else who read the manuscript and made suggestions along the way, including Judy Miller, Sandra Riordan (my wife), my children (Sarah, Timothy, Jonathan, Anna, Esther, and Mary Kathryn), Rebecca Ryals, Libbie Claire Eaker, Jackie Fuller, and others I am sure I am inadvertently omitting. Also thanks to Jenn Riggs for designing the cover.

CONTENTS

Appendix

PREFACE

"Yea though I walk through the valley of the shadow of death, I will fear no evil for Thou art with me..." The young, Jewish boy quoted this most familiar Psalm as he sat huddled in fear in a shelter in the heart of London. While Hitler and the Third Reich sought to destroy England and her allies during yet another bombing, at least one child reached into his memory and found solace and hope in the Shepherd's Psalm. Little did this boy know at the time, but he would later trust Jesus Christ as his Savior, grow to be a man, and eventually teach me systematic theology at Southwestern Baptist Theological Seminary in Ft. Worth, Texas.

Who has not found comfort and encouragement from the Psalms during some time of difficulty or personal failure in his or her life? The book of Psalms has been called humanity's hymnbook for a reason. It seems that regardless of one's religious persuasion, the Psalms have been a resource for which people have reached during times of great tragedy and upheaval. Through this book, people have encountered God, found comfort, and discovered the courage needed to take the next step into the unknown.

While this wonderful book of the Bible is loved and cherished, it is also misunderstood and overlooked. One could spend the rest of his life mining out the riches contained within jewel encrusted caverns known as the Psalms, and though he would come to the end of his days with a rich life and a full heart, he would discover the quest for understanding the Psalms had barely begun.

The Psalms contain for us a glimpse into the personal lives of the followers of God as they poured out their hearts to God in song. As they were originally written, the Psalms provided a resource to use in Jewish worship during times of festival as well as times of personal anguish and reflection.

For us today, we find a rich resource that still expresses the burdens of our lives and the desires of our hearts. The reader will find that while reading through this treasured book of Psalms, he will see a reflection of himself on every page and read the prayers within his own heart in every verse. The challenge for us is to understand the Psalms and to know how to use them today in worship and life.

Songs from the Heart is offered as a resource to help us in our quest to mine out the spiritual wealth contained in this treasure trove of inspired Jewish poetry. We will discover a clearer picture of God and a distinct call to worship.

In order to get the most out of this book, it is best for you to understand my original intent. I have divided the book into two parts. The first part is a brief overview of the book of Psalms. This is in no way comprehensive, and there are numerous other books available that will guide you deeper in gaining a firm grasp of the Psalter. I have sought to equip us to better understand the context of the 150 chapters of Psalms.

In the first chapter, you will see the Psalms put into the context of Old Testament Jewish worship. Have you ever thought about how the Psalms were originally used? The first chapter contains a story of a family who lived around 800 B.C. in a thriving city about forty miles south of Jerusalem. While the story of the family is fictional, I sought to help us see historically how a family would have used the Psalms in personal worship and corporate worship at a festival celebration. It is my prayer that this story will whet your appetite to dig deeper into a more in-depth study of the Psalms.

The second chapter provides for us a focused study on the big picture of the Psalms by looking at some of the unique qualities of Jewish poetry and presenting an overview of the whole book. This chapter will offer some foundational truths that will help you put much of the Psalms into its proper context. While this section will be a bit different from the other chapters, you will discover it to be helpful as you study the Psalms. The background information provided in the first three chapters will illuminate your heart to the spiritual truth contained in the book.

Chapter Three guides us in learning how to use the Psalms in our contemporary worship experience. Again, there are other authors whose sole purpose was to provide a resource to help readers make a modern-day application of the ancient book of Psalms. One such author, Tremper Longman, III, wrote a wonderful book worthy of study entitled *How to Read the Psalms*. There are other numerous resources available as well, but this brief chapter is offered to help us build a personal context for the study that will follow.

Part Two is the heart of this book. I originally began writing these chapters for devotional reading, and certainly they can be read in that fashion. Some of the chapters will focus on an entire Psalm while other chapters will focus on a portion of a longer Psalm. The particular Psalms I chose to discuss in this book are meaningful to me and provide a balanced overview to the overall intent of the book of Psalms.

It is my hope that by studying a random selection of Psalms in some depth, you will be challenged to engage the remaining Psalms and use them in your personal and corporate worship. You may want to read this part of the book for your daily devotions. If the chapters seem a bit long for a day's devotion, you may want to use one chapter for two days. My original intent was to provide a daily devotion that could be used five days a week for six weeks. You will see that my math is a little off (thirty-three instead of thirty), but, hopefully, you will be encouraged and challenged by what you read.

You will see at the end of each chapter is a section entitled "Further Thought." I have provided a list of questions and statements that will challenge you to make personal application of the truths of Scripture. It is my prayer that your worship of our Creator and God will be enhanced through a careful study of this book of songs.

I believe that through this study, we will find that God Himself is the greatest treasure of all. The Psalmists will help us come to know

God better as they have provided an inspired resource that will enrich our worship and deepen our knowledge of God.

Praise is a deficit in the modern-church today, and a study of the Psalms will challenge us to move praise back to its place of prominence. I believe that worship is the believer's first priority because God is first. God has given us the Psalms as a textbook on how to worship and a resource to be used in worship.

At times we will feel as if God is speaking to us, while at other times, we will find ourselves speaking to God. It is my prayer that through reading *Songs from the Heart*, God will place a song in your heart that bursts forth in praise of Almighty God.

PART I

Introducing the Psalms

CHAPTER ONE

Once Upon A Time...

David and Benjamin could scarcely sleep as they anticipated their annual trek to Jerusalem with their family to celebrate the Feast of Tabernacles. The two-day trip around the Western side of the Dead Sea would culminate with a steep climb up to the wonderful city of Jerusalem filled with excitement and adventure for two little boys. Though many of the festivities would be more meaningful to adults, the two boys relished the time they would sleep in the makeshift house that was really no more than a pole structure covered with palm leaves. They would enjoy the stories about Israel's sojourn and temporary dwellings during the wilderness wanderings, but their greatest delight would be playing with their old friends from around Judah as well as making new friends among the boys and girls encamped around the capital city.

David loved growing up in En Gedi and thanked God often for the privilege of living in the largest oasis in all of Israel. It was located nearly forty miles in the desert south of Jerusalem nestled against the tall slopes rising from the western shore of the Dead Sea. The fertile community was fed by four, refreshing springs that made this region quite popular through the years, even though it sat about 1000 feet below sea level. Some people called the area "The Garden of Eden in the Wilderness."

As far as David was concerned, En Gedi was most popular for being the place where his namesake hid out from King Saul, around 200 years earlier, after the King flew into a jealous rage when he felt his throne was threatened by the young giant killer. It was said that the future king of Israel hid out in a cave just above a beautiful stream the community had begun to call the *River of David*, and little David and

Benjamin loved to swim in the pool at the bottom of a beautiful waterfall everyone called *David Falls*.

During the journey and through the week of the Festival of Tabernacles, David, the oldest son in the family, would have certain responsibilities in caring for his younger brother and sister, Benjamin and Sarah. David carried a feeling of pride in not only being the eldest son, but also in carrying the name of the greatest king of Israel. His grandfather, a bent but strong eighty-two-year-old man, swore on the Torah and on his father's phylactery that the cave in which David hid from King Saul was on his property. David and Benjamin had played in the cave many times and had always felt a sense of reverence when they entered the cool embrace of the ancient cavern.

When David thought back to his previous trips to Jerusalem, what he really remembered most was the singing. His father, Hilkanah, loved to sing in his deep, baritone voice that seemed to reverberate between the low walls of the wadi, or dry river bed, near their home and carry over the vast arid plains above the city. David's father led his family in robust worship at every possible chance. The whole family made the trip to Jerusalem twice a year, for the Feast of Tabernacles and for Passover, and as soon as the wagon was pulling out from their home in En Gedi, Hilkanah would begin to sing.

He always started the trip with what he called his traveling song: "*How lovely are Your dwelling places, O LORD of hosts!*" Once this first line was sung, the whole family would join in on the second phrase: "*My soul longed and even yearned for the courts of the LORD; my heart and my flesh sing for joy to the living God.*" Hilkanah typically stopped when the song came to the phrase, "*How blessed are those who dwell in Your house! They are ever praising You.*" He said it was his opinion that when the Psalmist wrote "Selah" in the text, it not only meant to pause and take a breath, but it meant to pause and reflect. David was not sure the Psalmist really meant that, but he never tired of hearing his mother and father recount their blessings.

On their last trip to Jerusalem for Passover, his father had even expressed his gratitude for David's pet goat, Yierdi. David was sure that Yierdi would not make it through another year before being slaughtered, but his father seemed to have compassion on his tender son and allowed the goat to live. After making this choice, Yierdi seemed to sense his worth, and when he was of age, he fathered several kids. At least, David thought he was the father and insisted as much to his family. Once the family blessings had been thoroughly rehearsed, Hilkanah would pick up with the remaining part of the Psalm: *"How blessed is the man whose strength is in You, in whose heart are the highways to Zion…"*

While the children immediately sat up straight as soon as their father began to sing, it was the sweet, delicate voice of their mother that always seemed to make their hearts melt. David often thought that when his mother began to sing that God surely must have taken special notice. Her favorite traveling song was a Maskil that Hilkanah accompanied on the lyre. He would usually call David from the back of the wagon to take hold of the reins so he could prepare his favorite eight-string instrument for the beautiful soprano solo: *"As the deer pants for the water brooks, so my soul pants for You, O God. My soul thirsts for God, for the living God; when shall I come and appear before God?"* The way his mother sang this beautiful Psalm led David to long for God to work in his life and in the life of Israel.

David enjoyed watching his father melt before his very eyes as his mother sang from deep within her soul. When she sang the last phrase, *"Hope in God, for I shall yet praise Him, the help of my countenance and my God,"* Hilkanah would always pause at the conclusion of the song, and the family would ride in silence for a few moments.

David caught something out of the corner of his eye the previous year that nearly made him fall out of the wagon. Had he not been holding the reins, he was sure he would have been out on his head. He carefully studied his father this year, and his father did it again. Though a tear rolled down his dust covered cheek, David's father winked at his mother, and his mother seemed to blush a bit. It warmed David's heart to see the love in his father's eye, and he could not help but allow a smile to cover his entire face.

As David returned to the back of the wagon, he heard his little sister giggling. He wondered if Benjamin had tickled her or if she had seen the show of affection from his father.

David pulled out his small knife and sat on the back of the wagon with his masterpiece. He had been carving a donkey out of a small piece of wood from the Jericho Balsam tree his uncle had given him. Uncle Zedekiah said that King Solomon gave his ancestor the tree that started his balsam tree orchard. David knew that the Queen of Sheba had given King Solomon such a wonderful tree as a gift, but he was not sure if his uncle's orchard had really come as a result of this gift. Nevertheless, the ancient orchard was revered far and wide, and people gave his uncle much money for the ointment he would extract from his trees.

It was rare to carve on a piece of such a valuable tree, but his uncle gave him a branch that had broken off when a camel broke loose from a caravan and had run carelessly through the orchard. David's father had told him that if he did a good job on the carving, they would sell it in the market in Jerusalem, and David could have the money.

As small pieces of wood began to drift toward the ground that appeared to be moving under his dangling feet, David pondered the meaning of the tear on his father's cheek. David had heard his father and uncle talking about the king, which was rare indeed. Hilkanah informed Uncle Zedekiah that King Joash was turning the hearts of the people away from God.

"How can this be?" Zedekiah had asked. "I thought his uncle, Jehoida the High Priest, had raised him to honor the Lord."

"He did," Hilkanah had replied, "but as soon as Jehoida died, our King Joash seems to have forgotten the God of Israel. There is talk that judgment is coming to our people because of his rebellion. He even emptied the treasury of the temple and gave it to the king of Aram in order to form an alliance."

"Did he not know the words of King David? *"Some trust in chariots, and some in horses: But we will remember the name of the LORD our God."*

"I'm sure he knows the scripture," Hilkanah had sadly replied, "but he chooses not to obey it."

As the wagon rolled on toward the capital city and the joyous celebration that awaited them, David knew that deep in his father's heart was a growing sorrow over the waywardness of his people. Why did Israel continue to wander away from God? Had they not learned from the sins of the past and the judgment of God? Surely the King would awaken to God's truth and lead the people to honor the Lord.

By a little after noon the following day, the road to Jerusalem began its steep ascent. This was always a signal for Hilkanah to begin another song. David knew it to be a Song of Ascent that was meant for the climb up Temple Mount, but for Hilkanah, the climb began long before entering Jerusalem. *"I will lift up my eyes to the mountains; from where shall my help come? My help comes from the LORD, Who made heaven and earth."* This began a series of songs pouring from his father as he anticipated worshiping the Lord in the glorious temple Solomon built. Music appeared to be inbred in the hearts of the Jews, and it filled every expression of Jewish life. There seemed to be a song for every occasion, and David could not remember ever hearing of a Jew who could not sing.

Before setting up their temporary dwelling place outside the walls of Jerusalem, Hilkanah led his family through the beautiful temple gate just before evening sacrifices were made. They stood in hushed silence as the priest began to sing: *"Why do You hide Your face and forget our affliction and our oppression? For our soul has sunk down into the dust; our body cleaves to the earth. Rise up, be our help, and redeem us for the sake of Your lovingkindness."* David saw his father's lips move as he prayed the final words with the priest: *"Rise up, be our help, and redeem us for the sake of Your lovingkindness."* David bowed his head and joined with his father in praying for Israel's redemption.

The family quickly hurried to the site where they would erect their booth or tabernacle. Because Hilkanah had been constructing this temporary dwelling for years, he knew exactly what he was to do. In previous years, there had been a problem in finding enough palm leaves for their covering, so this year, Hilkanah had tied bundles of palm leaves to one of the donkeys following along behind the cart. As the structure was built, Hilkanah reminded the children of Israel's wandering in the wilderness for forty years.

The family would spend the week in what the Jews called a "booth" as a reminder that their ancestors did not have permanent dwellings for forty years because of their disobedience. The structure was completed just in time for the family to sit down to enjoy the Sabbath meal. For the Jews, the Sabbath began at sundown of the sixth day and was completed on sundown of the seventh day. The meal not only marked the beginning of the day of rest established by the law of God, but it also offered the Jews a weekly time of celebration and thanksgiving for God's blessings.

The Feast of Tabernacles specifically invited participants to reflect upon God's provision through the summer and a celebration of the harvest. This meal was always a favorite of David's as it seemed more like a party than a time of worship. As he considered this idea, the thought entered his mind that maybe worship was not just supposed to always be solemn. God obviously wanted them to celebrate and enjoy one another as well.

The following day, the conclusion of the Sabbath, was to be a time of rest, recreation, and preparation for the festivities of the week. While the family would worship together, they would also play together. Because they were surrounded by other Jews from all around Judah, they met in the early morning hours for worship in the temple, and the worship was typically led by the priests.

David and Benjamin could hardly contain their excitement as the group began to process through the gates of the city toward the temple steps. There were people from everywhere imaginable, and even though David did not know most of them, he felt as if he were among members of his family. He looked to his right and saw his sister, Sarah, walking hand-in-hand with a small girl he had never seen before. She had dark, shoulder-length hair, very much like his sister, large, brown eyes, and the olive-colored skin that was so common among the Jews. She was a bit shorter than Sarah, so David decided she must be a little younger. Since Sarah was seven years old, her new friend must have been about six. She looked over at David and smiled a big, toothy smile at him, but she was missing a tooth right in the middle of her smile. David smiled back and looked behind him to see a long processional of people making their way to the temple.

Someone in the front of the group began to sing, *"I was glad when they said to me,"* and then everyone joined in on the next familiar phrase: *"Let us go to the house of the Lord."* The group continued to sing: *"Our feet are standing within your gates, O Jerusalem, Jerusalem, that is built as a city that is compact together; to which the tribes go up, even the tribes of the LORD—an ordinance for Israel—to give thanks to the name of the LORD."*

The sounds of song echoed off the walls that bordered the narrow streets, and David found great comfort in hearing the sound. He couldn't help but feel that even as the people were glad to go to the house of the Lord, God would be glad to meet them there. His mother reached down and grabbed his hand, and he seemed to feel her excitement as well. They processed into the outer court of the temple as another song was coming to a close: *"Our help is in the name of the LORD, Who made heaven and earth."*

The morning was filled with singing and worship. Eventually, a priest took out a large scroll and began reading from the law: *"Now this is the commandment, the statutes and the judgments which the LORD your God has commanded me to teach you, that you might do them in the land where you are going over to possess it, so that you and your son and your grandson might fear the LORD your God, to keep all His statutes and His commandments which I command you, all the days of your life, and that your days may be prolonged."*

He continued reading the next scriptures, and David immediately recognized them as the *Shema*: *"Hear, O Israel! The LORD is our God, the*

LORD *is One!*" The priest paused and crowd echoed the last phrase: "*The* LORD *is One*!" While the word *Shema* simply meant "hear" in David's native tongue, it came to represent one distinctive of Judaism: Israel believed in only one God. This was quite different than the polytheistic nations surrounding the Israelites. David repeated the words with the rest of the group as they continued on into the next part of the passage. His mother had helped him to memorize this important passage just in the past year, and he beamed with a feeling of accomplishment as he spoke these words aloud declaring his love for the law of the Lord.

The rest of the Sabbath was filled with laughter, games, and food. The families who were encamped around them were also from En Gedi, and David knew them all. His good friend, Joshua, was camped right beside them, and David, Benjamin, and Joshua enjoyed spending the afternoon playing a game with pebbles and cloth that Joshua's father had taught them.

The Sabbath concluded with another wonderful meal and a quotation from the writings of King David: "*O* LORD, *our Lord, how majestic is Your name in all the earth, Who have displayed Your splendor above the heavens!*" David and Benjamin looked up in unison at the darkening sky, and the stars twinkled above. David thought about how far away these stars seemed to be and wondered what other things might be up in the heavens that declared God's glory. Eventually, David snuggled down under some blankets as his whole family began to turn in for the night.

The first day of the feast, following the Sabbath, was an exciting time for all of the festival participants. After the morning sacrifices, the people lined the streets for the processional of the Ark of the Covenant.

Every year, the Festival of Tabernacles began with a reenactment of the return of the Ark to Jerusalem. As the family ate the morning meal, Hilkanah told the family the familiar story of King David dancing before the Lord in the front of the processional as the Ark was brought back to the city of God about 200 years earlier. This year, the crowd buzzed with excitement, and David told Benjamin that he imagined it to be just the same 200 years earlier when King David was alive. Before the processional began, a priest stood on the open second floor of a building located on the road to the temple, and with a loud voice, he began to sing a psalm:

> O come, let us sing for joy to the LORD, let us shout joyfully to the Rock of our salvation. Let us come before His presence with thanksgiving, let us shout joyfully to Him with psalms. For the LORD is a great God and a great King above all gods, in whose hand are the depths of the earth, the peaks of the mountains are His also. The sea is His, for it was He who made it, and His hands formed the dry land. Come, let us worship and bow down, let us kneel before the LORD our Maker. For He is our God, and we are the people of His pasture and the sheep of His hand.

As the song concluded, there was a shout from the south, and the processional began. The people cheered and sang as the Ark made its way through the narrow streets and up the stairs leading to the temple. Even though David had seen the processional before, he marveled once again at the grandeur of the whole experience.

Each day during the Festival, the people gathered at the temple as songs were sung and scriptures read. Many of the songs were written by King David, but all of the Jewish people seemed to understand that they were more than just the words of a man.

The day always started and ended with sacrifices made by the priests, and in between the sacrifices, the people worshipped, ate, and enjoyed the common fellowship with gratitude for being blessed by God to be His chosen people. The Feast of Tabernacles was not only for the purpose of remembering the wilderness wanderings, but it was also a celebration of thanksgiving for God's provisions for the year, a commemoration of King David's coronation, and a reminder of God's place in the life of Israel. While the Ark of the Covenant symbolized several things, David told his brother that the main thing it symbolized was simply God's presence.

"The priests process with the Ark as a reminder," David told his brother.

"A reminder of what?" Benjamin asked.

"It is a reminder to all of Israel that we are nothing without God. We are the only people in the world who worship only the one, true God. The Ark is the picture of our agreement with God and His agreement with us."

"How do you know that?" Benjamin asked skeptically.

"Father told me, and he knows everything. The tablets of the commandments are inside the Ark along with a bowl of manna and Aaron's rod that budded."

"Wow. There's real manna inside?"

"Yes, and once a year, the blood of the sacrifice is spilt on top of the Ark. It's sort of like God sees the blood of the sacrifice instead of the commandments. He knows that we have a hard time obeying everything, so the blood kind of makes up for it."

"Makes up for it? I don't get it."

"I really don't either, but one day, we'll be smart like Father and we'll understand everything."

As the Jews worshipped and expressed their gratitude for God's provisions throughout the year and the gathering of the crops, numerous songs were sung. David knew some of them, but others were new to him. His favorite was sung in the courtyard of the temple when all the people were gathered. Their voices blended together, and David really felt as if God were sitting in heaven listening to His children sing: "*Shout joyfully to the LORD, all the earth. Serve the LORD with gladness; come before Him with joyful singing. Know that the LORD Himself is God; it is He who has made us, and not we ourselves; we are His people and the sheep of His pasture.*"

The week ended far too quickly, and as David pulled the covers over himself at the close of the final Sabbath, he could not help but feel sorrow that the week was coming to a close. He knew that the following day would be filled with busy packing and sad goodbyes. They would leave for home just after sharing a noon meal with all their friends. David was sad to leave Jerusalem, but he knew he would be returning for Passover in the spring.

David closed his eyes and lay quietly thinking about the music and the grand temple. He knew that he was somehow a part of something very special. As he drifted off to sleep, the final words of his favorite song floated through his mind: "*For the* LORD *is good; His lovingkindness is everlasting and His faithfulness to all generations.*"

CHAPTER TWO

Getting the Big Picture

Understanding the big picture is always important. My family and I have enjoyed putting puzzles together through the years, and in the early years of our marriage, my wife and I would leave an unfinished puzzle lying out for weeks at a time so we could stop and work on it for a few minutes whenever we had the chance. Before putting a puzzle together, I typically studied the picture on the front of the box. I have heard of people attempting to put puzzles together without looking at the picture, but I cannot imagine doing this. The big picture helps the little pieces make sense. I have a greater appreciation for a small, brilliant blue piece in a strange shape when I realize the far right side of the puzzle contains a glimpse of the tropical waters surrounding a beautiful, island paradise. Before we spend some days studying through various selected Psalms, I would like us to take a chapter to pause and look at the big picture of the glorious book of Psalms.

Psalms is one of the most loved and most read books of the Bible. It is difficult to fully grasp the impact that this central book of God's Word has had upon humanity.

One can approach this beloved, inspired writing from various perspectives and find instruction, comfort, inspiration, and encouragement. It is both a textbook on worship and a resource for worship. It is a word from God while also offering words to God. John Calvin reflected upon the challenges of adequately describing the value of the writings of the Psalmists: "The varied and resplendent riches which are contained in this treasury are no easy matter to express in words." Ambrose of Milan called the book of Psalms "medicine for our spiritual health," and Martin Luther articulated,

"Every Christian who would abound in prayer and piety ought, in all reason, to make the Psalter his manual."

While this centerpiece of Holy Scripture is both familiar to us and loved, we find it difficult to fully understand its meaning and a challenge to adequately read its pages. Part of the confusion comes from the fact that we live so far away from this antiquated culture and often times do not even understand the basic structure of this genre of writing. While creating the story in chapter one was my attempt to help us place the Psalms into the context of Old Testament life, there is much about the use of the Psalms that is still misunderstood.

Though Psalms would be considered Hebrew poetry, there are actually a number of sub-genres represented within the 150 chapters. Readers must seek to understand the purpose and intent of the original writers of the Psalms if they are to fully grasp the value of reading this inspired book. There are actually a number of ways in which the Psalms could be read, and certainly each way would offer some value. If this treasure of Hebrew poetry is only studied for its literary value, however, God's intent for including it within the pages of His inspired Word will be completely missed.

This chapter is included as a guide for those seeking to better understand the Psalms and for those who desire a thorough application of the Psalms to his or her spiritual journey. As we seek to gain a greater comprehension of this ancient text, we will first seek an overview of the book, and then, in the following chapter, we will consider the practical task of determining how to read the Psalms so as to best enjoy the riches of God's Word.

An Overview

The "Book of Psalms" gets its title from the Greek translation of the Old Testament and comes from a word that literally means "to pluck a string." The closest Hebrew word to "psalm" means "a song sung to instrumental accompaniment." From this title, one can see that the collection that we simply call *Psalms* was, from the very beginning, intended to be a collection of poems that was put to music and sung.

From our experience, we know that there are a number of songs that are basically poems put to music. We could be talking about today's country hits or something featured on a top forty radio station. It would also include anything included on Broadway or some beautiful aria sung at the Metropolitan Opera. It is the translation of the Hebrew title that gives us great clarity as to the purpose of this book of the Bible: "songs of praise."

Psalms is the first book in the third section of the Jewish Scripture, and this section is called *"The Writings."* It may have been given this title by ancient students of the Bible because it stood in contrast to *"The Law"* and *"The Prophets."* While *The Writings* are not given specifically as commands of God, like *The Law* or as verbatim oracles of God, like *The Prophets,* they have great value for Old and New Testament worship as well as worship in our modern Church. *The Writings* not only provide patterns of prayer and praise, but they also offer insight and understanding as to how God works in the history of humanity and how people should respond to a sovereign God.

Psalms is a bit unusual when compared to the other books falling into the broader category of *The Writings.* This selection of songs was written in response to the writer's personal encounter with Almighty God. Some of the Psalms are very personal in nature and reflect the interaction and struggle of one individual with his or her God while other selections reflect a corporate interaction with the Almighty. Though other books included in the biblical text known as *The Writings* reflect the wisdom of God and insight into one's personal encounter with the Transcendent, Psalms is undoubtedly considered the most personal and intimate of any of the books of the Bible. While many books speak *about* God, the Psalms speak *to* God. While many Bible books teach us theology, it is the Psalms that help us to experience theology.

The Psalms also reflect a literary style known as Hebrew poetry. You can open your Bible and read a Psalm and then compare that chapter to one found in Leviticus or Exodus. There is a stark contrast.

Knowing that the Psalms are poetry also creates a little bit of a struggle in our minds because we immediately begin looking for rhyme, as we might find in our own poetry. While we know that poems do not have to rhyme, we are still tied to our English understanding of poetry as we try to review the words of the Psalmists. Rhyme is not the keynote quality of Hebrew poetry. The focus of this type of poetry is rhythm, parallelism, and repetition. Sometimes the poetic quality of the Psalms is not as readily seen in English as it might be experienced in Hebrew.

We will often see one phrase repeated by another phrase that has similar, if not exact, meaning. For example, Psalm 19:1 says, *"The heavens are telling of the glory of God; and their expanse is declaring the work of His hands."* Note the two parallel phrases in this passage. This could be described as the Psalmist's means of emphasizing a thought or underscoring a concept. The truth is stated: *"The heavens are telling of the glory of God,"* and then it is emphasized with a duplication that is a variation on the initial theme: *"and their expanse is declaring the work of His hands."* As your read through the Psalms, you will begin to realize the reiteration of a thought with the repetition of the Psalmist's words. Sometimes we try to see the two phrases as containing unique thoughts or concepts, but if we understand Hebrew poetry, many times we will realize that the repetition is simply God's means of emphasizing a point or of giving greater clarity to a previously mentioned idea.

Just like in other books of the Bible, God used human beings to pen His inspired words. Second Timothy 3:16 says, *"All scripture is inspired by God,"* and it shares with us the concept of the human authors being *"carried along"* by God's Spirit as He guided the words that were written on the ancient scrolls. The human authors include kings, priests, leaders, and followers who lived and died over a period of about 300 years.

We know a few details related to some of the Psalms because of the titles that are included at the beginning of selected chapters. While it is difficult, and really impossible, to know the exact origins of the titles, most scholars seem to agree they are quite ancient. Though they appear to have been added in an editorial kind of way after the Psalm was written, this addition was done long before the Septuagint was written (the Greek translation of the Old Testament), which happened during the third century B.C.

King David is credited for seventy-three of the Psalms while two of them (72 and 127) are attributed to King Solomon. Psalm 90 is probably the oldest Psalm, and it was written by Moses. The family of Asaph wrote twelve of the Psalms (50, 73-83), and the sons of Korah wrote eleven Psalms (42, 44-49, 84-85, 87-88). In addition to some other named human authors, fifty of the Psalms do not designate an author. This variety of human authorship provides a rich background from which we can find encouragement and personal application. While we may think that we cannot relate to a king, we can certainly connect to what it means to have trouble.

It may be that it is because of the variety of authorship and circumstances behind the writing of each Psalm that we can so easily connect this scripture to our lives. It seems that the writers allow us to peer deep into the recesses of their souls so we can come to know their struggles, fears, doubts, and faith. Not only do we become intimately acquainted with the human authors, but we also become intimately acquainted with the God of the authors as God's character and activity is related to each circumstance.

The Psalms can be divided into five different categories or books: Psalms 1-41; 42-72; 73-89; 90-106; 107-150. Many scholars believe these five books follow a pattern established by the first five books of the Bible, called the Pentateuch, and each section ends with a doxology. For example, you can see this in Psalm 41:13 *"Blessed be the LORD, the God of Israel, from everlasting to everlasting. Amen and Amen."* It is interesting that Psalm 150 seems to be nothing but a doxology as it brings a close to the whole book of Psalms.

Even though we refer to this book as poetry, there are actually numerous literary types, or genres, included in this over-arching category. Understanding these different types of Psalms will help you better grasp the modern-day use of the selection. While we will look at the varied uses of these different styles later in the next chapter, consider briefly a definition and explanation of a few of these sub-genres.

Hymn

A hymn is a psalm of praise, and it was used as if the worshiper was standing face-to-face with God declaring His praise. It usually includes a call to worship, a description of God's attributes, and a final call to worship and praise the Lord. Consider Psalm 103:1-2: *"Bless the LORD, O my soul, and all that is within me, bless His holy name. Bless the LORD, O my soul, and forget none of His benefits."*

Lament

A lament will communicate the worshiper's sorrow and struggle with a problem that has yet to be solved. The Psalmist typically expresses deep distress, complaint, and even frustration. They also usually communicate faith in the midst of the spiritual battle as the worshiper cries out to God with a petition for His deliverance. There are times you can determine the source of the Psalmist's struggle, but at other times, determining the source is only conjecture. Note the opening words of Psalm 22: *"My God, my God, why have You forsaken me?"*

Processionals

The songs of procession communicated the longing and anticipation of the worshipers as they approached the temple for worship. As these Psalms are read, one may readily see the struggles of the journey to Jerusalem and the excitement in the heart of worshipers as they anticipated meeting with God. Some of these Psalms are referred to as "Psalms of Ascent" and they carry the idea of climbing the hill to the temple of God. This pattern is seen in Psalms 121-134. These songs were often sung by pilgrims on their way to Jerusalem to celebrate one of the festivals.

Royal Psalms

This is a title given to a number of Psalms that refer to either Israel's kings or to God, as the King of Israel. These songs were used during public gatherings, such as the coronation of a king, and declared Israel's faith in God and the king's submission to God as the true King of Israel. Unfortunately, few of the kings of Israel truly saw themselves as subservient to their Creator. The opening words to Psalm 21 reveal the royal nature of this Psalm: "*O LORD, in Your strength the king will be glad.*"

Thanksgiving Psalms

Thanksgiving Psalms go hand-in-hand with Psalms of lament in that they are a response to God's deliverance from times of struggle. The most familiar chapter of the Bible (at least according to the opinion of some) falls into this category: Psalm 23. This type of song usually includes a proclamation of love and praise, a summary of the Psalmist's time of need, a brief explanation of God's deliverance, and a closing expression of gratitude and praise.

Reflection Psalms

A number of Psalms reflect back to God's redemptive acts in the past. The two most prevalent events mentioned are the Exodus (God's deliverance of the Children of Israel from Egypt) and King David's reign. These songs were a reminder to the worshipers that God is a God who acts in the lives of His people. As the people reflected upon God's past activities, they were assured of His future blessings. Consider the opening words of Psalm 105: "*Oh give thanks to the LORD, call upon His name; make known His deeds among the peoples.*"

Wisdom Psalms

The wisdom writings in the Bible are usually considered to be books like Proverbs and Ecclesiastes. These include specific ways God wants His people to live and react to the circumstances of life and often present consequences for those who choose to disobey God's commands. A few Psalms fall into this category as well, and I mention it here because the longest chapter of the Bible, Psalm 119, would be considered a *Wisdom Psalm*.

Valuing Ancient Terms

As you read through the pages of the Psalms, you may discover several unfamiliar words. As strange as these words are to us, they were quite familiar to the Old Testament followers of God, especially to those who led Hebrew worship. Most of them are musical terms giving instructions as to how the Psalms were to be sung in worship, and many of them are translated into English in our Bible translations.

Selah

This is a musical term that gives the musician the instruction to pause. We might equate it in modern day music to a breath mark. In the public reading of this passage, the word *selah* would not be spoken, just like we would not sing the word "breathe" when we see a breath mark in a modern day song.

Mizmor

This Hebrew word is found in the title preceding verse one in our English translations, and it is typically translated as "psalm," as in Psalm twenty-three: "*A Psalm of David.*" It seems to be a direction to the musician, or worship leader, to accompany the song on a stringed instrument.

Maskil

This word is used in the title of thirteen Psalms and probably refers to using the song for "instruction" or for "contemplation." The word literally means "enlightened" or "to ponder."

Shir

This Hebrew word is usually translated as "song," like in the title for Psalm 121: *"Song of Ascent."* There are twenty-seven Psalms labeled as a *"shir,"* which seems to indicate this particular song was written to be a vocal piece. One would think any of the Psalms were written as vocal pieces, but a lot of them were intended to be accompanied by instruments. These "songs" are specifically for vocalists. There were probably times when these songs could only be sung without accompaniment because it would have been impractical to use instruments. For example, as the faithful made their way up the mountain to Jerusalem, the *"Songs of Ascent"* were sung in anticipation of the festival.

In addition to these words, a number of other Hebrew terms are typically translated into English. These terms provide direction for the musicians to use stringed instruments or have someone play the flute. There are a few places where the young maidens were instructed to sing alone or a special note was included "to the choir leader."

How were the Psalms used in Ancient Times?

This is an important question and one that is a little difficult to answer. The Psalter, or book of Psalms, was a continuing compilation, so the use of these inspired words was gradual as God inspired others to write His word.

As was stated in chapter one, the Jewish people were a singing people. Music was a vital part of their culture, and the Psalms became the songbook of their worship. The Psalms were incorporated into the daily life of Jewish people as well as into the corporate gatherings of the faithful for worship. Some of the Psalms were incorporated into the morning and evening sacrifices while other Psalms were reserved for specific events in Israel's religious calendar. You can imagine the significance of a song that was reserved for one particular event, and when that song was sung, there was no doubt as to what the song meant for the worshipers. For example, the priests would sing Psalm 95 during the processional of the Ark of the Covenant during the Festival of Tabernacles (or Booths).

While in the opening story, I had the priest sing the song from a rooftop near the temple road, we do not know where the singers positioned themselves for this important processional. We do know, however, that this psalm was sung as a part of this historical parade. It was a reminder of the time David returned the Ark to Jerusalem with singing and dancing. Every time a Jewish person heard Psalm 95 sung, I am sure he or she immediately thought of the value of the Ark and the picture it offered to Israel of God's abiding presence and continuous blessing.

Some of the Psalms were sung in the courtyard of the temple as the Jewish people gathered corporately for worship. It is possible that some of them were sung antiphonally (two groups facing one another across a great space singing almost as if one echoed the other). Psalm 136 is an antiphonal song. You can probably imagine a choir of singers standing on top of one wall of the temple singing, "*Give thanks to the LORD, for He is good,*" and another choir on the other side of the temple grounds echoing, "*For His lovingkindness is everlasting.*"

Other Psalms were more personal in nature and may have never made their way into a corporate worship experience. I would imagine that some of the songs of lament would have been used individually as one person cried out to God for help. I can imagine a Jewish man getting the news in 722 B.C. that the northern ten tribes of Israel had fallen to the Assyrians. He may have then broken out in a song, a lament that expressed his prayer to God: "*O LORD, how my adversaries have increased! Many are rising up against me.*" Some of these personal songs may have been sung from a parent to a child to remind the child of God's activity among the Children of Israel. Others were teaching Psalms used to instruct children on how to follow God and the consequences for choosing not to do so.

When my children were young, I made up a song about brushing their teeth. It was a real hit. The little game was that I would have to sing the entire song (to the tune of *Jingle Bells*). By the time I came to the grand conclusion – "Come on Brush Your Teeth," my child had been still in my lap long enough for me to accomplish the task.

Some of the Psalms were valuable in teaching the young Jewish children important truths about Jewish history and God's activity among His people. I am sure the melodies were useful in helping the children sit still long enough for these important truths to sink deep into their little, impressionable minds.

Although there is much more that could be said about the Psalms and there are some wonderful resources available for those who want to dig further into the topic, this information will at least provide you with some of the basic concepts upon which this book of songs was created. There is still one more topic that must be considered before delving deeper into some of the individual songs of the ancient Hebrew poets.

CHAPTER THREE
How can the Psalms be used today?

While most of us do not process up Temple Mount, parade around with the Ark of the Covenant, or fret over being attacked by King Saul, all of the Psalms can be applied to our modern-day circumstances. God gave us the Psalms to assist us in worship and to enrich our lives, so the reality is that we can use the words to the songs in about any way imaginable to help us encounter God and His glory. One great challenge in studying the Psalms is to force ourselves to move beyond seeing these passages as archaic words that applied to a group of people that lived thousands of years ago and see the relevance of the text to our experiences we may have had this morning.

One reason the Psalms are so loved is that they were written out of personal experiences, and they can just as easily be applied to your own personal experiences. While they laid bare the soul of the Psalmists, God can use them to lay bare your soul as well. We will probably all discover that in many instances our broken souls cannot be healed until they are first revealed. The Psalms can provide for us just such a tool to accomplish that task.

We can learn several basic principles from a study of the Psalms that will help us to be better worshipers, and then there are some specific applications of ancient practices that may strengthen our worship in churches around the world today. Let's consider some of the principles first.

Transferable Principles

The first principle is that God has made us to be worshipers. There is a reason that singing was incorporated into the life of God's chosen people, and this singing should be reflective of God's people today. Sadly, music has become an option in the lives of many believers, but the fact is God has made us to sing! Do you realize that when you sing, you are reflecting the nature and activity of God? God is a singer. Read carefully the words of Zephaniah 3:17 as translated in the New International Version: "*The LORD your God is with you, He is mighty to save. He will take great delight in you, He will quiet you with His love, He will rejoice over you with singing.*" WOW! This verse gets me pretty excited. It humbles me to think that God takes great delight in me (and you). This is a picture of us crying like a baby, and God, our Heavenly Father, is easing our anxiety with quiet whispers of love. As He gazes tenderly at us, He is flooded with joy and overflows with singing. Did you get that? God overflows with singing as He lovingly watches over you.

After bringing my newborn son, Timothy, home from the hospital, I had to take Sandra back because she was having some complications. Unfortunately, that meant Sandra was not there to enjoy the first few days of our son's life. Fortunately, I got to experience every moment with him. Unfortunately, I had a problem nursing him. Fortunately, he loved it when I held him. Unfortunately, he did not love it when I put him down. Fortunately, he slept when I rocked him. Unfortunately, he awakened as soon as I quit rocking. I think you get the picture.

The first few days of Timothy's life became a nightmare for me. I remember one night, after promising to buy him a new car if he would please go to sleep and let me sleep, he seemed to stare into my eyes with his dark, liquid pupils. I would have sworn the child smiled at me. My heart melted, and I began to sing over my beautiful son. He then ruined the moment with a messy diaper. Don't lose the significance of this. God sings over you.

When we sing, we are simply being like our Father. He made us to be singers. Do you realize that you are commanded to sing? Psalm 95 says, "*O come, let us sing for joy to the LORD.*" We are not only supposed to sing, but we are to "*sing for joy.*" That's right. Mouthing the words with pretend interest is not what God had in mind. The principle (and command) of singing is emphasized all throughout the book of Psalms, as well as other parts of the Bible.

The second principle is God-centered worship. It is so easy for us to forget that worship is for God and not us. We leave worship sometimes thinking, "I didn't get a thing out of that. I should have stayed at home and watched re-runs of *I Love Lucy*." While it is hard for us to get this concept in our entertainment driven society, we do not go to worship primarily to get anything out of it. It is true that when we do really worship, we *do* get something out of it, but that is not our primary purpose. We go to a worship service to *give* something – worship to God.

All through the Psalms, we see that God is the focus. God is the V.I.P. of every gathering. There is no evidence that anyone complained because someone traded in the sackbut for a lyre (look it up). There were no committee meetings called because some young whippersnapper got carried away on the high sounding cymbals. No one even seemed to be bothered that band members were playing "skillfully" on their instruments. There's no evidence of any repercussions over someone dancing, shouting, clapping their hands, raising their hands, falling on their faces, being quiet, or being loud because worship was not about the worshipers. Worship is about God.

The third principle is that worship is a verb (there is actually a great book with that title by Robert Webber). Worship is something we do. Psalms worship can be loud and expressive. We probably better start practicing here on earth because Heaven is going to have some pretty involved experiences where everyone is celebrating. It's not just going to be the young people on the front four rows. There will be some senior saints three miles back from the throne of God that are going to get "*glad in the Lord and rejoice*," and then they are going to actually "*shout for joy*." The thing is, no one is going to turn around and look at them real strangely because we're all going to be doing the same thing.

It is time for the Church of the Lord Jesus Christ to figure out how to celebrate our salvation. I know there are times for contemplation, but I guess I come from a tradition that seems to specialize in the contemplation department, so we do not really need a lot of help with that. The truth is, we probably do. Contemplation does not really mean sitting on the back row with our arms crossed. Worship is about engaging the mind and connecting the heart as we encounter God in a life-changing experience of recognizing His glory, declaring His worth, and proclaiming our love for a God Who sings over us.

The fourth principle is that worship is a lifestyle and not an event. Unfortunately, we have defined worship as a day on our calendars and a location on our GPS. Worship is what we do. Worship is who we are. We should wake up in the morning with "glory" on our hearts and drift off to sleep at night with "hallelujah" on our lips. We should sing when we walk down the road (whether we're climbing the hill to church or not), when we feel sorrow over our failures, when we feel abandoned by God in our grief, and when we are overwhelmed by His grace. We can find God in every moment. Every day is a twenty-four-hour experience in God's school of theology as the experiences of life teach us constantly about the nature and character of our Creator. To learn of God is to break out in singing and praise of the One Who has redeemed us and called us as His own.

Ancient Practices for Modern Expression

Other than the principles mentioned above, there are some specific ways we can apply some of the Old Testament practices to our twenty-first century worship. As you move into the next section of this book, I hope you will study each Psalm and look for ways you can meet God and worship. You may want to sing the Psalm back to God. I know you are thinking that you do not know the tune. Who cares? Make one up. God really doesn't care how you sing. He even commanded you to *"make a joyful noise."* We can all handle that. You can also consider the particular literary type of a Psalm, or genre, and think of modern ways to employ the ancient practices of worship. Let's consider a few of these ideas and get creative in how we can turn a type into a worship expression that brings a smile to the face of our Heavenly Father.

The *Hymns* of Psalms not only offer to us a wonderful vehicle for expressing praise to God, but they also teach us much about God's nature. When I grew up, we had a book called a "hymnal," but the fact was that most of the songs in this book were really not technically hymns. Most of the songs we sang at my church growing up were gospel tunes. I don't mean gospel like, "Put it on my Master Charge and charge it to Calvary" or something about a "cabin in the corner of Glory land." I don't mean to knock those songs, but we might be amazed by the number of songs we sing in "worship" that are really about what we get out of being a Christian. Even some of the great "hymns of the faith," are more man-centered than God-centered. Consider "Love Lifted Me," or "Surely Goodness and Mercy Shall Follow Me." It would do us well to study some of the old hymns that are really hymns: "Great is Thy Faithfulness" or "Holy, Holy, Holy." Look for ways to sing some of the hymns found in the Psalms back to God in order to declare His nature and character.

Laments can be used in worship as we lay our souls bare before the Lord. If you are struggling with some issues in your life, I feel sure that you can find a Psalm, or two, that expresses your need before the Lord. You will find in each lament that the Psalmist not only expresses your "complaint" before God, but he also expresses the kind of faith that you should have in the midst of your trouble. A song of lament will actually build your faith and not just undergird your frustration.

Processionals may be a little harder to contemporize, but maybe not. The fact is that if we are going to meet with God in worship at 10:00 on a Sunday morning, we better start much sooner to prepare our hearts for this encounter. Our preparation should take place all week. If we are meeting with God in personal worship six days a week, our Sunday experience would not be able to be contained. Can you imagine what it would be like if even 100 people encountered God every day and prepared for worship on Sunday? What would happen if a number of us would spend a little time on Saturday night singing some of the songs of procession? We could conclude our Saturday night preparation with going to bed early so we would be refreshed and ready to meet with God Sunday morning with renewed energy, mental alertness, and emotional excitement. What if we arose early on Sunday morning and began with some quite meditations on the nature of God and our redemption through Christ? What if we spent the morning singing songs of ascent as we prepared to "ascend" our own temple mount and meet with God? I'm telling you that worship at our local churches would never be the same.

I'll never forget being in the drive-thru one Sunday morning at a fast food restaurant (okay, my body being the temple of God is for another chapter). There was a family in the car in front of me who was obviously on their way to church. The kids in the back seat were fighting, literally. Mom and Dad had been arguing (while Mom was putting on her makeup), but the argument had to stop so Dad could order the food. In between placing the order, he did the old group slap procedure to stop the fighting in the back seat, but one quick son managed to avoid the large hand of discipline. I imagined this "saintly" family arriving at their church, getting out of the car, and entering into the building for worship with smiles on their faces and jelly on their shirts.

While we do not have an earthly king, the *Royal Psalms* could still be sung as we acknowledge to God that He is our King, and we submit to His sovereign rule over our lives. No doubt we could sing songs of thanksgiving and pause in between verses so family members could express things for which they are thankful.

We could contemplate the activity of God in our lives through the *Reflection Psalms*. While the Exodus does not specifically relate to us, we have all had experiences where God has delivered us. Maybe in family devotions, we could read some of the songs of reflection and then relate our own stories as to how God has worked in our lives. I think that every Christian family should incorporate stories of God's activity into their family story.

Wisdom Psalms could easily be utilized in both personal devotions and family worship as we study the contrast between obeying God and going our own way. The *Wisdom Writings* can be times of instruction for us followed by expressions of commitments as we reinforce our pledge to follow after God throughout our lives. I do not believe that tough decisions of faithfulness are made in the heated moments of temptations, but rather spiritual battles are won before we ever enter the battle field. Wisdom Psalms can be used, read or sung, as reminders of God's call upon our lives to be faithful.

I know that throughout the last paragraphs I have talked about singing the Psalms. Some of you are thinking that you really can't sing the psalms unless someone teaches you the melody. You really can make up your own music, but I am aware that if you do not have a musical background, you might find that a little challenging. Several Christian artists have written numerous songs from the Psalms, and that could be a good place to start. You could challenge your family to write some music. Honestly, my *Brush Your Teeth* song will not win me a Grammy, but my children still know it and could sing it for you today. I bet I'll have grandchildren reminding me of the powerful lyrics one of these days because their parents (my children) use the same tactic to help them avoid cavities. The same could be true with the Psalms. In addition to singing them, even though the Psalms are really songs, you can also speak them.

Regardless of how you incorporate the Psalms into your life and experiences with God, become a student of this wonderful section of God's Word. As you study the Psalms and use them in your prayer life and worship life, you will find that the Psalms speak to us, and the Psalms speak for us. You will discover that you can meet God in the Psalms, and you can seek God through the Psalms. At one moment, you will be overcome with tears, and the next you will be overwhelmed with joy. I invite you on a journey over the next weeks as you study through the selected Psalms in this book, but I invite you on a pilgrimage over the remaining years of your life as you practice and perfect a life of worship.

PART II

Meeting with God through the Psalms

PSALM 1
The Source of my Blessing

People pursue it and most people can't find it: happiness. According to a Harris Poll from June of 2013, only one in three Americans consider themselves to be very happy. If happiness is one of the main goals of Americans, there is a sixty-seven percent failure rate. People are quite interested in topics that will lead to personal fulfillment and happiness, but evidently their attempt at experiencing this fulfillment does not measure up.

Can you imagine how successful we could be if we could invent something that would guarantee people's happiness? Imagine a P90X program for personal happiness that was guaranteed to work. Actually, God gave us such a program about 3000 years ago found in the opening chapter of one of the most loved books of the Bible: Psalm 1:

> *How blessed is the man who does not walk in the counsel of the wicked, nor stand in the path of sinners, nor sit in the seat of scoffers! But his delight is in the law of the LORD, and in His law he meditates day and night. He will be like a tree firmly planted by streams of water, which yields its fruit in its season and its leaf does not wither; and in whatever he does, he prospers. The wicked are not so, but they are like chaff which the wind drives away. Therefore, the wicked will not stand in the judgment, nor sinners in the assembly of the righteous. For the LORD knows the way of the righteous, but the way of the wicked will perish.*

"*How blessed!*" These two words carry a wealth of meaning. The word "how" is a descriptive word that seems limitless and limited at the same time. "How" opens the lid to the well and offers us a peek into the bottomless pit of God's grace. There is no means by which one could measure the depth of the blessings of God: "*How blessed is the man…*" While "how" appears to be limitless, it is also presenting an attempt to describe the indescribable: "How blessed."

The word "blessed" is a wonderful word in the Hebrew language. You can find its Greek counterpart in the Beatitudes of Matthew 5. The Hebrew word that is translated as "blessed," carries with it the idea of happiness or joy that does not waver regardless of circumstances. It does not just mean a feeling of bliss that comes from everything lining up in our favor. We have a tendency to experience happiness as if we are on a rollercoaster. At one moment we are experiencing a high with everything going our way, and at another moment, we find ourselves in the valley of sorrow having lost all signs of our happiness as the winds of circumstances have changed. This passage indicates to us that this is not the kind of happiness God is talking about. While our happiness tends to be temporary, God's is permanent. While ours is tempered by emotions, God's is constant, regardless of our emotional state. I cannot imagine anyone in their right mind not wanting to swap the ebb and flow of circumstantial happiness with the constant reality of abiding joy. The question is, "How do you get it?"

The Psalmist begins by telling what we should not do. We should not *"walk in the counsel of the wicked, nor stand in the path of sinners, nor sit in the seat of scoffers."* Do you notice a digression in those three statements? Just compare walking with standing and sitting. It is similar to how we may get into a cold swimming pool. You first get your foot wet, then you get in up to your waist, and finally you take the full plunge as your head slips under the water. Happiness will not be found by listening to the counsel of those who do not know the Lord, and especially those who offer us counsel contrary to God's Word. Nor will we find happiness when we take a similar course (or path) as people living willfully away from God's will. Finally, we will throw happiness to the wind when we choose to hang out on a regular basis with the cynics and scoffers who outwardly reject God and His truth.

If you consider this digression, you will see the downward slide does not begin with sitting with the cynics, but rather it starts with walking in the counsel of the ungodly. I cannot imagine anyone volunteering to become a scoffer of God. It is usually a slow digression that happens as we start by listening to counsel that leads us away from God. We get more comfortable with disobedience and the ways of our world as we stand, or become familiar, with those who disregard God's truth. Eventually, we too become a scoffer. We will not find happiness, real happiness, unless we get off the cycle that leads to cynicism.

Our choice must be to *"delight in the law of the Lord"* and to meditate on this law regularly. The secret to happiness is not accomplishing your financial goals, finally reaching your weight aspirations, or securing that lasting relationship that leads to a "happy-ever-after" marriage. Happiness is connected to your thoughts and experience with God's Word. We will find happiness when we are "delighted" with God's Word.

How often are you delighted? What is it that brings you great pleasure? Imagine walking in from a long work day and discovering your wife has just prepared your favorite meal. Is that "great pleasure?" How amazing would it be if you came home after a night away on a women's retreat and discovered that your husband had completed everything on the "to do list" you asked him to do just last week? Have you ever secretly observed your child doing something very selfless and admirable? Surely these things would bring true delight. God says that real happiness does not come from the delight experienced by the fulfillment of those things, but rather, it comes from delight with the Word of God. Since God says happiness is connected to our feelings about His Word, we must determine what is necessary in our lives to bring about such reaction to the Scriptures.

Finding great pleasure in the Scriptures comes first by developing a plan for regular Bible intake. We will never learn to love God's Word unless we first of all receive God's Word. This may require developing the discipline just because you know it's good for you. That was sort of my approach to eating collard greens, and after a while, I have come to like them—sort of. Of course I think the Bible has far greater value than collard greens, and we will immediately *"taste and see that the Lord is good"* child 7.!

favorite meal, chores done, compassionate

as we read through the pages of God's Word. When we regularly read and study the Scriptures, we will come to see the Bible's value to our lives, and we will come to love it. Real delight will only happen as we read, study, and live out the Word of God. While reading the Bible may start out from simply a discipline, over time it will become a passion.

Sharing the Scripture is another way to develop delight in God's Word. As we speak with our friends and family about the truths contained in the Bible, the value and reality of the truths of Scripture become more solidified in our minds and lives. I have found it is actually through discussing and studying God's Word in the context of relationships that we come to more fully understand the meaning of Scripture. This is one value of being in a small group who meets regularly to study the Bible and to fellowship.

Delight is also found when we actually put the truths of Scripture to work in our lives through consistent obedience to God's commands and application of God's truths. We are more prone to become delighted with "*The Lord is my Refuge and Strength; a very present help in trouble*" when we have found ourselves in a needy spot in our lives and held to the truth of Scripture regarding God's strength, protection, and sufficiency. When we choose to trust in God's strength because we are convinced of God's truth, we will find great delight as God does indeed prove Himself to be our Refuge and Strength. It is an interesting paradox. Not only do we delight God in our obedience, but ultimately, we find delight ourselves as we put to practice the life-changing truth of God's Word.

Our delight will show as we "meditate" on it day and night. This means that we keep it on our minds and in our hearts constantly. This may require memorizing God's Word as well as coming up with various ways to keep Scripture in front of us. We may want to sing the Scripture or display art in our homes that contains Scriptural themes. Whatever we need to do to meditate on God's Word day and night, we must do it.

When we delight in God's Word in this way, the Bible says we will become like a firmly planted tree beside a life-giving stream of water. We will be vibrant, full, and purposeful. We will bear fruit in season. Other people will be blessed by our lives and encouraged to seek the Lord. Whenever we follow God's leadership and take steps in ministry and life, we will find great success where God is honored and lives are changed. We will also find that while those who do not know the Lord will fall in judgment, we will stand strong and true because we have been bought by the blood of Jesus, sealed by the Spirit of God, and justified by the grace of God.

So, the next time you take a test to determine your level of happiness, put on a mood ring (ok, so those probably aren't around anymore), or look at the Zodiac symbols at a Chinese restaurant and try to decide if you should marry a tiger or a bear, just remind yourself that real, lasting happiness comes only from God. We will enjoy this state of existence only as we find our delight in the law of the Lord and meditate on it day and night.

Further Thought...

- On a scale of 1 to 10, with 1 being not very high and 10 being the highest of the high, how would you rate your current state of happiness?

- What have you sought to do in the past in order to find happiness in your life?

- What are some things that bring you great pleasure (delight)?

- On a scale of 1 to 10, how would you rate your level of delight with the Word of God?

- What are some things you are willing to do to increase the "delight quotient" with God's Word in your life?

PSALM 3   7-6-20

When Life Crumbles

O LORD, how my adversaries have increased! Many are rising up against me. 2 Many are saying of my soul, "There is no deliverance for him in God." Selah. 3 But You, O LORD, are a shield about me, my glory, and the One who lifts my head. 4 I was crying to the LORD with my voice, and He answered me from His holy mountain. Selah. 5 I lay down and slept; I awoke, for the LORD sustains me. 6 I will not be afraid of ten thousands of people who have set themselves against me round about. 7 Arise, O LORD; save me, O my God! For You have smitten all my enemies on the cheek; You have shattered the teeth of the wicked. 8 Salvation belongs to the LORD; Your blessing be upon Your people! Selah

Have you ever felt like your whole world was crumbling around you? You can be blind-sided by many things, such as job loss, personal conflicts, or financial setbacks. Regardless of the source, troubles can be persistent and painful. If you have lived long enough, you have come to realize the issue is not "Will trouble come?" but rather "When will trouble come?" Trouble is as certain as the setting of the sun or the rain in spring. While looking at the source of our troubles can be instructive, the real issue has to do with what we will do in the midst of that trouble.

King David understood trouble, and many of the Psalms are written out of the context of overwhelming challenges that threatened him. Psalm 3 was written in response to some kind of serious problem, and David cried out to the Lord for help. Some think the problem had to do with a coup attempt by David's son, Absalom, and this story is recorded in 2 Samuel 15-17.

Absalom secretly built favor with the people and developed a strategy to steal the kingdom of Israel from his father, David. Not only did David lose the kingdom, but he also lost a son. He was forced to

run for his life. It was possibly out of this context that David said in
Psalm 3:1 "O LORD, *how my adversaries have increased! Many are rising up*
against me."

Though you may not be fleeing from someone trying to kill you,
there are still some serious enemies in your life who desire nothing
more than your demise. Satan, our greatest enemy, wants to rob your
joy, destroy your hope, weaken your faith, and disturb your peace.
While Satan may offer a full, frontal attack on us, many times his
attacks are subtler but equally as deadly. Sometimes he uses people and
circumstances to bring discouragement and failure.

Verse two of the chapter says, "*Many are saying of my soul, 'There is no*
deliverance for him in God.'" People often predict our failure and captivate
us with discouraging thoughts. King David had the experience of
hearing people say that he had no hope. Discouragement from others
can sometimes lead us to feel even greater hopelessness and despair.
We must remember that just because people may say, "*There is no*
deliverance," that does not mean the statement is true. Remember Job's
friends? They basically told Job to give up and die, but we later learned
their advice was not godly advice.

Notice that David quickly moved his thoughts from his problems
to the Problem Solver:

> *But You, O LORD, are a shield about me, my glory, and the One who*
> *lifts my head. I was crying to the LORD with my voice, And He answered*
> *me from His holy mountain. I lay down and slept; I awoke, for the LORD*
> *sustains me. I will not be afraid of ten thousands of people Who have set*
> *themselves against me round about. Arise, O LORD; save me, O my God!*
> *For You have smitten all my enemies on the cheek; You have shattered the*
> *teeth of the wicked. Salvation belongs to the LORD; Your blessing be upon*
> *Your people!*

It is interesting to note what words David used to describe God
and His work on David's behalf. He declared that God is "*a shield about*
me." That's really an interesting thought. Shields did not typically wrap

around a soldier. It seems David should have said "a shield before me" or something like that, but instead he described God as being a shield "about" him. This was no ordinary shield. Instead of God providing minimal protection, He was a full covering providing total protection from David's enemies. God offers this same protection for you and me. The Scripture says, "*You are a shield about me,*" and not "You could be or will be or might be a shield about me."

David also calls God, "*My glory,*" and "*the One who lifts my head.*" The only radiance David possessed was the glory of God. That is quite a story from the most powerful man in the world. It is a statement of humility and recognition of God's greatness. He says that God is his glory. The truth is, we have nothing impressive to bring before people. We really have no glory in ourselves, but Jesus Christ, the Light of the World, is the One who shines His glory into our lives.

Since God is the One who lifts our heads, we can assume that our heads are drooping from the overwhelming strain of our trouble. God holds our head up for sustenance, encouragement, and renewal. It is God Who gives us confidence and grace so our heads do not droop in shame or despair.

In desperation, David cried out to God, and God answered him. When you study the prayers of the Bible, many of them are prayers of desperation and fervor. It is rare to find gentle, passionless prayers that are recorded in the Scriptures. Usually, we find people wrestling with God and with circumstances, and their prayers reflect their grief, struggle, or pain. In response to David crying out to God, he seemed to almost whisper in contrast, "*I lay down and slept.*" That is an amazing statement. Usually our problems keep us from sleeping, but David knew that it was God who sustained him. He could rest with great confidence in knowing that while he was sleeping, God was not.

I mentioned earlier that the word "Selah" is like a breath mark, and singers would recognize it as an instruction to pause. Even though one should not read the word *Selah* out loud, it is interesting to think of the concept of Selah and how God alone is the One who makes true rest possible for His children.

David concluded this Psalm with a declaration of faith: "*Salvation belongs to the Lord.*" He trusted God with his circumstances and leaned upon God for his strength. Are you able to do that when you go through the deep valley of difficulty? Can you, by faith, acknowledge that you are not hopeless, but salvation belongs to your God?

Further Thought...

- Can you think of a time when you were in such a desperate state that if God did not do something, all would be lost?

- What did you do? What do you do when you move into seasons of difficulty and problems overwhelm you?

- How can David's declaration of God's qualities apply to your life and to your situation? What are some benefits of having God around you as a circular shield?

- Since God "lifts your head," what do you think He will do next?

- What will it take for you to be able to "lie down and sleep" in the midst of your troubles?

PSALM 5

Prayer for the Desperate

Give ear to my words, O LORD, Consider my groaning. 2 Heed the sound of my cry for help, my King and my God, for to You I pray. 3 In the morning, O LORD, You will hear my voice; in the morning I will order my prayer to You and eagerly watch. 4 For You are not a God who takes pleasure in wickedness; no evil dwells with You. 5 The boastful shall not stand before Your eyes; You hate all who do iniquity. 6 You destroy those who speak falsehood; The LORD abhors the man of bloodshed and deceit. 7 But as for me, by Your abundant lovingkindness I will enter Your house, at Your holy temple I will bow in reverence for You. 8 O LORD, lead me in Your righteousness because of my foes; make Your way straight before me. 9 There is nothing reliable in what they say; their inward part is destruction itself. Their throat is an open grave; they flatter with their tongue. 10 Hold them guilty, O God; by their own devices let them fall! In the multitude of their transgressions thrust them out, for they are rebellious against You. 11 But let all who take refuge in You be glad, let them ever sing for joy; and may You shelter them, that those who love Your name may exult in You. 12 For it is You who blesses the righteous man, O LORD, You surround him with favor as with a shield.

Desperation. We've probably all been there at one time or another. It may be the desperation for money to pay a bill or for healing in a relationship. It could be desperation for a job or desperation to be healed from a disease. The fifth Psalm was inspired by God and written by the quill of a desperate man. We can assume the problems King David was facing are the same ones written about earlier from Psalm 3: Absalom's coup attempt.

What do you do when you're desperate? Usually, we try to study our circumstances and come up with a plan. What did the King do? It seems that he went straight to the Source for solutions: God. In the opening verses of the Psalm he said, *"Give ear to my words, O LORD, Consider my groaning. Heed the sound of my cry for help, my King and my God, for to You I pray."* The Hebrew word that is translated as *"groaning"* is only used twice in the Old Testament (see Psalm 39:3 where it is translated "musing" or "meditating"). It has a double meaning. It means to think and also to make a dull noise. It could be translated as "meditate," but the second part of this meaning combined with the context indicates that David was not only contemplating his situation, but he was also moaning with dread as his reality sank into his heart.

David's son had betrayed him, and he had lost the Kingdom of Israel. The last little phrase of verse two says it all: *"for to You I pray."* I also love the fact that verse three indicates that he not only prayed, but he prayed consistently and with faith. He said, *"In the morning, O LORD, You will hear my voice; in the morning I will order my prayer to You and eagerly watch."* He prays, and he eagerly watches. His words indicate a note of expectancy that God will move and act in response to his prayers.

His prayer moves into a section where he declares the character of God. He says that God does not take pleasure in wickedness. Stop for just a moment and think about that statement. God has some pretty strong feelings about our sin. The Scripture even says God *"hates"* all who do iniquity. That is a disturbing statement and difficult for me to handle. It doesn't get any easier with the next phrases: *"You destroy those who speak falsehood; the LORD abhors the man of bloodshed and deceit."* It is easy for us to focus on 1 John 4:8: *"God is love."* God is love, but God also hates the wicked. That feels awkward to say, but the fact is that God is holy and cannot tolerate sin or the ones who practice sin. I would feel better if I could say God hates sin, but He loves the sinner.

Consider additional verses such as Psalm 11:5; Leviticus 20:23; Proverbs 6:16-19; Hosea 9:15. There is a challenge here because the Bible also says, *"For God so loved the world..."* (John 3:16) and *"But God demonstrates His own love toward us, in that while we were yet sinners, Christ died for us"* (Romans 5:8). How can God love the sinner and hate the sinner at the same time? We can only assume that God is using strong language to describe His righteous and holy reaction to that which is totally contrary to His nature. Whereas, we associate strong, negative emotions with the word "hate," it is difficult for us to grasp a holy reaction to sinful man by a sinless God.

Here's an additional New Testament thought we should consider. When you repent of your sin and trust Jesus as your Savior, God no longer sees you as a sinner, but rather He sees you as a forgiven saint. You have been justified (Romans 5:1), and you are not condemned (Romans 8:1). Because of God's grace and a Christian's acceptance of His salvation, we are cleansed by the blood of Jesus. With that said, we must still understand that God hates sin because it put His Son on the cross.

In contrast to God's response to sin and the sinner, God led David to reflect upon the abundance he experienced because of God's goodness. He used the word "lovingkindness" in verse seven: *"But as for me, by Your abundant lovingkindness I will enter Your house, at Your holy temple I will bow in reverence for You."* This is a wonderful word in the Hebrew language that could be translated as steadfast love or an overflowing mercy. He proclaimed God's "overflowing mercy" is "abundant." It is a picture of a never-ending, gushing, cool, mountain spring. It is because of this abundant mercy that we can enter into a relationship with God. We can *"enter [His] house."*

Because we do belong to the Lord, He leads us in righteousness. He makes His way straight or easier for us to follow. As believers, we can find great joy in the comfort of God's refuge. We can sing for joy because we are sheltered by the Almighty. Our rejoicing, however, is not in our benefits or in our blessing. Our rejoicing is not in our deliverance and it's not in our abundance. Verse eleven says we *"exult in You."* It is God Whom we praise. It is God Who blesses the righteous person, so it is God Who is worthy of our praise.

Do you remember the surrounding shield of Psalm 3? It is interesting that David carries that concept into this Psalm as well in verse twelve, but he says the shield that surrounds us is God's favor: *"For it is*

You who blesses the righteous man, O LORD, *You surround him with favor as with a shield.*" When you have God's favor, you have all you need.

This thought took me back to a memory that is probably inadequate for this truth, but nevertheless, it seemed to open my mind up to this concept more fully. When I was a 6th grader playing football for the park league, there was a boy playing in the backfield for another team. His name was Andre, and whenever Andre was given the ball, he scored. It really wasn't fair because Andre was like a man among boys or a giant among ants. I remember scoring with Andre one time, when I was playing defense, because he ran down the field with me holding onto his back. Needless to say, I didn't feel much like spiking the ball because the score went to the other team. We didn't have a chance. When God is on your team, He is all you need. When God's favor surrounds you, it doesn't really matter who the enemy is or what kind of weapons they may wield.

What kind of person is surrounded by God's favor? This Psalm says it is the righteous person. We must consider this from two perspectives. The New Testament says our righteousness is in Christ, so we will never enjoy God's favor unless we are first in Christ. Theologians call this "imputed" righteousness. Romans 4:1-5 describes the righteousness Abraham enjoyed as being "credited" to him. This is righteousness that belongs to God that has been graciously given to Abraham. I defined imputed righteousness in my upcoming book, *Immovable: Standing Firm in the Last Days,* as "the right standing God chooses to give us, thereby making us right, clean, and forgiven in His sight."

The other kind of righteousness is "imparted" righteousness. Imparted righteousness means we die to ourselves and allow Jesus to impart or live out His righteousness through our surrendered life. It is the Galatians 2:20 concept of being crucified with Christ and dying to self so He can live His life through us. It is righteousness, both imputed and imparted, that allows us to be surrounded with God's favor.

When we have this concept of God and of ourselves and when we pray these kinds of prayers, we really can eagerly watch for God's deliverance and greatly anticipate His favor. Will you trust Him in your desperate times? Will you receive and live out the righteousness of Christ and be consumed with and surrounded by the favor of Almighty God?

Further Thought…

- Have you ever had a time of real despair where you could only groan before the Lord?

- What would it take for you to pray ordered and focused prayers during times of crisis?

- How have you experienced God's abundant lovingkindness? Can you make a list of some of these abundant, overflowing blessings from God? Why not pause to thank God for His goodness and blessings in your life.

- Is there sin in your life that does not reflect the character of Christ in you? Are you willing to repent and turn from that sin?

- Would you say you are enjoying the favor of God? If not, why not? What are some changes you should make in your life so you can live your life in such a way that God can bless it?

PSALM 8

Contemplating God's Majesty

O LORD, our Lord, how majestic is Your name in all the earth, Who have displayed Your splendor above the heavens! 2 From the mouth of infants and nursing babes You have established strength because of Your adversaries, to make the enemy and the revengeful cease. 3 When I consider Your heavens, the work of Your fingers, the moon and the stars, which You have ordained; 4 what is man that You take thought of him, and the son of man that You care for him? 5 Yet You have made him a little lower than God, and You crown him with glory and majesty! 6 You make him to rule over the works of Your hands; You have put all things under his feet, 7 All sheep and oxen, and also the beasts of the field, 8 the birds of the heavens and the fish of the sea, whatever passes through the paths of the seas. 9 O LORD, our Lord, how majestic is Your name in all the earth!

Some years ago, my wife and I heard that there would be a meteor shower during the night, and we awakened all of our children to see the heavenly production. We laid down on our driveway motionless in the wee hours of the morning as we stared up into the heavens waiting patiently for a unique fingerprint of God to be displayed before our eyes. While I think we missed most of the meteor shower, we didn't miss the handy work of God. The sky was covered with both bright and dim twinkles, and occasionally we would see a shooting star plummet toward the earth.

I wonder if the Psalmist had been lying on a grassy hill outside the city of Bethlehem looking up into the heavens, as I did from my driveway, when God led him to think of the words of this Psalm. I can imagine David thinking of the majesty of God as he considered the vastness of the heavens. This view, and God's Spirit, inspired David to say, *"O LORD, our Lord, how majestic is Your name in all the earth, Who have displayed Your splendor above the heavens!"*

David began with a declaration of God's place in his life: "*O Lord, our Lord.*" While the word "Lord" is repeated twice, it is two different Hebrew words. The first word is the personal name God gave to Moses at the burning bush. Moses told God that when he told the Children of Israel that God had sent him to deliver them, they would ask for God's name. God told Moses that His name was Yahweh, or "I Am that I Am." This name became the personal name of God to the Jewish people. In this passage, David first referred to God with His personal name emphasizing both his eternality and his current reality.

The second word could be translated as "sovereign" or "one who rules and commands." It was as if David was saying that the God whom Israel knew as their Creator and Deliverer was also the God who ruled over them as their Sovereign King. David just didn't say "O Lord, the Lord," but rather he used the word "our." When we enter into a covenant relationship with our Creator, that we call Christianity, God really does become our God. Christianity is an intimate, personal relationship with God.

He then says, "*How majestic is Your name in all the earth, Who have displayed Your splendor above the heavens!*" The Hebrew word that is translated "majestic," literally means wide or great. It points to the vastness and uniqueness of our Creator. God is majestic and excellent; He shares no rivals when considering His glory. Have you ever used the word "majestic" to describe something that seems to be in a category all its own? I once described the Rocky Mountains as being "majestic and incredibly beautiful." The only problem with this comparison is that the Rockies are not the only majestic mountains in the world. Just a little north of the Rockies are the Grand Tetons. North of that is Glacier National Park. You could go south into Mexico or South America or go west to Mount Everest and find more examples of majestic mountain peaks that might even make the Rockies look less majestic. When you speak of God's majesty, He stands alone when compared to other things that are vast, wide, or great.

God's majesty is reflected in the heavens as they really do declare the glory of God (see also Psalm 19). Suppose we have a scale wherein an inch equals a million miles. How far do you suppose it would be to the nearest star apart from our sun? 100 feet? 300 feet? Now remember that in our illustration, one foot will equal twelve million miles. 100 feet would be over a billion miles. If one inch equals a million miles, the closest star would be 20,661 feet away. While that's the closest star, the galaxy that is farthest away, to our knowledge, is 1,302 billion light years away. A light year is 5,878,499,810,000 miles, so you will need to multiply that number by 1,302 to understand how vast space is. Keep in mind, however, that we haven't found the end of space yet and probably never will. God has truly displayed His splendor in the heavens.

When you consider these numbers from our 21st century understanding of space, it makes verses three and four even more significant: *"When I consider Your heavens, the work of Your fingers, the moon and the stars, which You have ordained; what is man that You take thought of him, and the son of man that You care for him?"* Though the Psalmist had never heard of the Big Bang Theory or of Charles Darwin, he had no doubt that God was the one who created the earth. It was as if David was picturing God, sitting at a potter's wheel, modeling the earth with His fingers. He was the One who spoke the world into existence, flung the stars into space with a single utterance, and created mankind in His image. In light of these startling facts, isn't it amazing to think that God has considered us and cares for us? God made us just a little lower than Himself and crowned us with glory and honor.

Have you ever shared David's query: *"What is man that You take thought of him...?"* I can't really wrap my mind around how or why a God that is so big would take thought of me. It is difficult for me to try to find a comparison, but a weak illustration would be like me taking a personal interest in every ant in my ant bed laden yard. While it seems hard to grasp, I accept the fact that God really does care about me. He is not so busy as to be unaware of my personal needs and concerns.

He makes an interesting statement that is translated in different ways. Note how the New American Standard translates verse five: "*Yet You have made him a little lower than God, and You crown him with glory and majesty!*" While some translators prefer to use the word "angels" instead of "God," the Hebrew word is actually "Elohim," which is one of the words for God in the Old Testament. It says that God has crowned humanity with "glory and majesty." These are the same words used to describe God's uniqueness. While mankind does not share God's glory and majesty, God is saying that there is something really special and unique about humanity. No other animal is like mankind. God made every other animal to be subjected to people in that God "*put all things under his feet.*" We really are special to God. You are special to God.

This is one reason that Satan has worked so hard to lead modern day people to accept the theory of evolution. This theory, which is shot full of more holes every day by new discoveries, says that human beings are here because of a cosmic accident. The Bible says we are here because the Creator of all things thinks so highly of us that He made us and individually knows everything about us.

David concluded this song of praise by reiterating his opening phrase as if it were the second piece to a matching set of bookends: "*O LORD, our Lord, how majestic is Your name in all the earth!*" While David used this Psalm to communicate his praise of Almighty God, the words should express our prayer of praise as well. We should reflect upon God's vastness but also upon God's personal interest. Just when we think that we are insignificant, we can remind ourselves that God made us just a little lower than Himself. When we think that God has abandoned us, or at least is not aware of our struggles, we can be reminded that God is very mindful of us and knows every detail of our lives.

Further Thought…

- Have you personally responded to God's offer of grace and salvation so that God is not just "the Lord" but "our Lord?" If not, why not now tell Him that you believe that Jesus died for your sins and rose again, that you want to turn from your sin and follow Him, and that you want Him to be the King over your heart and life?

- What does it mean to you to be in a covenant relationship with God? Can you think of examples of other covenant relationships? Do you know of any Bible verses or Bible stories that give examples of this special, close relationship that is built upon a covenant? If you don't know how to answer this, you may want to do a Bible study on the concept of covenant.

- Have you ever tried to count the stars? How does it make you feel about God when you consider the vastness of space?

- What thoughts of God do you have when you consider that God in His majesty takes thought of you?

- Do you have any struggles in your life right now that you should trust to God's keeping? He really does care and understand all the issues of your life. Will you let Him help you carry your burdens today?

PSALM 11
Confidence

In the LORD, I take refuge; how can you say to my soul, "Flee as a bird to your mountain; 2 For, behold, the wicked bend the bow, they make ready their arrow upon the string to shoot in darkness at the upright in heart. 3 If the foundations are destroyed, what can the righteous do?" 4 The LORD is in His holy temple; the LORD'S throne is in heaven; His eyes behold, His eyelids test the sons of men. 5 The LORD tests the righteous and the wicked, and the one who loves violence His soul hates. 6 Upon the wicked He will rain snares; fire and brimstone and burning wind will be the portion of their cup. 7 For the LORD is righteous, He loves righteousness; the upright will behold His face.

Mark Twain quipped, "To succeed in life, you need two things: ignorance and confidence." What do you suppose he meant? I think it is easy to understand the part about being confident for that is a great and necessary quality, depending upon in whom you place your confidence.

King David opens up this Psalm with a statement about this quality: "*In the LORD, I take refuge.*" His confidence, however, was not in himself; it was in the God of Israel. He specifically used God's personal name, Yahweh, so there would be no mistaking Who was the object of his confidence. It was as if he were saying, "No other place of safety or person of means can really provide protection. My confidence is in Jehovah, God!" When you consider all the military prowess of David, the giant killer, and all the weaponry at his disposal, David's statement has an even stronger ring. It may be that David's circumstances reminded him of how vulnerable he really was, or maybe he had concluded that the only thing that gave his sword power was the strength offered him by his Creator. Regardless, David knew that his success was tied exclusively to the power and presence of God in his life.

"*Refuge*" is a great word that is used repeatedly throughout the Psalms, and it is one focal point of this Psalm: "*In the* LORD, *I take refuge.*" It could have been used to describe a safe harbor for a ship during a storm or a dry cave for a soldier during a spring rain. It could also have been used to describe the place of safety created within a fortified city as a community of people stood against the threat of attack. The fact that David found refuge in the Lord meant that he stood in need of protection and he understood there was no comparison to the strength found in God Almighty.

David's confidence in the Lord was so great that when people suggested he try another alternative, he turned a deaf ear to their suggestion. God's detractors may say things like the words found in verses one through three: "*Flee as a bird to your mountain; for, behold, the wicked bend the bow, they make ready their arrow upon the string to shoot in darkness at the upright in heart. If the foundations are destroyed, what can the righteous do?*" Do you see the fear that could be put into the heart of a believer if we listen to the enemies of God? It's almost as if I can hear someone saying, "There's no way you can make it. The obstacles are too great. You don't have enough money. You better figure out a different strategy." The only thing we need to figure out is God's will. We just need to make sure that we are following God's plan and submissive to His will.

This moves me to the second part of Mark Twain's quote: ignorance. To succeed in life, you must be ignorant. Really? Ignorant of what? While Mr. Twain is not around for me to question, I'm going to take a bit of a leap and say that I think he was saying that success comes when someone is ignorant to the fact that something can't be done. Imagine the comments President John F. Kennedy received on May 25, 1961 when he said we would put a man on the moon by the end of the decade. One thing that was so astounding about this goal was that when President Kennedy made this prediction, the technology necessary to put a man on the moon had not yet been invented. While I do not know of any specific examples, I am sure there were plenty of naysayers verbalizing the impossibility of such a feat.

Consider the Wright brothers. The impossibility of flying was a foregone conclusion, but these two brothers somehow managed to beat the odds. How was that possible? It was possible because they seemed to be ignorant of the impossibilities. We, too, must be ignorant of the impossibilities, because with God, all things are possible (see Matthew 19:26).

David seemed to be saying that the odds of success did not really matter as long as God was on His throne. He said, "*The LORD is in His holy temple; the LORD'S throne is in heaven.*" This is to say that God is King of kings and Lord of lords. Since God is on His throne, nothing else really matters. God is totally trustworthy, and He is looking for people who will put their trust in Him. The conclusion of verse four says, "*His eyes behold, His eyelids test the sons of men.*" God is searching for people who will trust Him and live rightly before Him. 2 Chronicles 16:9 says, "*For the eyes of the LORD move to and fro throughout the earth that He may strongly support those whose heart is completely His.*" God is searching the earth for men and women, boys and girls, who are sold out to Jesus Christ. He will strongly support them. He will be their refuge. He will be their success.

God presents a contrast in this Psalm, and verse five presents the two options: "*The LORD tests the righteous and the wicked, and the one who loves violence His soul hates.*" He compares the righteous and the wicked. Once again, God says His soul "*hates*" the one who loves violence. As I said in a previous chapter, this concept is difficult to grasp and muddied by the fact that we are forced to view the concept of hate from our own perspective. Because God is holy, He has no alternative but to be revolted by that which is contrary to His righteous character. We need to hold to that concept as we make choices every day. We must choose obedience and righteousness so we can reflect His character and walk in His blessing.

God says there will be negative consequences for the one who lives wickedly: "*Upon the wicked He will rain snares; fire and brimstone and burning wind will be the portion of their cup.*" Surely, God is speaking of eternal judgment with those thoughts, but there is probably a description of the results in this life of making decisions without the guidance and blessing of the God, Who is all wise.

The righteous, however, *"will behold His face."* What is God saying? He is saying that those who walk in obedience to God's commands will see God. These words seem to be somewhat repeated by Jesus in John 14:21: *"He who has My commandments and keeps them is the one who loves Me; and he who loves Me will be loved by My Father, and I will love him and will disclose Myself to him."* Do you really want to see and experience God? One of the keys is simply obedience. The question is, "How will we see God?" We will see God by developing knowledge of the person of God, by developing a heightened awareness to the activity of God, by developing sensitivity to the voice of God, and by developing an understanding of the Spirit of God. God is righteous, and He loves righteousness. If you want to see God, obey His commandments and walk intimately with Him through a personal relationship.

God specifically said we will behold His *face*. This must have shaken the Jewish readers because everyone knew you could not see the face of God and live. Even Moses was not allowed to see God's face (see Exodus 33:20), but now God is saying that it is possible to have such a relationship with our Creator that we can actually behold His face. It is a picture of intimacy, accessibility, and transparency. Not only do we want to know God, but He wants us to know Him.

You can place your confidence in a lot of things, but many of those things will let you down. God, however, will never let you down. As we face the uncertainties of tomorrow, let's join the Psalmist and say, *"In the LORD, I take refuge."*

Further Thought...
- What does confidence mean to you?
- Do you agree with Mark Twain's statement that success comes from both confidence and ignorance?

- Do you think there are negative consequences for wickedness in this life? If so, what?

- Why do you think God loves righteousness?

- What do you think it means to "behold God's face?"

PSALM 13
What to Do When You Don't Know What to Do

How long, O LORD? Will You forget me forever? How long will You hide Your face from me? 2 How long shall I take counsel in my soul, having sorrow in my heart all the day? How long will my enemy be exalted over me? 3 Consider and answer me, O LORD my God; enlighten my eyes, or I will sleep the sleep of death, 4 and my enemy will say, "I have overcome him," and my adversaries will rejoice when I am shaken. 5 But I have trusted in Your lovingkindness; my heart shall rejoice in Your salvation. 6 I will sing to the LORD, because He has dealt bountifully with me.

Forgotten. Have you ever been forgotten? I going to Ft. Pierce, Florida to visit my grandmother remember when I was about six years old. My parents, sister, two brothers, and I made the long trek to south Florida to see my mother's side of the family and to enjoy some time at the beach. One morning, we all loaded into the car to make the short drive over the causeway to go swimming in the Atlantic Ocean. When we parked the car and began filing toward the bathhouse, my mother realized we had left my sister. She had been forgotten in the mayhem of gathering swimming gear, packing a lunch, and cramming kids and grownups into the car. My mother raced back across the bridge to my grandmother's house and rushed into the house expecting to find a distraught little girl. Instead she heard the very exasperated, shouting voice coming from behind the closed bathroom door, "Mama, bring me some toilet paper." I wonder how long it would have taken her to realize she had been forgotten.

David felt forgotten. In the midst of his dire circumstances, he found hope in the midst of conflict and despair. During the first two-thirds of the Psalm, it seems that despair wins, but in the final two verses, hope eventually triumphs. Notice his opening words: "*How long, O LORD? Will You forget me forever? How long will You hide Your face from me?*" Can you relate to David's struggle? He actually felt as if God had hidden His face from him. While we do not know how long he struggled with feeling abandoned by God, it must have been quite a while.

Note the next couple of questions he asked God in this prayer of despair: "*How long shall I take counsel in my soul, having sorrow in my heart all the day? How long will my enemy be exalted over me?*" Have you ever gone through a real challenging experience that seemed to have no end? I have walked with people through terminal illnesses, economic reversals, and severe family problems, and, at times, it really did seem as if there was no hope in sight.

If David really felt so alone, it must have been because he had gone through a significant period of time where negative circumstances were being heaped upon him in a relentless flourish. In times like that, we might wonder why God would allow such struggle in our lives. Why would God "*hide [His] face from me?*" While we could argue the fact that God had not really hidden His face, sometimes our circumstances cause us not to be able to realize God is actually there beside us. So, even though God has not actually forgotten us, it sure seems to feel that way. Once again, I ask the question, "Why would God allow such struggle in our lives?"

There are several reasons why trials are allowed to crash into our otherwise contented lives. First of all, we must be careful and not blame God for everything. For that matter, we can't blame Satan for everything either. Let's get honest and acknowledge that sometimes trouble comes because we invited it. We were all born with a sin nature that continues to influence Christians, even after our salvation. It is true that we are dead to sin, but the influence of that old sin nature is still felt in our lives. This natural tendency to go our own way can get us into trouble and lead us to ignore things that would actually lead us to a path of honoring God.

If this Psalm was written in response to Absalom's rebellion, David might have to put some of the blame upon himself for his parenting failure. Second Samuel 13 tells of David's oldest son, Amnon, raping his half-sister, Tamar. Some translations indicate in 2 Samuel 13:21 that

David not only became angry, but he did nothing about it because he loved his son. The variation in translation comes because the phrase was added to the Greek translation of the Old Testament, but it is not included in the Hebrew text. Regardless of whether or not this phrase was included in the original text, one can see that David did nothing about his son's crime.

While David did nothing, Absalom, David's second-born son, took matters into his own hands to defend his sister's virtue. Absalom killed his older half-brother, Amnon. Because David did not discipline his son and deal with this crime properly, he now had a raped daughter, a murdered son, and another son who had committed the murder. Fast-forward to Absalom leading a coup attempt to take the Kingdom from his father, and you may realize that some of David's grief was self-inflicted. Don't be so quick to blame God or Satan for your troubles. You may only need to look in the mirror to see the one most responsible.

Other people can sometimes be responsible for our troubles simply because they are broken by sin, and broken people sometimes act like they are broken. Should we be surprised when a spiritually fallen person does something that reflects his spiritually fallen nature? When that happens, we might get caught up in the cross-fire and find ourselves wounded. We certainly can't blame God for that either. While we could blame Satan, because of the sin factor, he is not really off to the side creating havoc. Sometimes, our troubles are simply caused by others.

Whether problems are caused by us, by others, or by Satan, God allows them and chooses to use them for our benefit. That's why Romans 8:28 says, *"And we know that God causes all things to work together for good to those who love God, to those who are called according to His purpose."* Remember that God's greatest goal for Christians is Christlikeness; therefore, He is more interested in your character than your comfort. God is willing to let us get uncomfortable if it will grow us to be more like His Son.

After rolling around in his sorrow for a bit, David finally declares his faith in God in the final two verses of the Psalm: *"But I have trusted in Your lovingkindness; my heart shall rejoice in Your salvation. 6 I will sing to the LORD, because He has dealt bountifully with me."* He reminds himself of God's *"lovingkindness."* Again, that is such a wonderful word. It means steadfast love or unfailing mercy. It is as if David is saying, "Even though it looks like You have abandoned me, I know you haven't. I am trusting in your mercy and grace that are never ending and your presence that is never fading."

As he reflects upon the mercy of God, it seems as if his spirit lifts and his perspective changes. He is led to think of the salvation that God has given him, and this thought moves his heart to rejoice. He is catapulted into a spirit of worship and adoration. He reflects upon the fact that even though bad things were happening, God has still dealt "bountifully" with him. The Hebrew word that is translated as "bountifully" means "to deal fully." It made me think of a card game, like Spades, where the dealer gives out all the cards in the deck. David is saying that God has given everything to him. Basically David is saying that on his worst days, he is extremely blessed. Can you relate to that? If you got what you deserved, it would be hell – literally. You and I deserve death and hell, yet God offers us life and heaven. We deserve misery and judgment, yet God offers us joy and forgiveness. What a deal! We've got the best hand of all because God has given us everything! We, too, can sing to the Lord because He has dealt bountifully to us. Praise His name!

Further Thought...

- Have you ever felt forgotten or abandoned by someone in your life? Have you ever felt abandoned by God?
- What do you do when you feel all alone in the midst of your trouble? Do you get overwhelmed by the problems or do you eventually end up acknowledging God's goodness?

- Can you look back in your life and remember times of difficulty that God has used in positive ways? How did you benefit or what did you learn from your times of difficulty?

- Make a list of all the ways God has blessed your life. Would you say that He has dealt bountifully with you?

- How should you respond to God during times of loneliness when you feel abandoned by everyone, including God?

PSALM 16
Filled and Overflowing

Preserve me, O God, for I take refuge in You. 2 I said to the LORD, *"You are my Lord; I have no good besides You." 3 As for the saints who are in the earth, they are the majestic ones in whom is all my delight. 4 The sorrows of those who have bartered for another god will be multiplied; I shall not pour out their drink offerings of blood, nor will I take their names upon my lips. 5 The* LORD *is the portion of my inheritance and my cup; You support my lot. 6 The lines have fallen to me in pleasant places; indeed, my heritage is beautiful to me. 7 I will bless the* LORD *Who has counseled me; indeed, my mind instructs me in the night. 8 I have set the* LORD *continually before me; because He is at my right hand, I will not be shaken. 9 Therefore my heart is glad and my glory rejoices; my flesh also will dwell securely. 10 For You will not abandon my soul to Sheol; nor will You allow Your Holy One to undergo decay. 11 You will make known to me the path of life; in Your presence is fullness of joy; in Your right hand there are pleasures forever.*

"Oh wow. That's plenty; as a matter of fact, that's more than I can handle." Have you ever made a similar statement? Your child may have been serving you ice-cream or your spouse may have been loading your arms with firewood. The Psalmist felt like his portion was more than he could ever hope for, but his feelings were positive, not negative. Verses five and six of this chapter seem to reflect a heart of gratitude as if an individual is looking at the will of a deceased relative: "I can't believe he left all this to me; this is quite an inheritance."

David begins by describing his inheritance as simply *"the Lord."* Although there are several Hebrew words he could have used that would be translated as *"Lord,"* he chose the word that meant God's personal name: *Yahweh.* It was a term reflective of God's actions in Israel's history. It was a name that spoke of intimacy, nearness, deliverance, and sufficiency.

When he said, *"the lines have fallen in the pleasant places,"* he was speaking symbolically of his inheritance by thinking of how a surveyor would draw out the lines defining the boundaries of a piece of property. He reflects upon the blessing of his inheritance, which is the Lord, and he says *"it is beautiful."*

Have you ever thought of God as being beautiful? It is easy to see beauty in a sunrise or in the opening of a fragrant rose in early spring, but do you really think of God as beautiful? I see God as big, creative, and powerful, but I've not really thought often of Him as beautiful.

As David considered the fact that he had *"no good besides [God],"* he pondered the beauty of his inheritance. Maybe one could think of piles of glistening gold or bags of sparkling diamonds as beautiful. David was thinking about the striking beauty of his Creator, Who was the portion of his inheritance.

Nothing else matters when you have God, because God is enough. Do you ever wish you had more? Maybe you got a raise this year, but wouldn't it be nice if it were more? Maybe you bought a 2008 vehicle, but a 2010 would have been better. How often have you spoken phrases or heard phrases like "If my health were better..." or "If my circumstances were just a little different...?" David exclaimed, "I am so satisfied with my portion because God is enough!" We really need to learn this same contentment. Is it possible that we are sometimes not content because we do not realize what we have? David understood the value of his relationship with God.

David declared that his portion is good because of several reasons. One is that he saw God as the Counselor Who always gave perfect counsel: *"I will bless the LORD who has counseled me; indeed, my mind instructs me in the night."* Is God your counselor? What would it take for your mind to instruct you in the night with godly, perfect counsel? The obvious answer is that our minds must be filled with the Word of God, but we must also be sensitive to the voice of God.

Why do you suppose David would be up in the night listening to God's counsel? The only reason I can think of is that he was either facing the threat of attack, or he was troubled by his problems and unable to sleep. Either issue would cause David to need counsel, and he knew the best One to approach for wisdom about future direction. When you awaken in the night, what comes into your mind? It is easy to lie in bed at night and worry about your problems, to be angry over being slighted, or to be troubled about a decision. God says that He never abandons us, and if we need wisdom about a matter, we should ask Him (see James 1:5).

Not only is David's inheritance good because of God's counsel, but it is also good because of God's strength. It is rare to find a person who can declare, "*I will not be shaken,*" but David did: "*I have set the LORD continually before me; because He is at my right hand, I will not be shaken.*" God is the source of his joy, strength, help, and wisdom because David has set the Lord continually before himself. He doesn't just occasionally set the Lord before him, but he continually sets the Lord before him.

What is David's secret for strength and fortitude? The secret is God. Because God is continually set before him, he can say with certainty, "*I will not be shaken.*" Can you say that? Can I? If we are honest with ourselves, we might have to say, "Sometimes I set the Lord before me, and upon those occasions, I am not shaken." David makes this statement and connects the historical past with the uncertain future. He has set the Lord before him (past/present), and "*I will not be shaken*" (future). If we can learn to continually set the Lord before us, we will find great strength, determination, and perseverance while facing the greatest challenges.

It is because David understands his priorities that he then says, "*Therefore, my heart is glad and my glory rejoices; my flesh also will dwell securely.*" Anytime you see the word "*therefore,*" you need to ask, "What is the 'therefore' there for?" It is a connecting word. David is saying that because he daily makes the decision to keep God before him, his heart is glad, and he finds great security. I cannot imagine anyone not wanting joy and security. We live in a time when our security is constantly threatened and depression is constantly seeking to become our best friend. God says that we can find joy in the midst of sorrow, help in our times of greatest need, and security when we feel most vulnerable. It will come as a result of placing God continually before us. This is speaking of an ongoing, intimate relationship with our Creator. We do this by daily walking with God and constantly filling our minds with the things of God.

I love David's final declaration in verse eleven: "*You will make known to me the path of life; in Your presence is fullness of joy; in Your right hand there are pleasures forever.*" The only way we will ever hope to know the "*path of life*" is if God reveals it to us. The only way we will experience joy in its fullness is if we dwell in God's presence. And the only way real pleasures will be ours is if we stay in the "*right hand*" of God. All of these things point to our need to walk daily with God. This means that we seek Him in His word, and we please Him with our actions. It means that we practice daily what it means to "*die to self and live unto Christ.*" For some of us, the joy meter has bottomed out and our life compass no longer seems to point to true north. God says that He is the One who makes all things right and helps us to find our way. We must simply return to His presence.

It is true that God is everywhere, so how must we return to His presence? I like to think of it as God's factual presence and God's realized presence. The fact is, God is everywhere. There is nothing you can do to get away from God. Jonah made this surprising discovery when he tried to flee God's presence by running to Tarshish.

Even though God is everywhere (omnipresent), sometimes we do not realize He is with us. Knowing that God is with us and experiencing His promised presence grows within us a feeling of security and sensitivity to God that we might otherwise never know. David realized the constant presence of God in his life, and because of this, he could declare things like, "*I will not be shaken,*" and "*in Your right hand there are pleasures forever.*"

Further Thought...

- Are you satisfied with your portion, or would you say that you have been cut short?

- How would you describe your spiritual inheritance? Is it true that we many times think of our inheritance as a place or a reward and not as a Person?

- What can you do to fully grasp the depth and width of God's blessings?

- Is there something in your life right now that is causing you to be shaken?

- What must you do to be able to declare with David, "*I have set the LORD continually before me; Because He is at my right hand, I will not be shaken?*"

- Are there some things in your life right now about which you need counsel? What must you do to prepare your mind to receive the counsel of God? What will you do the next time you awaken during the night with troubles on your mind?

- To which of the two can you most easily relate? God's factual presence or God's realized presence? What changes do you need to make in your life so God's realized presence becomes a part of your normal existence?

PSALM 17

The Apple of God's Eye

Hear a just cause, O LORD, give heed to my cry; give ear to my prayer, which is not from deceitful lips....6 I have called upon You, for You will answer me, O God; incline Your ear to me, hear my speech. 7 Wondrously show Your loving-kindness, O Savior of those who take refuge at Your right hand from those who rise up against them. 8 Keep me as the apple of the eye; hide me in the shadow of Your wings...15 As for me, I shall behold Your face in righteousness; I will be satisfied with Your likeness when I awake.

Have you ever gone to court? If not, I'm sure you have at least seen a trial on television. In the courtroom, you will find a prosecutor and a defense attorney, a witness stand, the judge's bench, and the jury box. The lawyers present the case, the judge presides over the trial, and the jury decides the verdict. In some cases, there is no jury, and the judge is required to pass judgment.

Psalm 17 seems to start out in an imaginary courtroom, and David is presenting his case. While we do not understand all of the circumstances, David is presenting a character witness for himself: "*Hear a just cause, O LORD, give heed to my cry; give ear to my prayer, which is not from deceitful lips.*" He considers his cause to be just and his motives to be pure. Verse five of this Psalm says, "*My steps have held fast to Your paths. My feet have not slipped.*"

I had a thought as I read over this Psalm again. When crying out to God, my motives and cause have not always been pure or just, but God still answers. Even though righteousness honors the Lord in the courtroom of the Almighty, 1 John indicates that we actually have an Advocate who steps out on our behalf before the Judge (see 1 John 2:1). The just hearing we receive from the Judge is actually based upon His mercy and not our actions or motives. Praise the Lord!

Consider the words of verse six: "*I have called upon You, for You will answer me, O God; incline Your ear to me, hear my speech.*" David concluded that he calls upon God for God *will* answer. Let's consider this for a moment. Once again David used a word for prayer that is not delicate or gentle: "*call.*" It literally means "to shout," so David is saying he shouted out to God. Think about that for just a moment. When do you ever shout? I shout when someone is a long way off, and I need to get his or her attention.

I may shout when I get passionate about something, or I could shout, though I shouldn't, if I lose my temper. Shouting seems to indicate some kind of desperation or unbridled passion. I think David is saying that he threw delicacy to the wind and shouted out to God in his desperation. I think God wants passion from His children. We are told throughout the Bible to cry out to God.

Note that David gave us the reason he shouts to God: "*for You will answer me.*" God is an answering God. Jeremiah understood this when he wrote of God's message to him: "*Call to Me and I will answer you, and I will tell you great and mighty things, which you do not know*" (see Jeremiah 33:3).

In his prayer, David makes several requests. First, he asks God to "*incline Your ear to me, hear my speech.*" In other words, he is asking God to please listen to the things that are on his mind. Isn't it interesting that David first says he called out to God because God will answer, but then he follows it up with a request for God to listen. It is almost like he knows that God will answer him, but he still wavers a bit at the beginning of his prayer. Have you ever felt that way? There is a main part of your brain and your heart that knows that God hears your prayer, but then in a moment of desperation, you cry out again, "Please hear me God for I am so desperate for you."

The second request is found in verse seven: "*Wondrously show Your lovingkindness.*" I love the Hebrew word that is translated as "*lovingkindness.*" It is the Hebrew word *hesed,* and it can be translated as steadfast love and mercy. It is the same word used in Lamentations 3:22 and 1

Chronicles 16:34. It is a combination of words that include mercy, kindness, grace, and compassion.

The first two words of this request are critical for our understanding: "*Wondrously show*." The word *show* literally means "to separate." It is like David is asking God to make a distinction between His lovingkindness and the kind of mercy the world shows. Here is a very loose translation: "Make the contrast between the world's love and grace and Your love and grace ridiculously obvious to those of us who can so easily miss it."

The next request is "*Keep me as the apple of the eye*." Isn't it interesting to find a little saying that has become a part of our language actually came from the Bible? Have you ever thought of anyone as being "the apple of your eye?" This phrase has come to mean that someone is cherished by you, but in the Old Testament days, it literally meant "the little man of the eye." You and I know that when you look at an object, your eye receives it as a miniature reflection of the actual object. It is almost as if there is a mirror in our eyeball reflecting whatever it is we are looking upon to our brains. This phrase could simply be a request for God's resolute notice.

David indicated he had been the apple of God's eye, and now he wants to continue being treasured in this way. To be the little man (or woman) of God's eye means that God is always watching you. The fact is we *are* always reflected in God's gaze because we never step away from His notice. Psalm 32:8 says, "*I will instruct you and teach you in the way which you should go; I will counsel you with My eye upon you*." In other words, God always sees you and is fully aware of your circumstances. This says you and I have incredible value to God. He cherishes us.

David then asks, "*Hide me in the shadow of Your wings*." As he wrote these words, he was obviously thinking back to a barnyard scene he must have witnessed. Maybe it was a moment of danger, at least from a chicken's perspective, and all the little chicks ran quickly under the extended wings of the mother hen. For a little chick, there is no better place of safety than under the wings of mother hen. You know, it's sort of the same way for people.

I was always a little nervous about my mama watching my football games when I was a teenager because I had a secret fear that she would come running out of the stands onto the field after someone on the defense gave me an exceptionally painful blow. As a kid, there is nothing like the safety of a mother's arms. David understood this in relationship to his heavenly Father. While a hen's wings are not really all that strong and a mother's arms have limitations, God's wings are impenetrable and God's strength is limitless. If you need safety at a moment of great weakness, there is no better place to be than snuggled up next to the breast of Almighty God listening to the rhythmic pulsation of His strong heart that says "I love you" with every beat.

The prayer concludes with a declaration or resolution: "*As for me, I shall behold Your face in righteousness; I will be satisfied with Your likeness when I awake.*" Isn't it interesting that David begins by asking God to look at him, and he concludes with his commitment to look at God. It is almost as if David acknowledges the fact that he will forever be found within the steady gaze of his heavenly Father, but for God to be forever in David's gaze, he must make a steadfast commitment. He also seems to point out that beholding God's face will only happen if we are walking in righteousness. This almost seems to say that while God sees everything, including my sin, it is my sin that causes me to turn my face away from God. Maybe it is saying that we cannot sin unless we first move our gaze from the loving face of God. This is why he says he will be satisfied with God's likeness. He is saying I will resolve myself to always look into the face of God.

Further Thought...

- If God's notice of you depended upon your character, would you ever have His attention?

- How does it make you feel to think that you have an Advocate in Jesus Christ and that God's mercy and grace are not dependent upon your actions?

- Do you ever feel like you do not really understand God's mercy? Is it possible that the true definition of God's love is made confusing because of the world's definition of love and mercy?

- Meditate for just a moment on being the "apple" of God's eye. How does it make you feel? What do you think that means for you?

- Has there ever been a time when you ran to God for shelter? What was it like? What did He do?

- Can you make the same commitment the Psalmist made in the final verse (to be satisfied with God's face, to look upon God in righteousness)?

8-28-20

PSALM 18:1-19

Finding Help on the Narrow Path

I love You, O LORD, my strength. 2 The LORD is my Rock and my Fortress and my Deliverer, my God, my Rock, in whom I take refuge; my Shield and the Horn of my salvation, my Stronghold. 3 I call upon the LORD, Who is worthy to be praised, and I am saved from my enemies. 4 The cords of death encompassed me, and the torrents of ungodliness terrified me. 5 The cords of Sheol surrounded me; the snares of death confronted me. 6 In my distress I called upon the LORD, and cried to my God for help; He heard my voice out of His temple, and my cry for help before Him came into His ears...16 He sent from on high, He took me; He drew me out of many waters. 17 He delivered me from my strong enemy, and from those who hated me, for they were too mighty for me. 18 They confronted me in the day of my calamity, but the LORD was my stay. 19 He brought me forth also into a broad place; He rescued me, because He delighted in me.

"I love you." There's nothing quite like hearing those words from someone special in your life. One of my sons recently sent me a text with a picture of a construction project he had completed. I was quite proud of him for his accomplishment, but the best part of the text was the way he ended it: "I love you, D" (for some reason in Riordanese, "D," "T," and "J" are easier to say than Dad, Timothy, and Jonathan). As a father, there's nothing like hearing those words from your children.

David starts out the eighteenth Psalm with those words: "*I love You, O Lord.*" Think for just a moment about how unusual this was for an Old Testament follower of God. While we know that Christianity is an intimate relationship with God, many of the followers of God in the Old Testament saw their Creator as Someone to be feared, not Someone to be loved. David seemed to get it. God wanted an intimate relationship and not just strict obedience.

If you look in your Bible, you will notice the title of this Psalm: "*A Psalm of David, the servant of the LORD, who spoke to the LORD the words of this song in the day that the LORD delivered him from the hand of all his enemies and from the hand of Saul.*" While David may have written this Psalm later in life, he was reflecting back upon all the times God delivered him from trouble, including the trouble he experienced with King Saul.

One part I like in this introduction are the words, "*who spoke to the Lord.*" Being that this is a song, David obviously spoke the words to God through a song. Note that in his worship, he didn't just sing about God or about what he got out of following God, but rather, he sang songs of worship *to* God. When you worship, do you sing to God? If we understand worship to be an encounter with our divine Creator and loving Father, I think it will change our passion and fervor for worship.

Next David said, "*I love You, O Lord, my Strength.*" It is interesting to note how many of the Psalms are written out of times of desperation and weakness. David was obviously helped by God to overcome a great challenge. It is almost as if using the word "*strength*" as a synonym for God opens the door for a litany of nomenclatures for the Almighty: "*The LORD is my Rock and my Fortress and my Deliverer, my God, my Rock, in whom I take refuge; my Shield and the Horn of my salvation, my Stronghold.*" Wow! Do you see that a significant part of worship is praise? David is giving praise to God by declaring God's character and nature. Praise is focusing on Who God is while thanksgiving is focusing on what God has done. They can both overlap, but they are also both distinctly different. You can use these names of God in your own expression of praise. Why don't you stop for just a moment and read verse two back to God in a prayer of praise? You can expound upon it a bit by giving examples of how you have experienced that aspect of God's character in your life.

Now move down to verse six: "*In my distress I called upon the LORD, and cried to my God for help; He heard my voice out of His temple, and my cry for help before Him came into His ears.*" He described his trouble as being "*distress.*" The Hebrew word means to be "wrapped up, enveloped, or tied up." David was saying he was fully encompassed by his trouble and unable to get out by his own devices. Have you ever felt that way? To be "wrapped up" by your problems can really be an overwhelming feeling. What do you do when you are distressed? Hopefully, you do what David did: call upon the Lord.

Notice also that he says he "*cried to my God for help.*" Again, he uses terms to indicate his anguish and desperation. Here's the awesome thing: when David cried out to God in his distress, God heard him! It's interesting how David determined that God heard him out of His temple. It was as if to remind us that even though God is removed from us, He is not really removed from us. Think about that for a moment. God is never far away.

Even while David used a variety of terms to describe God, in verses sixteen and seventeen, he reaches once again for synonymous repetition to describe his deliverance: "*He sent from on high, He took me; He drew me out of many waters. He delivered me from my strong enemy.*" Take just a moment to meditate on these terms. What does it mean to be "taken by God" or to be "drawn by God out of many waters?" Maybe you feel as if the waters are nearly covering your head. God can draw you out. It doesn't really matter how strong your enemy is, God can deliver you. He delivered David.

We must also be reminded that sometimes God's deliverance does not necessarily fit our definition of "deliverance." Remember the disciples? Knowing they would encounter a life-threatening storm, Jesus sent them out onto the lake anyway. Jesus ultimately walked out on the water and calmed the storm. This is a gripping and troubling thought: Jesus sent his disciples into the storm. We need to be reminded, as I once heard someone say: God doesn't always deliver us from the storm, but sometimes He delivers us through the storm.

While everything around David seemed to be unstable and precarious, God was David's steady ground. He said in verses eighteen and nineteen: "*But the LORD was my stay. He brought me forth also into a broad place; He rescued me, because He delighted in me.*" What does it mean to say that God is your stay? It is really an interesting Hebrew word. While it can be translated in a variety of ways, it literally means "to" or "towards." It insinuates support or strength, but it is literally saying that God is directed towards you. When you are going through trouble, God's back is not turned to you, but rather, God is fully aware of your circumstances. He is your stay. No one else is your stay – only God.

Do you see what happened as David realized that God's attention and power was directed towards him? God brought him to a broad place. I love that. It reminds me of some of the hikes I've had on the Appalachian Trail where the trail may have meandered over a mountain and run in narrow fashion along the side of a steep drop off. While the trail has never become something like the width of a balance beam in a gymnastics meet in the Olympics, it has gotten narrow enough to make me a little nervous with an unstable, precarious fifty-pound pack resting upon my back. It is a good feeling when you get past the narrow part and find the wide path. David wrote that God took him through the tight place and put his feet upon the wide path. God can do that for you too.

The last part of verse nineteen is so powerful to me. Why does God face you and me? Why is He our Rock, our Fortress, our Deliverer, and our Shield? Why does He rescue us from the tight spots and put our feet on the wide path? It is because He delights in us. That is amazing. The Creator of the universe delights in me. I can't fathom it. I can't understand it, but I believe it. God says He delights in me as His child. I do not deserve His delight. I have not earned His delight. I am His child, and I relish His grace and mercy. Join with David today in reflecting upon your place with the Almighty. Call upon the LORD, who is worthy to be praised, and declare your sufficiency in Him.

Further Thought...

- Think back to a time when someone special told you they loved you. How did that make you feel? Are you a parent or grandparent? How does it make you feel when your children or grandchildren express their love for you?

- When was the last time you told God that you loved Him? Do you think He enjoys hearing of your love?

- Read again the synonyms David used for God: *my Rock and my Fortress and my Deliverer, my God, my Rock, in whom I take refuge; my Shield and the Horn of my salvation, my Stronghold.* Take a few minutes and think back to times in your life when God has shown Himself in a similar way to you.

- Can you remember a time when you were walking on a narrow path? How did you feel? How did God move you to a broad place? What was your response to God?

- How does it make you feel to think that God delights in you?

PSALM 18:30-36 ✓

Stable and Prepared for What Comes my Way

As for God, His way is blameless; the word of the LORD is tried; He is a shield to all who take refuge in Him. 31 For who is God, but the LORD? And who is a rock, except our God, 32 the God who girds me with strength and makes my way blameless? 33 He makes my feet like hinds' feet, and sets me upon my high places. 34 He trains my hands for battle, so that my arms can bend a bow of bronze. 35 You have also given me the shield of Your salvation, And Your right hand upholds me; and Your gentleness makes me great. 36 You enlarge my steps under me, and my feet have not slipped.

Have you ever blamed God for something? Do you remember the words of Martha to Jesus in John 11:21, "Lord, if You had been here, my brother would not have died." Has her comment ever struck you as being odd? She starts out by saying "Lord," as if Jesus is her Sovereign, but then she proceeds to rebuke Him as if she were His sovereign. While we may not always verbalize it, we too can blame God for letting us down. It may have been the death of a loved one or the loss of a job. It could be deaf ears to a fervent prayer or unmoving arms to a desperate need. "God, if you would have just answered my prayer, all of this wouldn't have happened!"

First of all, I am glad that God is big enough to handle our immaturity and gracious enough to overlook our mistakes. He has a totally different view of our circumstances than we have, and we can always trust Him to do the right thing. David understood this and expressed it with the opening words of verse thirty: "*As for God, His way is blameless.*"

What does it mean to say God's way is "*blameless?*" The Hebrew word means "unscathed, perfect, or intact." Ezekiel 43:25 translates the same Hebrew word as "without blemish" (NAS). In other words, whatever God does is always right. His decisions and actions are not even marginally wrong. If we find ourselves in a place of blaming God, it means that our perspective is limited, and we are in the wrong place. God is not to be blamed, but at that moment, we are.

Look at the second phrase in that verse, "The word of the LORD is tried." This is actually a picture of the work of a refiner. It could be someone refining gold where the gold is melted in a fire so as to remove the impurities. The word literally means to be refined or sifted so the finished product has no impurities. The wonderful thing for us is that God never has to sift His words. They are perfect or flawless from the beginning. God is totally trustworthy, and His word is always right. That is difficult for us to grasp sometimes, but we can always act on God's word and know it is the right thing to do. You can probably think back to times in your life when you acted on God's word and found it to be right, or tried.

If we believe these first two thoughts and act upon them, God's way is blameless and His word is tried, we will find "*He is a shield to all who take refuge in Him.*" He is your protection and a place of hiding for you when you don't understand what is going on or do not know the right thing to do. Have you ever been in that particular spot? Maybe you're there now. If you just need to stop for a bit and rest, God is there for your protection and renewal.

It is almost as if David begins to focus upon the Lord in these verses through expressions of worship when he says that God is "*the LORD…a rock*" and "*the God who girds me with strength.*" An amazing thing happens when we turn our gaze fully upon God. We gain a better view of God and a clearer perspective on our struggles.

Notice the transition that happens in these verses. First, God is blameless, and His word is tried. When I focus on Him and realize His character and nature, He "*makes my way blameless.*" Truly to focus upon the Lord impacts our daily lives. Everything about us comes into clearer focus, and even our motives bend to the will of the Almighty. Maybe it's time to quit looking at your circumstances and start focusing on the One Who is bigger than any circumstance.

When we do that, we can sing with the Psalmist, *"He makes my feet like hinds' feet, and sets me upon my high places."* The hind, to which David is referring, is a sure-footed deer that can stand in difficult terrain. We will find renewed strength and a ready reserve deep within us that will help us to soar above our circumstances. I can't help but believe that as God "sets us upon high places" that we will gain a whole new perspective of our issues. It is important to emphasize that as we fix our gaze upon God, our problems get a lot smaller. It reminds me of the old hymn: "Turn your eyes upon Jesus; look full in His wonderful face, and the things of earth will grow strangely dim in the light of His glory and grace."

Look at the next line of encouragement: *"He trains my hands for battle, so that my arms can bend a bow of bronze. You have also given me the shield of Your salvation."* Once again, note the progression. First God's way is blameless and His Word is tried, but as we move our gaze to Him, our way becomes blameless. While we first hide in the strong embrace of our heavenly Father for protection and security, we eventually find ourselves becoming prepared for battle. It is like God is picking us up, dusting us off, and refitting us to go out and face the enemy once again. Can you imagine the strength you would need to bend a bow of bronze? God will give you strength for your circumstances. The shield He offers us for our protection is the shield of salvation. From a New Testament perspective, we can think about the security and strength we have from the One Who is Faithful and True, the God Who will never leave us or forsake us; the One who makes our salvation sure through Jesus Christ our Savior and Lord.

The result of all of this is confidence, steadiness, and success: *"And Your gentleness makes me great. You enlarge my steps under me, and my feet have not slipped."* I do not think God is saying He will boost our ego and make our esteem swell among our peers, though that could happen. I think God is saying He will expand your life and your heart. He will magnify Himself within your life and help you to understand that with God, you stand above the world and its trials. He will whisper in your ear, *"Greater is He that is in you than he that is in the world."* He's going to give you "big feet" so that your personal foundation is strengthened.

When you receive the blows of life, you will find that you are more stable. Those size sevens are going to become size sixteens, and you will find new strength to withstand the attacks of the enemy. Though you may have fallen in the past, you will find renewed energy so as not to slip the next time. God really does make all things new. He really does turn things around. He turns you around, and puts you on the high places, so in the future, your first gaze will be at His face and not at your problems.

Further Thought…

- Have you ever blamed God for something? Did it make you feel any better or help you resolve your problem?

- What might be a good way for you to move your attention from your problems to the Problem Solver?

- Do you remember a time when you chose to be obedient to God's word, even when you didn't want to? What were the results? Did you find yourself warming to the task of obeying God once you took the first step?

- Have you taken a seat on the battlefield and given up in the midst of the battle? God wants to refit you for war. What do you think you need to do first so as to be readied by God for the next attack?

- What would being "great" look like to you? Can you imagine having "big feet" during the next storm of life? Can you picture a surer foundation in your life? How might that help you respond differently to the trials of life?

8-27-20

PSALM 19:1-6
Encountering the Glory of God

The heavens are telling of the glory of God; and their expanse is declaring the work of His hands. 2 Day to day pours forth speech, and night to night reveals knowledge. 3 There is no speech, nor are there words; their voice is not heard. 4 Their line has gone out through all the earth, and their utterances to the end of the world. In them He has placed a tent for the sun, 5 which is as a bridegroom coming out of his chamber; it rejoices as a strong man to run his course. 6 Its rising is from one end of the heavens, and its circuit to the other end of them; and there is nothing hidden from its heat.

From ancient history, mankind has been fascinated with the study of the heavens. Twenty-six years ago, the Goseck Circle was discovered in Germany, which Archeology Magazine referred to as "possibly the world's oldest solar observatory." While it is difficult to pin an exact date on the original construction, it appears that ancient man was seeking to create a means by which he could study the solar system. If the dating system is correct for this discovery, it was built long before David became king of Israel.

It should not surprise us that David makes mention of the heavens as if they had been studied, and he mentioned the fact that the heavens speak a language of its own. What do you suppose the heavens are talking about? They are declaring their Creator's glory: *"The heavens are telling of the glory of God; and their expanse is declaring the work of His hands."*

Space is such a fascinating mystery to us, and every time we look up into the heavens, the glory of God is declared. It is difficult for us to fathom this declaration because space is beyond our knowledge. Just think for a moment about how big space is.

Because most of us can imagine the size of our own planet, let's start with the earth. The earth is about 8000 miles wide, so if you were able to bore through the middle of the earth and travel from one side to the other at sixty miles per hour, it would take you about five and one-half days to make the journey. The moon is 240,000 miles away from earth, so it would take us 167 days to get there in our space ship going sixty miles per hour. A trip to the sun would take 176 years, and a vacation across our galaxy, the Milky Way, would take a million, billion years at our designated speed of sixty miles per hour. Here's the thing. Scientists have determined that there are at least 100 billion galaxies and that space is infinite! Is it any wonder that God proclaimed the heavens declare His glory?

This declaration is a continuous, non-stop announcement of God's majesty as *"day to day pours forth speech, and night to night reveals knowledge."* When the Psalmist said every day *"pours forth speech,"* he used a word that meant to "gush forth," like the releasing of water that has been pent up behind a dam. Even as the water cannot be contained, the praises of God and the declaration of His glory cannot be stopped from this amazing aspect of His creation. Every night that passes reveals the infinite knowledge of God. Verses three and four indicate that while this speech is pouring forth, there are actually no words spoken. God's creation is a silent testimony to the power and knowledge of God. Is it any wonder that evolutionists are working so hard to cut out the tongue of this herald of God's truth?

Unbelieving scientists are so determined to remove the glory of creation from God that through the years, they have been willing to resort to distortions or outright lies. For example, the so-called *Nebraska Man* was discovered in 1922 when a Nebraska rancher discovered a tooth. In desperation to create the "missing link" to evolution, scientists applied some imagination (a lot of imagination) and created a jawbone, skull, skeleton, body, and fur. This creation was labeled *The Nebraska Man*. A London Newspaper took it a step further and created a *Nebraska Mom*. Sometime after this "great" discovery, an identical tooth was found, but this time it was still attached to a skull and a body...of a wild pig. One writer remarked, "Ironically, while scientists were attempting to make a monkey out of a pig, the pig made a monkey out of the scientists." I think Nancy Pearcey was right on target when she said, "The issue is not fundamentally a matter of evidence at all, but of a prior philosophical commitment" (*Total Truth*, 167).

Satan has been at work from the beginning to rob God of His glory, and the only way the proclamation of God's glory can be silenced from the realm of space is if secularists can somehow lead people to think the universe came into being as the result of a huge, cosmic accident. Time Magazine once summarized Darwin's assumptions with these words: "Charles Darwin didn't want to murder God, as he once put it, but he did." Regardless of what Darwin, or any other secularist attempts to do, the heavens continue to pour forth their silent witness to the authenticity of a Creator.

What does this passage mean when it says it is "*telling of the glory of God?*" The word *glory* means "praise, honor, or fame" in the English language. The Hebrew word that was used literally means "heaviness." It is as if the Psalmist is seeking to describe the indescribable, God, and he puts his finger on the one thing that can somehow express God's immeasurable vastness: space. As hard as we try to understand space, there's just more out there than we can possibly grasp. The same is true with God. It has always amazed me that some people cannot believe in God because He does not neatly fit into their capacity for understanding. Job concluded, "*How great is God—beyond our understanding*" (Job 36:26 NIV).

What does this mean for you and me? Because God is glorious and the heavens continually make this declaration, we should experience what I have heard called "appropriate smallness." We should understand our place before Almighty God and understand our only acceptable action is to bow in surrender to the One who spoke the stars into existence.

Thoughts of the heavens should also lead us to marvel at what I will call "unimaginable grace." The fact that this God, the One who spoke and everything came into being, has stooped to come to earth as a human being so He could die on a cross on our behalf and rise again from the grave should lead us to marvel and worship before a God of such abounding mercy. When we pause to consider our appropriate smallness compared to God's unimaginable grace, we come to a conclusion of His immeasurable bigness of heart. Yes—heart. God obviously thinks a lot of you and me to choose to come and live among us. The fact that the infinite God put on the limitations of man for us is mind blowing. Imagine this God needing a diaper change because He chose to become a baby so He could eventually die on a cross for me. It is indeed mind-boggling.

Tonight, as I gaze into the heavens, I will think of God's bigness, but not just the bigness of his power. I will ponder long the bigness of His heart, of His grace, and of His mercy. The heavens declare the glory of God, and it brings me to my knees in awe of this God Who loves me.

Further Thought...

- When was the last time you paused to really gaze up into the heavens? How does it make you feel?

- What is the most amazing thing about space to you? Can you think of a way that this aspect speaks specifically to the glory of God?

- How do you think the heavens reveal the "heaviness" of God?

- Is it appropriate to feel small before God? Do you think that people are sometimes too proud before God and "bigger" than they ought to be? How?

- Have you ever become proud or self-sufficient? What should you do the next time you begin to feel inappropriately big?

- Pause for a few moments and tell God how big He really is to you and what it means to you that He has been willing to embrace you for eternity.

PSALM 19:7-11
Embracing the Law of the Lord

The law of the LORD is perfect, restoring the soul; the testimony of the LORD is sure, making wise the simple. 8 The precepts of the LORD are right, rejoicing the heart; the commandment of the LORD is pure, enlightening the eyes. 9 The fear of the LORD is clean, enduring forever; the judgments of the LORD are true; they are righteous altogether. 10 They are more desirable than gold, yes, than much fine gold; sweeter also than honey and the drippings of the honeycomb. 11 Moreover, by them Your servant is warned; in keeping them there is great reward.

"More desirable than gold..." Many people will do anything for wealth. I recently read a Yahoo poll asking the question, "What would you do for a million dollars?" The answers were interesting, and sometimes funny. One man answered in a way that probably many people feel: "Just about anything."

In 1991, James Patterson and Peter Kim wrote a book called "The Day America Told the Truth," and they reported the disturbing results of a survey regarding wealth. One question posed was, "What would you do for ten million dollars?" Twenty-five percent determined they would abandon their families, twenty-three percent would become a prostitute for a week, and seven percent would kill a stranger. That means that when you are shopping at Walmart, there are at least seven to fourteen people in the store who would be willing to kill you, if the price was right. Wow!

Can you imagine anything more desirable than wealth? The Psalmist said God's law is more desirable. It is *"sweeter also than honey and the drippings of the honeycomb"* (vs. 11). Really? Do we cherish God's law that much?

What was David talking about? He begins this section with the following words: *"The law of the LORD is perfect, restoring the soul."* It seems like an abrupt transition from the previous section, but with a little study you will see the topic flows smoothly from the previous line of thinking. Whenever we read the words "*law of the Lord,*" we automatically think of the Law of Moses, the Ten Commandments, or even the whole Bible. Think about it from David's perspective. He was probably writing this around 1000 B.C., and his access to the Law of Moses was somewhat limited. I know he was the king and could have scribes read him the law whenever he wanted, but he probably did not have a leather bound copy that he read every morning for his quiet time.

We have a tendency to see the "*law of the Lord*" as either being chiseled on a stone, rolled up in a scroll, or bound up in a leather book. I think David had another thing on his mind. I'm not saying that the words that were on the stone or would have been included in a book were not part of the big picture, but for David, "*the law of the Lord*" was seen more as the "rule of life" as handed down by the Creator. Literally, the word means "instruction" or "doctrine." It is important that we get this. As we expand our understanding of "*the law of the Lord,*" we will gradually come to understand that the rule of life to which David was referring could be translated as simply "the Truth." This concept expands Psalm 19:7-11 to more than just the part of the Bible that was written during David's life, which was the Torah. It must include all of the truth of God, which means we can place all of the words from the Old Testament and New Testament into this category.

This idea must be expanded to include more than just the words on the pages of our Bible. If "the rule of life" or "God's instruction to humanity" was what David had in mind, then understanding real truth would be the very thing that would bring us our greatest joy. Jesus affirmed that it is truth that will set us free (see John 8:31-32). Understanding and receiving truth is such a critical thing that Jesus came into the world to make truth known.

Look again at what Jesus said to Pilate at His trial: "*In fact, for this reason I was born, and for this I came into the world, to testify to the truth*" (John 18:37). Jesus' mission in the world was to testify to the truth. Isn't this what King David was doing a thousand years earlier? He is saying that God's truth is perfect, and it restores the soul.

The typical pattern of Hebrew poetry is synonymous repetition, and we certainly see that in this passage of scripture. While we could focus in great detail on each of these phrases, I do want us to briefly consider the second half of this first phrase: "*restoring the soul.*" David is saying God's law, or truth, is perfect and it brings restoration to our souls. The King James Version says "*converting the soul,*" and we automatically think of our salvation. The word really means "restoring from disorder and decay." The idea is that our lives have become a disordered, spiritual mess, and it is God's truth that helps us to make sense out of life and what it means to be right with God. It is God's truth that helps us to understand the twistedness of the society around us, and it is God's truth that makes our paths straight as we walk through a crooked world.

What about your life? Is it disordered and in need of repair? Maybe you need to immerse yourself, your patterns, and your beliefs into the reservoir of God's truth. It is possible that you have begun adopting the philosophy of this age with the results being a topsy-turvy life that is missing the blessings of God and the joy of the Lord.

Can you now see the connection of verses seven through eleven to the first six verses of this chapter in the Bible? God inspired David to reflect upon the order of the universe, which moved him to think about the order of life. Even as God created everything with symmetry and purpose, our lives too have purpose and design that is built upon this underlying fact of truth. While the universe has order, sinful humanity has become disordered and broken. The only way we can be restored to God's intentional design is through adhering to the truth of God.

Now let's think for just a moment about the remaining couplets. Remember that each phrase begins with a synonym for the truth of God, and the second half shares a result of God's truth applied to our lives. You could break down each description and uncover various nuances of the truth of God, and that study would be very worthwhile. The first phrase says that God's testimony is *"making wise the simple."* This of course means the simple of mind, and it is saying that God's truth can make sharp the dullest mind. James 1:5 says *"But if any of you lacks wisdom, let him ask of God, who gives to all generously and without reproach, and it will be given to him."* God, who is Truth, gives us wisdom for daily living, and all we must do is ask for it.

Note the next two results. God's precepts are *"rejoicing the heart,"* and God's commandments are *"enlightening the eyes."* I have had so many people indicate to me throughout my life that following Christ was a burden, as if Jesus is a giant killjoy. Actually, the opposite is true. God said that ultimately keeping His law is not burdensome (see 1 John 5:3).

The Psalmist points out in our scripture for today that God's truth brings joy to the heart. It really does set us free, and after filling our hearts and our minds with God's truth, we may find ourselves doing a little happy dance. Knowing the Lord really does bring joy to our lives.

Note also that it says our eyes will be enlightened. This made me reflect upon where God led the Apostle Paul to remind us that the god of this world has blinded the eyes of unbelievers to the truth of the gospel (see 2 Corinthians 4:4). When we immerse ourselves in the truth of God, we find that our understanding is heightened and our awareness to truth and reality are keen. While we can spend our time studying all of the false teaching available in our world today, the best approach is to fill our minds with the truth of God. When we do this, false teaching becomes quickly apparent to us because it registers as being contrary to what we know to be right. Basically, this means that we are seeking to interpret the world through the lenses of God's truth instead of the lenses of the philosophy of our day. You could call that a "biblical world view." When we look at the world from God's perspective, our minds are enlightened, and we know the paths we are to take in life.

Verse eleven brings some concluding remarks by reminding us of two great results we will experience when we pursue the truth:

"Moreover, by them Your servant is warned; in keeping them there is great reward." We are warned. Warned of what? While we could probably consider numerous things, one thing that must be considered is that we are warned of consequences – the consequences of a disordered life. By loving and pursuing the truth of God, we are learning the necessary steps in pleasing and honoring God. If we choose another path, we are choosing a path of sorrow and judgment. If we pursue the philosophy of our day, we will end up disillusioned and empty. Only through Jesus can we find true joy and abundance (see John 10:10).

He says that when we keep God's laws and apply God's truth, we will find *great reward*. We're not talking about something like the prize in a box of Cracker Jacks or even the $100 given when we return our neighbor's lost puppy. We are talking about a *great reward*. It is a reward that cannot be described nor can it be contained. It is a reward of joy beyond our wildest imaginations and peace beyond compare. It is the thrill of God doing exceedingly more than we could ask or think (see Ephesians 3:20). It is the anticipation of knowing that your life is somehow connected to God's grander purpose for humanity and that every day you live is somehow being used to accomplish the eternal purposes of God. The reward is GREAT! It is the reward of knowing that your heavenly Father is pleased and that you have pronounced His name great through a life that is well lived. It is the reward of knowing that others have found life in Christ through your silent, and not so silent, testimony of the love and grace of Christ. And finally, it is the reward of hearing God say, *"Well done, My good and faithful servant"* as you enter into the glory of heaven and your eternal home with a God who gave His life for you. The reward is truly GREAT!

Further Thought...

• What are your thoughts about the meaning of the "Law of the Lord?"

- How has embracing God's truth restored your soul? Can you think of times you allowed other things to direct your steps that caused your soul to be hurt or broken?

- How have you experienced the reward of knowing the Truth of God?

- What are some ways that you can pursue God's truth? Can you think of some changes you need to incorporate into your life so you can heed the warnings and experience the rewards?

PSALM 23
The Nurturing and Compassionate Shepherd

The LORD is my shepherd; I shall not want. 2 He makes me lie down in green pastures; He leads me beside quiet waters. 3 He restores my soul; He guides me in the paths of righteousness for His name's sake. 4 Even though I walk through the valley of the shadow of death, I fear no evil, for You are with me; Your rod and Your staff, they comfort me. 5 You prepare a table before me in the presence of my enemies; You have anointed my head with oil; my cup overflows. 6 Surely goodness and lovingkindness will follow me all the days of my life, and I will dwell in the house of the LORD forever.

David ran quickly to the side of the quivering, little lamb that had cowered in a small crevice. The helpless creature hopelessly sought refuge from the charging bear and certain death. David screamed out righteous anger as he flung a stone into the air from his taut sling hitting the bear squarely between the eyes. He quickly straddled the huge creature, pulled his knife from the sheath on his side, and he slit the bear's throat. As David knelt to lovingly pick up the frightened lamb, he thought of God's tenderness and care for him. It made David think that he was God's little lamb, and God was his faithful Shepherd.

We do not know for sure all of the events and circumstances that led to David being inspired to write what is probably the most familiar passage of the Bible, the twenty-third Psalm. We know, however, that at times David thought back to encounters he had with lions and bears as he reflected upon God's faithfulness to deliver him from his enemy (see 1 Samuel 17:34-37).

While David was inspired to write numerous Psalms, none have ministered to the hearts of men and women, boys and girls, quite like this chapter. David was a man who knew about danger and heartache, and it was in the midst of various trials that David learned of God's faithfulness. He learned the principle of repeated faithfulness: if God was faithful in the past, He will be faithful in the present and the future. Scientists might call it the "Law of Probability," but we can simply call it faith.

Though the imagery of shepherd and sheep is significant in the opening words, one of the most prominent words to me is the possessive pronoun "my." Think of the intimacy and warmth of those two letters that make up one of the smallest words in the English language, but consider the profound message those two little letters shout out for the entire world to take notice. God is not just *the* Shepherd or *a* Shepherd. God is *my* Shepherd, and He longs to be experienced up close and personal.

A lot of people speak of Christianity, or of God, with vague generalities, but David understood that to be a follower of God was to have a close relationship with a cherished father. There is so much more to Christianity than quoting creeds or attending religious functions. It's more than daily rituals or religious habits. Becoming a Christ follower moves us into a love relationship with God that is real, intimate, and personal. While this relationship affects our habits and may be expressed in creeds, it must be more than just form and function. It is a relationship, an experience that affects every part of our lives. Can you say that God is *your* Shepherd?

The shepherd/sheep relationship was one of the closest relationships known to the Jews, outside of the relationship between a husband and a wife. This relationship depicted gentleness, love, compassion, and provision. From the sheep's perspective, it represented dependence, need, and trust. It is interesting that of all the visual images God gave to describe His relationship with His followers, David was led to choose the imagery of a shepherd and sheep.

While a little lamb seems so cute and huggable, it is really a very dumb animal. It has a small brain and lacks the ability to reason and understand. It can quickly grow nervous and can easily die from fear, if circumstances grow dire. Sheep are totally dependent upon the shepherd for life and health. David confessed that God is his

Shepherd. Because God is his Shepherd, there is nothing in his life that he lacks. If you think about it, that is really quite a statement: *"I shall not want."* You can't say that unless you have a faithful Shepherd who loves you and is willing to give His life in order to meet your needs.

Look at the next series of statements describing God's faithfulness and provision: *"He makes me lie down in green pastures; He leads me beside quiet waters. He restores my soul."* The *"green pastures"* are a picture of God's provision while the *"quiet waters"* are a picture of God's peace. Sheep cannot, or will not, drink from rushing water. The noise and chaos of a loud stream brings confusion and fear. God takes us to *"quiet waters"* to meet our needs because He not only knows of our physical needs, such as water, but of our emotional struggles as well.

Our need for a restored soul speaks to the brokenness of our lives. There are so many things that cause us sorrow and heartache, but God restores our soul. We can look at this phrase from a New Testament perspective and even be grateful for the salvation our Shepherd has provided us through the cross. Our salvation brings an eternal restoration to our broken lives.

The next phrase moves us to spiritual considerations without doubt: *"He guides me in the paths of righteousness for His name's sake."* Again, it is impossible for us not to consider these words without Calvary on our minds. Because of Christ's death on the cross, we can know the righteousness of Christ. God led Paul to write in 2 Corinthians 5:21: *"He made Him who knew no sin to be sin on our behalf, so that we might become the righteousness of God in Him."*

Through our relationship with the Shepherd, we take on His righteousness, but He also leads us to choose righteousness. This does not mean that Christians never sin, but it does mean that God gives us a new nature and a new capacity and hunger for righteous living. Because He is our Shepherd, He really does lead us down the right path. May the words of Psalm 119:35 be our prayer and our declaration: *"Make me walk in the path of Your commandments, for I delight in it."*

David reflected on the fact that our Shepherd guides us in paths of righteousness *"for His name's sake."* This idea really carries two concepts. One idea focuses on our perspective and the other one upon God's. We are led down righteous paths because we carry God's name. Whatever we do flows out of our new nature and gives testimony to the authenticity of our God. Does it bother you when you see a Christian acting in a way that is in stark contrast to the name they wear? Sometimes our actions and our profession do not exactly agree.

I once had a guy get angry with me on I-285 because I momentarily forgot that even though the speed limit says fifty-five miles per hour, you are supposed to go seventy-five. What was I thinking? The guy tailgated me for a bit and then zoomed around me giving me the 'evil eye' when he passed. He probably learned the 'evil eye' from his mother or maybe he read about it in his Bible (it is mentioned a few times in certain translations). I think he had a Bible because when he got in front of me, I saw the Christian "fish" symbol on a bumper sticker on the back of his car. Maybe it was his wife's car.

The other perspective considers the word *"for"* a little differently. It could be used to indicate cause as if to say, *"He leads us in paths of righteousness because of His name."* This would say that God does certain things because of His nature and character. We know that to be true. There are certain things God must do and attitudes He must display because of His nature. Our inner character always shows, in one way or another. Because God loves us and because God is righteous, He must lead us on the best path, which is the path of righteousness. This is an important thought because we can always know that God's ways are always the right ways. He will never lead us in a direction that is not right, and He can never act in a way contrary to righteousness. This means that even when things God is doing do not seem right, they are. Even when His commandments do not seem to make sense, they are not only a suggested way for us to take, but rather they are the only way we are to take if we are going to follow our Lord.

Even when we go through circumstances that come close to our death, we will find God's comforting presence. David said that in those challenging circumstances when his death seemed close at hand, he would not be afraid. This is a statement of total trust in God's mercy, love, and sovereignty. While we should cherish life and do everything in our power to preserve it, death will eventually come, and at some point, death will be a part of God's plan for our eternity. For the Christian, death is the door through which we all must go to enter into our eternal life. I do know there will be some Christians alive at the return of Christ for His Church, and it certainly could be our generation, but if not, we will all die. It is a guarantee, as stated by Hebrews 9:27: *"It is appointed for men to die once and after this comes judgment."*

We may have more than one close encounter with death in our lives, and we can be certain that God is with us when the shadow passes over our lives. We need not fear evil. Our Shepherd will walk with us even through those dark nights of confusion and pain. It is because of this verse that I believe when we die, we will not cross over to the other side alone. I do not know how God will do it, but somehow He will walk with us during the moment when we seem to be most alone.

Verse five is an interesting verse and difficult for us to understand. Jewish custom led Israelites to value highly their guests. It gave a host significant responsibility for the guest's safety. Think back to the story of Lot in Sodom (see Genesis 19). When the angels came to his home to warn him of the impending doom, the men of the city wanted to take Lot's guests for immoral purposes. Lot replied to their demands by pleading for the men not to harm his guests by asking them to *"do nothing to these men, inasmuch as they have come under the shelter of my roof."*

In Psalm twenty-three, God is saying that we have entered into the protection and provision of His home. Even in the presence of our enemies, God holds them back and provides for us nourishment for strength and companionship for comfort.

When David said, *"You have anointed my head with oil; my cup overflows,"* he was saying that God has given us the best of everything.

The word *"anointed"* is not the same word used when describing the process of anointing a king, but rather the word literally meant "fat." It came to provide a picture of generously pouring perfume on the head of a guest in the midst of a joyous celebration. Surely, we find joy and celebration in the presence of our heavenly Father.

The final verse is a promise of God's steadfast love, consistent presence, and eternal provision. He says His *"lovingkindness will follow me all the days of my life."* This word *"follow"* literally means "pursue." Think about that. It is almost the picture of a lover wooing his beloved or a shepherd running after a wayward sheep. He will never leave us. His goodness and grace will pursue us all of our days, and we will ultimately find great joy in the eternal presence of our God who led us safely home.

Further Thought…

- Do you consider Jesus to be *your* Shepherd? What does the possessive pronoun, *my*, mean to you?

- What do you do when you find yourself in a time of need? In light of this passage of scripture, what should you do?

- Can you think of a time when God led you to "green pastures" or "quiet waters?"

- Do you find yourself in need of restoration? Brokenness can come from a lot of places, like sin, sorrow, or failure. What would you need to do in order to allow God to bring restoration?

- What does it mean to you to think about God's *"rod"* and *"staff"* comforting you? A rod or staff could have been used for a variety of purposes: guidance, discipline, or even protection. Have you ever seen God work in your life in one of these ways?

- Re-read the last verse. Can you say with David that *surely* God's lovingkindness is pursuing you? Take just a moment and think about what it will be like dwelling with God forever.

- Thank God for being your Shepherd.

PSALM 24

Becoming a Part of the "In Crowd"

*The earth is the LORD'S, and all it contains, the world, and those who dwell in it.
2 For He has founded it upon the seas and established it upon the rivers. 3 Who
may ascend into the hill of the LORD? And who may stand in His holy place? 4
He who has clean hands and a pure heart, who has not lifted up his soul to falsehood and has not sworn deceitfully. 5 He shall receive a blessing from the LORD
and righteousness from the God of his salvation. 6 This is the generation of those
who seek Him, who seek Your face—even Jacob. Selah. 7 Lift up your heads, O
gates, and be lifted up, O ancient doors, that the King of glory may come in! 8 Who
is the King of glory? The LORD strong and mighty, the LORD mighty in battle. 9
Lift up your heads, O gates, and lift them up, O ancient doors, that the King of
glory may come in! 10 Who is this King of glory? The LORD of hosts, He is the
King of glory. Selah*

Members only! Have you ever been a part of a select group with its
accompanying privileges? When I was twelve and thirteen years old, I
was a member of the Elks' Club swim team and diving team. Even
though I was a member of the swim team, my family and I were not
members of the Elks' Club. What this meant for me was that I was
allowed to come to practice every morning at 8:00, but as soon as
practice was over, I had to get out of the pool. Only members could
swim during regular hours.

Psalm twenty-four introduces some of the "members only" privileges of being a follower of God. Even as with the Psalms we have
considered up to this point, God inspired David to write this Psalm as
well. He began by writing of God's ownership of the world. The first
two verses almost seem to be separate from the section beginning in
verse three, but with some thought, you might see the connection.

There is a sense in which every creature on planet earth is a part of a special society simply called "God's creation." This is why David concluded, *"The earth is the LORD'S, and all it contains, the world, and those who dwell in it."* Whether you are a Christ-follower or not, you belong to the Lord. You are His creation thereby making you God's property. I recently built some book shelves. I'm actually kind of proud of them, but if you looked at them, you might not be so proud. I like them because I bought the materials, and then I constructed the shelves. I also like them because they work, and they were cheap, or rather "inexpensive." My point is that my book shelves are mine because I created them. God made you, so whether you acknowledge it or not, you belong to God. That does sort of make you a part of a special group.

Unfortunately, ownership by virtue of creation does not guarantee that heaven is your home. The Bible says that *"the person who sins will die"* (Ezekiel 18:20), which means that every human being is destined to eternal death, or separation, from God because *"all have sinned"* (see Romans 3:23). Though every person is a member of the human race, every person does not have the "members only" privileges of being a part of God's family. That comes through repentance and faith in Jesus Christ.

The second section focuses on what it takes to really be a part of God's family. Keep in mind that God is inspiring these words to be written about 1000 years before Jesus was even born. Though Jesus existed, because He is eternal, He had not yet made His grand entrance into humanity.

We can gain a full understanding of these words by connecting these truths to additional thoughts in the New Testament. Note how David began this section with a question: *"Who may ascend into the hill of the LORD? And who may stand in His holy place?"* What did the Psalmist mean by asking this question? The euphemism *"the hill of the Lord"* pointed to the geographical location of the temple. Though the actual temple was built by David's son, Solomon, the Ark of the Covenant was returned to Jerusalem during David's reign and placed in a tent.

This tent, and later the temple, was positioned on a raised portion of Jerusalem, which meant worshipers ascended the hill as they made their way to worship. This is why some of the Psalms are called "Songs of Ascent." As the words of this Psalm were written, however, David was speaking about more than just climbing the hill to have a religious experience. We could equate it in modern-day thinking to the fact that David was talking about more than just going to church.

In this passage, God is calling us to a personal encounter with Himself. He is basically asking the question, "Who can enjoy an intimate relationship with God?" The answer to this loaded question deals with one's character and personal holiness: *"He who has clean hands and a pure heart, who has not lifted up his soul to falsehood and has not sworn deceitfully."* If you think about this reply and compare these words to the actions of people, our conclusion might be that no one can ascend the hill and enjoy a personal relationship with God. The *"clean hands and pure heart"* is obviously talking about moral righteousness and clean motives. The follow-up statement also calls for moral purity as it relates to dishonesty. We should not be surprised that God says He cannot have fellowship and receive worship from one who is deceitful and dishonest. King Solomon was inspired by God to write in Proverbs 12:22, *"Lying lips are an abomination to the LORD, but those who deal faithfully are His delight."* Consider Proverbs 6:16-19 where God says He *"hates"* seven different things and calls them an *"abomination."* Two of these things deal with dishonesty: *"a lying tongue"* and *"a false witness who utters lies."*

Once again, we must ask who can climb the hill leading into God's inner chamber of intimate fellowship. Is there a human being alive who has not done something with a wrong motive at some point or been dishonest? I think we can all agree that all of our hands have been dirty with sin, so maybe we should consider another question. How do we get our hands clean? The only means by which our sin can be forgiven and our lives made clean is through repentance and faith. In the Old Testament, repentance and faith were tied to sacrifices of animals while in the New Testament (and today), repentance and faith are tied to the sacrifice of Jesus. Only through Jesus can we stand before God with clean hands. Romans 5:1 indicates that *"having been justified by faith, we have peace with God through our Lord Jesus Christ."* I would say that *"peace with God"* could be synonymous with ascending the hill of the Lord and standing in His holy place.

Verse five says that the person who enjoys fellowship with God will *"receive a blessing from the LORD and righteousness from the God of his salvation."* Can you imagine a greater blessing than enjoying fellowship with Jesus Christ?

This verse also points to the New Testament idea of imputed righteousness. It says that our righteousness does not come through our own efforts of perfection, but rather our righteousness is from God. This is a hard truth to grasp, but it is very liberating. As badly as we want to be righteous and obedient to God, you will probably always find ways that you fall short. Satan loves to remind you of all of your failures, and he seeks to create in you a defeated and hopeless spirit. You and I need to remind ourselves often that our righteousness actually comes from Christ and not from our own efforts. I do not want to minimize our desire and efforts to choose to obey Christ, and I do not want to minimalize the seriousness of sin in our lives. However, we must understand that we are made righteous through repentance and faith in Jesus Christ and His finished work on the cross.

There is another thing that the person will do who desires to worship our glorious God and enjoy His fellowship. This person will be a seeker. The Psalmist announced, *"This is the generation of those who seek Him, who seek Your face."* Do you really want an intimate relationship with God? The Bible says that the person who enjoys a close relationship with God is one who seeks God's face. I think there is something to the fact that God says we seek His *"face."* Remember, as stated in a previous chapter, that God said we could never see His face and live. Here we are told to seek His face. He is using a description that gives a ready picture of closeness and personal warmth. God is saying that we can know Him "face to face."

There are very few people in my life that can get face to face with me. Think about it for just a minute. I love the pastors with whom I work, but it would just be weird for them to get too close to my face. I suppose we could do that man hug thing and slap each other on the back two times, but that's about as intimate as it gets. Even when you hug someone in Christian fellowship, you're not really face to face. I guess your cheeks might get within close proximity as your face is moving toward the right side of your friend's head. I get face to face with my wife, and that gesture usually ends in a kiss. If you think about it, the only people you get face to face with are people you are about to kiss: spouse, children, and grandchildren. Seeking God's face is a picture of intimacy and love. It points to an unusually close fellowship and deep abiding love that you can have with your Creator.

Intimacy with God leads to the final expression of worship David emphasized in the last section of this Psalm by repeating the words twice: "*Lift up your heads, O gates, and be lifted up, O ancient doors, that the King of glory may come in! Who is the King of glory? The LORD strong and mighty, the LORD mighty in battle.*" Knowing God rightfully leads to worship. With David's opening words in this verse, one has a mental picture of the gates of the ancient temple swinging open so the real King of Glory can make a grand, regal entrance. It makes me wonder if we welcome in the King of Glory as we gather weekly to worship. Can you imagine the spiritual fervor and passionate worship if we really did welcome in the King of kings every time we gathered as a church? This idea also gives me a little spiritual lift as I anticipate another grand entrance by the King at His second coming.

When we welcome God's presence in our midst, it causes us to recognize Him as the "*King of Glory*" and as "*the Lord strong and mighty*" and "*mighty in battle.*" Once again, God chose to use His personal name, Yahweh, to describe Himself, and most editors use all capital letters for the word "*LORD*" to indicate this special Hebrew word. When we encounter our glorious Lord and deepen our walk with Him, we enjoy fellowship with the God Who loves us, and we worship the One Who is worthy of our supreme devotion and love.

Further Thought...

- Have you ever considered the fact that God owns everything? What does that mean to you?

- Make a list of some of the main things you consider yours, and remind yourself that they actually belong to God. Take a moment to tell God that you recognize these things as belonging to Him, and pledge yourself to be a faithful steward over His possessions.

- Are you included in the "members' only" group? If you have turned from your sin and placed your faith in Christ Jesus, you are a member of God's family. Are you part of the *"generation of those who seek Him?"* As God describes the people with whom He can have fellowship, would you be able to enjoy that kind of intimacy with God?

- How do you maintain clean hands and a pure heart?

- Are you regularly seeking the face of God? What are you doing to seek Him?

- Take just a moment to pray verses seven and eight back to God: *"Lift up your heads, O gates, and be lifted up, O ancient doors, that the King of glory may come in! 8 Who is the King of glory? The LORD strong and mighty, the LORD mighty in battle."*

PSALM 27

Overcoming Fear

The LORD is my light and my salvation; whom shall I fear? The LORD is the defense of my life; whom shall I dread? 2 When evildoers came upon me to devour my flesh, my adversaries and my enemies, they stumbled and fell. 3 Though a host encamp against me, my heart will not fear; though war arise against me, in spite of this I shall be confident. 4 One thing I have asked from the LORD, that I shall seek: That I may dwell in the house of the LORD all the days of my life, to behold the beauty of the LORD and to meditate in His temple. 5 For in the day of trouble He will conceal me in His tabernacle; in the secret place of His tent He will hide me; He will lift me up on a rock. 6 And now my head will be lifted up above my enemies around me, and I will offer in His tent sacrifices with shouts of joy; I will sing, yes, I will sing praises to the LORD. 7 Hear, O LORD, when I cry with my voice, and be gracious to me and answer me. 8 When You said, "Seek My face," my heart said to You, "Your face, O LORD, I shall seek." 9 Do not hide Your face from me, do not turn Your servant away in anger; You have been my help; do not abandon me nor forsake me, O God of my salvation! 10 For my father and my mother have forsaken me, but the LORD will take me up. 11 Teach me Your way, O LORD, and lead me in a level path because of my foes. 12 Do not deliver me over to the desire of my adversaries, for false witnesses have risen against me, and such as breathe out violence. 13 I would have despaired unless I had believed that I would see the goodness of the LORD in the land of the living. 14 Wait for the LORD; be strong and let your heart take courage; yes, wait for the LORD.

Have you ever really been afraid? It's one thing to experience the childhood fear of monsters, but how do you overcome adult fears? Even as adults, some of our fears are totally unjustified, but some adversaries are real and formidable. You may struggle with the fear of looming financial disaster or irreversible, terminal illness. It is possible that the uncertainties of the future have created great concern in your life, and your fear is not for yourself but for what could happen to your children. Your fear could even be a persistent phobia that is irrational to others but very real to you. What do you do with debilitating fear?

David faced this kind of enemy and conquered it with the Lord's help. In the opening verse of this Psalm, he made three declarations that give us a clue as to how David dealt with potential fear: *"The LORD is my light and my salvation; whom shall I fear? The LORD is the defense of my life; whom shall I dread?"* This declaration is key to how David dealt with fear in his life, so let's consider each statement individually.

"The Lord is my light." You could take this statement literally because God gives evidence to His physical radiance in a variety of places in the Bible (consider the Shekinah glory in the Old Testament and the pillar of fire for the Children of Israel in the wilderness). Deuteronomy 4:24 calls God a *"consuming fire."* Jesus even said, *"I am the light of the world"* (see John 8:12).

Though we could take this description literally, I believe David is speaking figuratively. He could have been referring to God as being a guide to his life. In Psalm 119:105, God's word is seen as a *"lamp"* to our feet and a *"light"* to our path. David could have been referring to times of potential darkness in which he had lived in the past. It could have been the darkness of despair and depression or the darkness of sin, but in the midst of these times, God always came forth to illumine his way. So, the light may have been beams of hope or rays of encouragement.

It is also possible that the Lord acted as light in David's life by illuminating sin during times of rebellion. Nathan, the prophet, came to David after David had committed sin with Bathsheba and insured the death of her husband. God used the prophet to confront the king and to call him to repentance. There is nothing quite as chilling as Nathan's words *"You are the man! Thus says the LORD God of Israel"* (see 2 Samuel 12). All of these thoughts are true, and maybe David had one particular application in mind. The fact, however, is that God is a light to us.

The Lord is also our *"salvation."* It is easy to imagine David's train of thought with this declaration. As he wrote these words, he could have thought back to his short, but very impactful battle with the giant, Goliath, in the Valley of Elah. It is possible he was thinking of the times God delivered him from the bear or the lion, or maybe he was thinking of his narrow escape from King Saul.

Regardless of the circumstances, David had been in serious trouble at various points in his life, and God saved him from impending doom. To say that *"the Lord is my salvation"* indicates that we stand in need of a Savior. It is significant the Psalmist didn't just say that God gives salvation but rather God *is* salvation. Saving is as much a part of His nature as creating or loving. God is your salvation because you need saving. God is your salvation because there is no other means by which you can be saved (see Acts 4:12).

David also declared that God is *"the defense of my life."* Again, consider all the things the King could have declared to be his defense. He could have spoken of his great army, his numerous chariots, his swift horses, or the wall built strategically around the city of Jerusalem. David recognized that all of this paled in comparison to the mighty strength of God Almighty.

Lloyd John Ogilvie, former pastor of First Presbyterian Church in Hollywood, once asserted, "What a person thinks about God will determine what he does about his problem." Do you look at your problem and think you have a big God or do you look at God and think you have a big problem? The Psalmist expressed it well in Psalm 20:7 *"Some trust in chariots and some in horses, but we trust in the name of the LORD our God"* (NIV). David, as well as the rest of Israel, learned from their history that the greatest army in the world was never enough. I'm sure the initial defeat at Ai (see Joshua 8) had been told many times throughout the years, and many Israelites were well aware of how important it was to trust in God as their defense.

In what do you trust? It is easy to trust in your own preparation or prowess. Your confidence may be in our nation's military might or in some particular weapon that may give us the upper hand in battle. If so, you will discover that every defense has its weakness, but God is all powerful and will never fail you.

Notice the different words used in verses two and three to describe David's adversaries: *"evildoers, my adversaries and my enemies, a host, and war."* These enemies were indeed formidable, but they did not strike fear into the heart of the king because he had placed his trust and hope in God. He said, *"in spite of this I shall be confident."* His confidence was not in his own strength, but rather it was in the Lord.

I know the value of confidence, and I can readily acknowledge that I have been able to accomplish certain things in life simply because I first believed that I could do it. When I was on the diving team as a young teen, I found that self-confidence was half the battle for learning new dives. Physical ability was important, but my feet would never leave the diving board if I did not first convince myself that the complex twists and turns could be accomplished.

While self-confidence is good, it is important that we go deeper and understand that we have these abilities only because God has given them to us. For example, a dive with two-and-a-half flips and a twist off the high dive could only be accomplished because God gave me the physical ability to do it. I had to learn that the best kind of self-confidence was a God-confidence. It is like what Paul avowed in Philippians 4:13: *"I can do all things through Him who strengthens me."*

Verses four through six take us a little deeper into the thinking of the Psalmist as we discover his real passion for life and motivation for victory. He had one great desire: *"That I may dwell in the house of the LORD all the days of my life, to behold the beauty of the LORD and to meditate in His temple."*

He began this section by saying, *"One thing I have asked from the LORD."* Think about that for just a moment. If you could ask only one thing from God, what would it be? I can think of quite a list, and I would have a hard time deciding which thing is the most important. David narrowed it down to the one most important thing. More than anything, he wanted to dwell with God so he could behold God's beauty. This does not sound like a hands-off, distant kind of experience, but rather it sounds like a "God, up close and personal" kind of relationship. King David learned to focus on God and not on his problems.

David understood that out of the context of his growing relationship with God, God would *"conceal me in His tabernacle; in the secret place of His tent He will hide me; He will lift me up on a rock."* It is as if the king understood that the only place that was safe was the presence of God. He wanted God to *"conceal"* him. Have you ever had a need to just hide away? David discovered that when God hides you, you will not only be protected, but you will be lifted up. Maybe you have fallen, or at least, you are teetering. You can find great comfort in knowing that God says when you hide in Him, He will lift you up on a rock.

This should lead to the most engaging and passionate worship of your life. It will possibly include *"shouts of joy"* and singing. Yes, you may shout, and even though you may be one who thinks he is unable to sing, you will be singing to the top of your voice to the glory of God. Whenever we lose ourselves in thoughts of God, singing and worship are natural by-products. The Bible says that singing is an evidence of being filled with the Spirit (see Ephesians 5:18-21).

Shouting, or at least emotional responses, are a natural by-product of joy and gratitude. Have you ever been so full of joy that you just had to shout? Christianity should lead to that on a regular basis. We need to choose not to be so dignified that we can't express our love and joy before the Lord. David told his critical wife, "I will become even more undignified than this" (see 2 Samuel 6:22) when she criticized him for his lack of dignity. She didn't like it when he danced through the streets of Jerusalem as the Ark of the Covenant was returned to the Jewish capital city. Do you think Christians today are ever too dignified to truly worship and celebrate God?

While speaking during one of the lowest points of the Great Depression, Franklin D. Roosevelt declared, "The only thing you have to fear is fear itself." I think he was saying that fear can be a great enemy as it can be debilitating. We need to put on faith in order to conquer fear. Our faith is in the Almighty, all consuming, gracious, and merciful Heavenly Father. Fear can be conquered when we realize God is always bigger than the obstacles.

How do we put on faith not fear? God offers two words of instruction regarding this. The first one is in verse eight, "*Seek My face,*" and the second is found in the final verse of this chapter: "*Wait for the LORD; be strong and let your heart take courage; yes, wait for the LORD.*" These two instructions overlap in that we seek God's face by waiting for the Lord.

An integral, faith-producing discipline that we should employ when seeking God's face is reading and studying God's word. Romans 10:17 says, "*So faith comes from hearing, and hearing by the word of Christ.*" Meaningful time spent in reading and listening to God's word will strengthen your faith and prepare you for the unexpected twists and turns of life. Often times Satan wants to cause us to think that something bad happened to us because we didn't have enough faith, as if faith is something we work up from within our hearts. We do not generate faith. Faith is a by-product of an intimate relationship with God. We cannot manipulate God by generating faith. Forcing faith out of a cold, distant heart does not result in an intimate relationship with God that forces Him to act on our behalf. It is a white-hot, love relationship with our heavenly Father that grows an undeniable, unstoppable faith. I once read, "Faith is the outer manifestation of an inner heart in communion with God."

Note the second part of the equation to overcoming fear: waiting on God. Isaiah 40:31 says that when we wait before the Lord, we will find new strength: "*Yet those who wait for the LORD will gain new strength; they will mount up with wings like eagles, they will run and not get tired, they will walk and not become weary.*" Unfortunately, we often think that God is supposed to bend to our wishes and act according to our schedules and agendas. We forget that He is God, and we are not. Being quiet and waiting before the Lord is a difficult discipline, but it is well worth it. I do not have space in this chapter to go into great detail about what we should do as we wait, but you should mark it down that your time of waiting involves prayer, fasting, worship, and Bible reading.

We are in much too big of a hurry, and we often determine that if God does not act quickly, His answer must be "No." We may think He must not be listening to our prayers today. I am convinced that we miss out on really knowing God because we create time constraints in which God must act. Waiting means that God is Sovereign, and we are not. It means we are on His schedule not our own. It means that we are willing to spend the rest of our lives patiently seeking Him, if that's what it takes. His response and answers are His prerogative and not our own. After spending time quietly waiting before the celestial throne of God, we will slowly begin to realize that the things that had once overwhelmed us have slowly become increasingly small. The once large mountain has been diminished to a small mound of dirt.

Fears are real and problems are intimidating, but God is bigger and faith is liberating. Will you allow God to be your light and salvation? Can God be the defense of your life? Of course, He can, but you must seek His face and wait patiently before Him. In the waiting, you will find that you are in the perfect place for His transforming work to be done in your life.

Further Thought...

- Have you ever thought about God as being your light? What would that mean in your life?

- Do you struggle with fear? Write down the top three things that bring fear to your heart. How does knowing God set up a defense in your life against these fears?

- What are some things you can do to seek God's face? Make a list. Are you doing these things now? If not, are you willing to incorporate them into your life now?

- When you contemplate the greatness and goodness of God, do you ever feel like shouting? Do you find that you are more expressive in your worship during personal worship or corporate worship (Sunday morning church)? What would *"shouts of joy"* look like to you in your times of worship?

- Are you a singer? If not, why not? God has made you to sing. Would you be willing to lift your voice up to God in a song of praise? Why not do so right now?

- Do you like to wait on someone? Is it difficult to wait on God? What are some things you can do that will make the waiting more productive?

PSALM 31:14-24

What to do When Your Surrounded

But as for me, I trust in You, O LORD, I say, "You are my God." 15 *My times are in Your hand; deliver me from the hand of my enemies and from those who persecute me.* 16 *Make Your face to shine upon Your servant; save me in Your lovingkindness.* 17 *Let me not be put to shame, O LORD, for I call upon You; let the wicked be put to shame, let them be silent in Sheol.* 18 *Let the lying lips be mute, which speak arrogantly against the righteous with pride and contempt.* 19 *How great is Your goodness, which You have stored up for those who fear You, which You have wrought for those who take refuge in You, before the sons of men!* 20 *You hide them in the secret place of Your presence from the conspiracies of man; You keep them secretly in a shelter from the strife of tongues.* 21 *Blessed be the LORD, for He has made marvelous His lovingkindness to me in a besieged city.* 22 *As for me, I said in my alarm, "I am cut off from before Your eyes;" nevertheless You heard the voice of my supplications when I cried to You.* 23 *O love the LORD, all you His godly ones! The LORD preserves the faithful and fully recompenses the proud doer.* 24 *Be strong and let your heart take courage, all you who hope in the LORD.*

I think that somewhere hidden within my life is a stifled cowboy. Maybe every little boy wants to be a cowboy, and every man has a secret wish to saddle up and ride off into the sunset. While I was in college, I read every one of Louis L'Amour's books in the Sacket series. I know I should have been reading about biology and western civilization, but at least I learned how to get out of a crunch when holed up in a boxed-in canyon. I haven't had to worry about a boxed-in canyon yet, but when it does happen, I'm going to be ready.

One of my favorite movies while growing up was *Butch Cassidy and the Sundance Kid*. Let's forget for a moment that these two were actually outlaws. One of the last scenes shows the two bandits in Bolivia after failing to leave a life of crime. They were discovered in town with stolen mules and money, and the Bolivian army surrounded them. The movie shows the outlaws going out in a blaze of glory with pistols drawn and bullets flying.

Have you ever felt surrounded? So maybe Butch Cassidy and the Sundance Kid deserved being apprehended by the authorities, but you're one of the good guys. What do you do when the "*besieged city*" is actually your life?

David started this Psalm off in verses one and two with these words: "*In You, O LORD, I have taken refuge; Let me never be ashamed; In Your righteousness deliver me. Incline Your ear to me, rescue me quickly; be to me a rock of strength.*" Have you picked up on the fact that David seemed to spend his life being attacked and surrounded? Is it any wonder that many of us feel so drawn to the Psalms? Our lives really are lived out on the battlefield, and we find that many days are spent simply firing and reloading. Hopefully, you're not *really* firing and reloading, but it sure feels like you are under constant assault. God offers us some encouragement during times we feel as if our lives are under siege.

Today's scripture picks up in verse fourteen of the thirty-first chapter of Psalms: "*But as for me, I trust in You, O LORD, I say, 'You are my God.'*" It is as if David is saying that it doesn't really matter how big the army is that is surrounding him, he will trust in the Lord. There are some days that our battles seem overwhelming, and we are not sure we can make it out alive. Our declaration must be like David's.

In the previous verse (13) he stated that he had been slandered, surrounded by terror, and his life had been threatened. In the midst of that, David pronounced his trust in God. When he said "*Lord,*" he used the personal name of God, Yahweh. I have already written about this name of God as being connected to Moses' experience at the burning bush. It is the name God chose for Himself that means "I Am Who I Am." In other words, He is the God of the present tense.

Note that within this verse, David used two different names for God: Yahweh and Elohim. The second name meant heavenly being or deity. With these two words, David speaks specifically of the God who delivered the Israelites from bondage and says that He is David's deity.

In a culture surrounded by false gods, it is significant that the most powerful man in the world declares that Jehovah God is the One he chooses to trust and serve.

We too are surrounded by numerous gods: materialism, naturalism, personal achievement, sex, etc. All of these gods, and more, are vying for our affection and devotion, but we must make our own declaration stating our devotion to the One true God. Can you connect to a time in your life when you may have felt surrounded? Can you really say with David, *"As for me, I trust in the Lord?"*

His next statement is significant, and we must share his conviction: *"My times are in Your hand; deliver me from the hand of my enemies and from those who persecute me."* First of all, it is difficult once again to determine exactly to which enemy he refers. It doesn't really matter, because we all have various enemies. I'm not speaking of a friend who treated us badly or a spouse who is not acting in love toward us. The Bible says we are in a spiritual battle, and our enemy is not made up of flesh and blood (see Ephesians 6:12). Without trying to fully define our enemy, can we acknowledge that our times are in God's hands?

When he used the word *"times,"* he was saying that both his entire life and the unique circumstances of his life were under God's control. If we are going to overcome all of our enemies, we must be able to state with David that we have fully trusted God with the days, minutes, and seconds of our lives. Life is lived in seconds and milliseconds, and spiritual battles are won in the tiny clicks of life's clock. We have a tendency to focus on the larger passages of time, but spiritual faithfulness and victories are experienced on a much smaller scale. If you want to win the spiritual battles, you must defeat the enemy in the seconds of life. These seconds of victory eventually make up an hour, a day, a year, and ultimately, a lifetime. All of your times must be in God's hands.

In this prayer, David calls out to God for help with what I will simply call a prayer for proximity. He is asking God to be near. The great news is that as Christians, we now have the wonderful abiding presence of the Holy Spirit in our lives, which means we always live in close proximity to God. We can thank God that not only does His face shine *upon* us, but He also shines from *within* us. I believe that David's prayer actually contains symbolic words asking for God's favor, but from a New Testament perspective, we know that God's favor comes as we yield to the urging and pleading of the Holy Spirit Who lives within our hearts. We realize this favor as we yield to God's sovereign control over our lives.

Verses nineteen through twenty-one present David as the supplicant and worshipper focusing on the character of God. He first declared God's *goodness,* which God has *"stored up for those who fear"* Him and for *"those who take refuge in"* Him. Think for a moment about a God who is good. This means that He does not have the capacity for anything contrary to goodness. To say God is good is to say He is pleasant, agreeable, excellent, valuable, benevolent, and kind. This means that there are no defects or contradictions in God. You cannot add anything to His nature to make Him more complete or to cause Him to act in a better way.

This truth also means that He is the source of all things that are good. James 1:17 says, *"Every good thing given and every perfect gift is from above, coming down from the Father of lights, with Whom there is no variation or shifting shadow."* This verse means that when something good comes into your life, it is a reflection of a good God who gives good gifts to His children. David exclaimed that God's goodness is *"great."* It is difficult to describe or categorize the goodness of God. It can't really be measured nor can it be understood. He could just simply say it is *"great."*

One thing God does out of His goodness is provide us protection. David said, *"You hide them in the secret place of Your presence from the conspiracies of man."* I wrote previously about being *"concealed"* by God, but note in this passage we are hidden in *"the secret place of Your presence."* This is really a great thought. We find security and protection from being in the presence of God. It is true that every human being lives in God's presence. Even the Psalmist pointed to the omnipresence of God in

Psalm 139:7-10: *"Where can I go from Your Spirit? Or where can I flee from Your presence? If I ascend to heaven, You are there; if I make my bed in Sheol, behold, You are there. If I take the wings of the dawn, if I dwell in the remotest part of the sea, even there Your hand will lead me, and Your right hand will lay hold of me."*

There is a difference between God's omnipresence and God's realized presence. God is everywhere at the same time, but while this is a reality, it is also true that not everyone realizes the presence of God. Even for us as believers, there are times that God's presence seems more real than other times. I do not think it is necessarily that God is actually more present at one time than He is at others, but rather, I think it is that we are more aware of His presence because our spiritual senses are more tuned in and cognizant of God's manifestation of Himself. It is this realized presence that offers comfort and security to the believer who is in the midst of a spiritual conflict.

The Psalmist overflows with gratitude and worship in verse twenty-one when he acknowledged, *"Blessed be the LORD, for He has made marvelous His lovingkindness to me in a besieged city."* The translation of the last two words has brought about considerable debate, and you will find translators use different English words in an attempt to capture the meaning of the Hebrew text. The word literally means "under siege," and this makes some scholars wonder if David is making a specific reference here to real struggles of Israel at a specific time. It is possible that the Psalmist was simply using the imagery of a city under siege to give the readers an image of the spiritual conflict that is inevitable for one who follows God.

God's mercy and grace is *"marvelous"* in response to the spiritual attacks and conflicts believers face every day. At times, our lives must feel like a besieged city, but God always comes through and brings deliverance. Do you ever feel surrounded by your spiritual enemy – kind of like a besieged city? While you could respond in a variety of ways, one of the best responses you can give is to stop and worship God.

In response to this spiritual siege, David challenged those who follow God to *"be strong and let your heart take courage, all you who hope in the LORD."* God wants us to be strong in the midst of conflict and challenge. He wants us to be courageous and not give in to the gentle calls and strong temptations around us. Instead of placing your hope in things that are sure to change and do not hold the answers for eternity, the Psalmist calls us to *"hope in the Lord."* If your hope is in other people, you will eventually be disappointed. If your hope is in the government, you will eventually be let down. We can take courage if our hope is in the Lord. What gives you hope? Your circumstances may be overwhelming and your future prospects may be less than optimal, but you will find great strength and courage when you place your trust in the Lord.

Further Thought...

- How would you describe the enemy in your life?
- Do you ever feel besieged or surrounded by the enemy? What do you do?
- Do you agree with the Psalmist that your times are in God's hands? What does that mean to you, and what difference does this knowledge make in your life?
- Can you think of a time when you put your hope in something or someone other than God? How did it go?
- What does it mean to you to put your hope in God?

PSALM 32:1-6 ✓
The Grace of Forgiveness

How blessed is he whose transgression is forgiven, whose sin is covered! 2 How blessed is the man to whom the LORD does not impute iniquity, and in whose spirit there is no deceit! 3 When I kept silent about my sin, my body wasted away through my groaning all day long. 4 For day and night Your hand was heavy upon me; my vitality was drained away as with the fever heat of summer. Selah. 5 I acknowledged my sin to You, and my iniquity I did not hide; I said, "I will confess my transgressions to the LORD"; and You forgave the guilt of my sin. Selah. 6 Therefore, let everyone who is godly pray to You in a time when You may be found; surely in a flood of great waters they will not reach him.

Isn't it amazing how television commercials can really stick with you? I can remember commercials from when I was a child, but I would be hard-pressed to tell you much about many television shows I happened to have watched. Commercials are such a big deal these days that some people make the sacrifice to watch the Super Bowl just so they can see the commercials. I do have an appreciation for a good commercial. There was a particular commercial that aired when I was a kid that sticks in my mind. It was so catchy that it was mentioned often in my home growing up. The advertisement was for milk, and it featured children in various stages of drinking a glass of milk. The last shot was of a little boy finishing his glass and saying, "It make me happy." It became a standard joke in the Riordan household to reflect upon an event or opinion by saying "It make me happy." Think about it for a moment. What does it take to make you happy? Happiness appears to be the number one pursuit of all people, so we have to determine what really helps us find this plateau of satisfaction.

David began Psalm 32 with a statement about happiness. While the word "happy" is not used, the word "blessed" is used, and the word "blessed" means deep levels of joy or happiness. I wrote about the wonderful Hebrew word that is translated as "blessed" in our chapter from Psalm 1. One writer defined it as "ecstatic delight."

While I have not done a nation-wide survey, I'm going to venture out and say that personal happiness is one of the great motivators of Americans. I have seen people give up incredible jobs with a big pay check because they weren't happy. I've seen families move across the country, change churches, buy cars, have children, and give stuff away in search of the sometimes seemingly elusive happiness. This Psalm opens with a statement that reveals at least part of the recipe for happiness: *"How blessed is he whose transgression is forgiven, whose sin is covered!"* David said that abiding joy and happiness comes when we know that our sins have been forgiven.

It is impossible to know exactly to what *"transgression"* David was referring, but some scholars have speculated that he was reflecting back upon his sin with Bathsheba. It might be helpful to read Psalm 51 (David's prayer of repentance) and then read Psalm 32 again. He uses three different words to describe his sin: *transgression, sin,* and *iniquity*.

The Hebrew word that is translated *"transgression"* is a synonymous word for sin, but it can be specifically translated as *"rebellion."* We must remember that God does not give sins a grade, but there are different types of sin with various effects on humanity. Some sins slip out of us and are not a result of premeditation. We are born with a sin nature, and we often times sin without even realizing it. Sometimes, we sin, and we even deceive ourselves into thinking our motives were pure and our actions were justified. The sin to which David refers, however, is not a small moral slip but rather an open act of rebellion. He confirmed that it brings great, abiding joy when these open acts of rebellion are *"forgiven."*

Forgiveness is an amazing thing. Have you ever known a person to forgive someone for a horrendous act? I've known wives who forgave their adulterous husbands, families who forgave drunken murderers who killed a family member by vehicular homicide, and children who forgave abusive parents. Martin Luther King, Jr. once declared,

"Darkness cannot drive out darkness; only light can do that. Hate cannot drive out hate; only love can do that."

I am challenged to forgive you, if you sin against me, but if your sin is against someone else, I am not personally offended or affected. God is offended and affected by every sin that is ever committed because every sin is an affront to His holy character. As horrible as our sin is to our perfect God, He extends to us the grace of forgiveness.

The word that is translated as *"forgiven"* in this passage means "to lift up or carry away." This means that when we repent of our sin before our Heavenly Father who is most offended by our transgression, He carries our sin away. Micah 7:19 says God will *"cast all their sins into the depths of the sea,"* and Hebrews 8:12 says God *"will remember their sins no more."* I read one blog that reminds us that God doesn't really forget our sin, because He might later remember it, but He chooses to *"remember our sins no more"* (http://odb.org/2006/12/11/does-god-forget). Stop for a moment and think about the difference of those two concepts. God really does remove our sins from us as far as the east is from the west (see Psalm 103:12).

The word *"sin"* in verse one means an offense that is deserving of punishment. While we could discuss a worthwhile punishment for different sins, God says that the person who sins must die (see Romans 6:23). Punishment for sin is eternal separation from God Who made us for relationship and eternal life.

While you can see the two words in verse one indicating sin, rest your eyes and feast your soul upon the two words describing what God will do for the repentant person. Not only does He *"forgive"* our transgressions, as stated above, but He also *"covers"* our sin. *"Cover"* means to *"conceal so it cannot be seen."* I can't help but see this word from a New Testament perspective. Our sin has been covered by the blood of the perfect sacrifice: Jesus. King David probably thought about the blood of the sacrifice being poured out upon the Mercy Seat of the Ark of the Covenant. Inside this carefully constructed box were three items: The Ten Commandments, a bowl of manna, and Aaron's rod that budded.

Think about the first item. The Ten Commandments condemns us as sinners and shows us that we are not worthy of a relationship with a perfect, holy God. The blood of the sacrifice covered the lid that concealed the law, so when God looked down at the law that condemned, He saw the blood that redeems. Now apply that concept to your life. The law still condemns but the temporary blood of the inadequate sacrifice of sheep and goats has been replaced with the permanent sacrifice and the sufficient blood of our gracious Savior, Jesus. We, too, have been covered by the blood of the sacrifice, only this time, the blood came from Jesus dying for our sins on a cross. Ephesians 1:7 says, *"In Him we have redemption through His blood, the forgiveness of our trespasses, according to the riches of His grace."*

Verse two of our Psalm goes into greater detail of our redemption and forgiveness: *"How blessed is the man to whom the LORD does not impute iniquity, and in whose spirit there is no deceit."* God presents a third word for sin: *"iniquity."* This word carries the idea of being perverse or crooked. It is a picture of a twisted limb. It portrays the concept of something being different than the way it is supposed to be. On my many backpacking trips through the mountains, I have seen numerous trees twisted by storms and ravaged by disease. Some of them look quite funny with very unusual shapes, while others seem to be so weak I feel I should run past them lest they fall on me. Regardless of their form, I know that it is not the way it is supposed to be.

Sin is not the way it is supposed to be in the lives of human beings. Immorality is a twisted version of life, and debauchery is an aberration of mankind as God intended. This passage says that even though we are twisted by sin, there is an option whereby our sin is not *"imputed"* or *"counted"* against us. This presents the beautiful picture of the justification that is possible for those who repent of their sins and follow Jesus Christ (see Romans 5:1).

Read verses three and four again to see what happens when we keep silent about our sin. David referred to the time he ignored his sin and refused to repent. The result was that he was physically affected by it and became emotionally distraught. Our natural inclination is to deny our sin and run from God, but God says we must run to Him and repent of our sin. Only then can we find emotional and spiritual healing from our wickedness. Verse four speaks to the fact that sometimes God brings discipline into our lives because of our sin (also see Hebrews 12:4-11).

Verse five shows us the right response to God regarding our sin: "*I acknowledged my sin to You, and my iniquity I did not hide; I said, 'I will confess my transgressions to the LORD'; and You forgave the guilt of my sin.*" We must own up to our sin before God. He already knows about it; we may as well acknowledge it. Do not hide your sin from yourself or from God. Confess it to the Lord and repent. The scripture says that God forgave the "*guilt*" of David's sin. This word is the same word that is translated "*iniquity*," which meant "crookedness" or "perversion."

We are guilty for the perversion of our lives as a result of sin, but God forgives us of our guilt. Satan, however, loves to shame us over our guilt and try to keep those feelings of shame and reproach fresh in our hearts. God says He forgives our guilt! This is the message of the cross: you are forgiven. When you repent of your sins and trust Jesus, God forgives you of all your unrighteousness (see 1 John 1:9). What do you suppose the word "*all*" means? It doesn't mean part or everything up to a certain point. It is because God forgives us of all our iniquity that we can be called children of God and even "*saints.*"

What then should be our response? Under God's inspiration, David pleaded, "*Let everyone who is godly pray to You in a time when You may be found...*" When we recognize sin in our lives, we must pray to God. Do not put it off for a more opportune time. The moment you realize you have sinned is the opportune time for repentance. The longer we wait, the harder our hearts become. We slowly minimalize our sin and quickly justify our behaviors. We begin to compare our sins to other people, and before long, we forget how serious our sin is before our perfect God. We must remember that other people are not the standard for righteousness; Jesus is. Do you want to experience abiding joy? Do you want your sin to be covered? The only right response to our sin is repentance. Not only does it *"make me happy,"* but it makes you happy and God happy. Fellowship is restored. Christians are re-engaged. The mission is fulfilled. Sin is covered.

Further Thought…

- What is your normal, first reaction when you are confronted with sin in your life? This confrontation could come from Scripture, from the Holy Spirit's prompting, or from a friend.

- Have you ever *"kept silent"* about your sin and not gone before God and dealt with it? How did that make you feel? Were you vulnerable to repeat offenses?

- Do you struggle with feelings of being unforgiven, even after repenting of your sin? Satan enjoys making you feel unforgiven, but God says you are forgiven. What can you do to defeat Satan's accusations and claim the forgiveness that is yours through Christ?

- Have you ever been disciplined by God? How did you respond? How does God's discipline confirm that you are God's child?

- Do you think it is sometimes difficult for a Christian to find God? Can our sin so block our mental and spiritual perceptions that we have a hard time "getting through?" What can you do if you find yourself in that predicament?

- Remember that God wants intimate fellowship with His children, and He is not holding Himself back. How can repentance and confession restore fellowship with God? What role do you think prayer, Bible reading, worship, fasting, and ministry have in restoring fellowship with God?

PSALM 33:1-7
Joy-filled Worship

Sing for joy in the LORD, O you righteous ones; praise is becoming to the upright. 2 Give thanks to the LORD with the lyre; sing praises to Him with a harp of ten strings. 3 Sing to Him a new song; play skillfully with a shout of joy. 4 For the Word of the LORD is upright, and all His work is done in faithfulness. 5 He loves righteousness and justice; the earth is full of the lovingkindness of the LORD. 6 By the Word of the LORD the heavens were made, and by the breath of His mouth all their host. 7 He gathers the waters of the sea together as a heap; he lays up the deeps in storehouses.

I stood in our kitchen a few nights ago and relished the sounds coming from upstairs. Two of my girls were cleaning their room, which was a thrill all by itself, but the thing that brought joy to my heart was listening to them sing. One sang melody, and the other was harmonizing. I not only enjoyed the quality of the unintended concert, but the sweetness of the joy in their hearts touched me. As I read over the first section of verses in the thirty-third Psalm, I couldn't help but think of the recent music from upstairs. Even as I enjoyed the sweet melodies from the hearts of my precious girls, God enjoys the melodies from the hearts of His precious children.

The opening verse of this Psalm calls us to worship: *"Sing for joy in the LORD, O you righteous ones; praise is becoming to the upright."* While we do not know who God used to write this Psalm, we do know that it was someone who had a heart for worship. It would be easy to attach this chapter to King David, as we have been able to do with all the previous Psalms of our study, but there is no sure indicator as to who wrote it. Nevertheless, the writer admonishes us to sing.

As you turn through the pages of the Bible, you will readily see that God not only created us to sing, but He commands us to sing. It is interesting to study the physiological aspects of singing and discover that God created us uniquely to be able to utter intelligible sounds in intentional ways to express incredible worship to our Creator. Just consider the issue of vocal vibrato. You may have never given thought to the presence of vibrato in a singer (the little tone wobble that happens), but it is an interesting phenomenon to consider. Vibrato begins in the brain stem, which contains the control center for a particular nerve that works with the vocal chords to create the small variation. You may be wondering about the significance of vibrato. That little wobble helps a person to stay on pitch, and it especially helps groups of singers to have a better blend.

Hopefully you get the idea that God has made you special in many ways, but one of those ways is that you have the ability to sing. Granted, some people sound better than other people, so in other passages, you are only admonished to *"make a joyful noise."* I figure whether you sound good or not, you can make a noise that brings glory to God. We should sing praise to God because it is *"becoming to the upright."* This underscores the fact that you are made to sing God's praise. It is fitting for a human being, who is made to sing, to lift his or her voice in declaration of God's nature.

In other places, singing is evidence of the Holy Spirit's presence (see Ephesians 5:18-21 and Colossians 3:16). Singing seems to be a natural by-product of a person who is surrendered to the work of God in his or her life. Worship flows effortlessly from a surrendered Christian's voice.

Note that the Psalmist commanded us to sing for *"joy."* I believe the word *"for"* is more of a result than a cause. In other words, sing because you are filled with joy. In our study of Psalm 16, we saw that living in God's presence brings us *"fullness of joy."* Since we are filled with joy in God's presence, overflowing with joyful praise is a natural result of walking with God. The converse of this concept would also be true as well. If you do not overflow with joyful praise, it may be because you are not abiding in God's presence.

I wonder what the Psalmist would have said in verses two and three if he had been writing this in 2014. While we do not usually play a lyre or harp, we do play keyboards, guitars, and drums. Regardless of the instrumentation, God is saying, "Play your instruments unto the Lord with skill and purpose." Play and sing out for joy your gratitude and worship of Almighty God.

The reason we are to worship in this way is because *"the word of the LORD is upright, and all His work is done in faithfulness."* Did you catch the significance of those words? We are to sing and play instruments to God because of Him and not because of us. Sadly, we have made worship more about us than about God. Kent Hughes gave a sad commentary on the Church in his book *Disciplines of a Godly Man:* "The unspoken but increasingly common assumption of today's Christendom is that worship is primarily for us—to meet our needs. Such worship services are entertainment-focused, and the worshipers are uncommitted spectators who are silently grading the performance."

What has brought us to the place to think worship is for us? We worship because God is faithful, and His Word is upright. Over 100 years ago, a Danish philosopher and pastor named Soren Kierkegaard compared worship to a drama with actors, prompters, and an audience. The problem Kierkegaard pointed out was that everyone seemed to misunderstand who played what role. He stated the actors were the worship leaders, God was the prompter, and the congregation was the audience. Pastor Kierkegaard said everything needed to be changed around so that the actors should be the worshiping congregation, the worship leaders should be the prompters, and God is the audience.

This Psalm gives us several more reasons why we should worship God. The writer already underscored the fact that God is faithful and has given us His Word, but he also declared that God *"loves righteousness and justice."* Have you ever thought about what it would be like if God were not righteous and just? Because God is righteous, He, by nature, must do what is right. That means that we can know without doubt that God never does anything that is wrong or bad. When He allows something to happen in our world or in our lives, we can be confident that it is right.

This truth also means that God not only cannot sin, but He cannot cause people to sin. When people sin against us, it was because they used their free will to make choices that are contrary to God's nature. Because God is righteous, He becomes the standard for right and wrong. It is the foundation of God's righteousness that led our forefathers to design a nation built upon the absolute truth of right and wrong. God's righteousness is the foundation of the whole concept of law and our judicial system. Because God is just, sin cannot be ignored.

It was because of God's justice, at least in part, that Jesus had to die upon the cross for the sins of the world (The other motivating factors for Christ's death were God's mercy and His love for humanity). It is God's justice that causes Him not to be able to tolerate sin. If you think about it, it is God's justice that can lead us to also marvel at His *"lovingkindness."* The Psalmist said, *"The earth is full of the lovingkindness of the* LORD.*"* It is because of God's mercy that we are not consumed (see Lamentations 3:22-23). The *lovingkindness* of God and the *justice* of God seem to be polar opposites, but in actuality, they each underscore the magnitude of the other. Because God is just, we marvel at how deep His lovingkindness must be. Because of His lovingkindness, we realize how thorough His justice must be.

Verses six and seven point to the power of God in that He is the Creator of all that exists: *"By the Word of the* LORD *the heavens were made, and by the breath of His mouth all their host. He gathers the waters of the sea together as a heap; he lays up the deeps in storehouses."* He is completely God over all that exists. Not only did He create everything, but He also sustains everything. Paul underscored this in Colossians 1:16-17 and pointed to Jesus' deity as the Creator and sustainer of the world: *"For by Him all things were created, both in the heavens and on earth, visible and invisible, whether thrones or dominions or rulers or authorities—all things have been created through Him and for Him. He is before all things, and in Him all things hold together."* The Psalmist's words run parallel with Genesis 1 when he said the world was created by *"the Word of the* LORD.*"*

When we consider the power of God's breath, the mercy of God's heart, and the faithfulness of God's acts, can we do anything but fall on our faces before Him in thankful adoration and worship? The attributes of God should lead us to even play our instruments or sing *"with a shout of joy"* and *"sing to Him a new song."* For all of those times we may have complained about the new song the worship leader introduced on Sunday, we might go back to this verse and be reminded that God takes pleasure in our fresh, unrehearsed expressions of worship. I jokingly say that this Psalm was not written to Baptists because we do not like singing new songs, but the truth is most people prefer staying in a musical territory that is more familiar. A new song, however, is one that is not known and might even be made up on the spot. I challenge you to try that sometime. You may want to wait until you are worshipping alone, but give it a try. Think about how awesome God is and just begin to sing to Him. I think you will find it to be very meaningful, and God will find it to be precious.

Further Thought...

- Do you like to sing? When you sing songs in worship, do you find yourself focusing on God or focusing upon yourself?

- Make a list of a few of your favorite worship songs. Do your songs focus upon God and His character or upon what you get out of having a relationship with God?

- Make a list of some worship songs that you think would best express praise to God (remember that praise is acknowledging the character and nature of God).

- Do you see yourself as the audience in worship instead of the performer? Do you have any attitudes that need to be changed so your worship is God-centered and not you-centered?

- What are some things you can do this Sunday in worship to help you sing *to* God in worship?

- Do you ever sing to God alone? Would you be willing to sing Him a *"new song?"* Give it a try and tell one of your good, Christian friends about your experience.

PSALM 33:8-22
A Blessed Nation

Let all the earth fear the LORD; let all the inhabitants of the world stand in awe of Him. 9 For He spoke, and it was done; He commanded, and it stood fast. 10 The LORD nullifies the counsel of the nations; He frustrates the plans of the peoples. 11 The counsel of the LORD stands forever, the plans of His heart from generation to generation. 12 Blessed is the nation whose God is the LORD, the people whom He has chosen for His own inheritance. 13 The LORD looks from heaven; He sees all the sons of men; 14 from His dwelling place He looks out on all the inhabitants of the earth, 15 He who fashions the hearts of them all, He who understands all their works. 16 The king is not saved by a mighty army; a warrior is not delivered by great strength. 17 A horse is a false hope for victory; nor does it deliver anyone by its great strength. 18 Behold, the eye of the LORD is on those who fear Him, on those who hope for His lovingkindness, 19 to deliver their soul from death and to keep them alive in famine. 20 Our soul waits for the LORD; He is our help and our shield. 21 For our heart rejoices in Him, because we trust in His holy name. 22 Let Your lovingkindness, O LORD, be upon us, according as we have hoped in You.

Do you remember the old E. F. Hutton commercials? In one of them, two men were walking through an airport, and one man asked the other, "My broker gave me some advice about a particular stock, what did your broker say?" The friend then replied, "My broker is E. F. Hutton, and E. F. Hutton says…" The men pause and suddenly notice that everyone in the airport baggage claim area has gotten silent so they could listen to what E. F. Hutton said. Then, the voiceover says, "When E. F. Hutton talks, people listen." While I do not know whether or not people listen to E. F. Hutton, I have known people in my life that carried that kind of respect. For example, when evangelist Billy Graham says something, it seems like everyone takes notice and listens. The Psalmist started out this section of Psalm 33 with a statement about the authority of God's words: "*Let all the earth fear the*

LORD; *let all the inhabitants of the world stand in awe of Him. For He spoke, and it was done; He commanded, and it stood fast.*"

All of the earth should "*fear*" the Lord. Does this really mean we are supposed to be afraid of God? We need to consider this word carefully because we may too easily water the term down to mean something much less significant than the original meaning intended. We are told over 300 times in the Bible to fear the Lord.

We must realize that we often times treat God very casually and fail to acknowledge the "otherness" of our Creator. God is not like us, and we need to realize God's deity stands in contrast to our humanity. I remember when I was a teenager; a Christian band of teenagers from another church came to sing for our youth group. I must first emphasize that these teens were serious about their faith and on fire for Jesus Christ. It's funny, however, that the only song I remember them singing contained the phrase, "Jesus is my buddy, and I'm a buddy to Him." I understand what they were trying to say, and I certainly agree that Jesus has called us to an intimate relationship with Himself. Jesus affirmed us in John 15:15, "*No longer do I call you slaves, for the slave does not know what his master is doing; but I have called you friends.*" We must also realize that Jesus is God. While God calls us to familiarity and intimacy, He is also Almighty God. The God Who warned, "*Do not hinder [the little children] from coming to me*" (Matthew 19:14), also announced, "*Whoever touches the mountain shall surely be put to death*" (Exodus 19:12). Somehow, both responses are appropriate. While God calls us to intimacy, He also deserves reverence and respect.

These two perspectives are especially shaped by one's relationship with God. If someone is not a Christian, then he or she should be quite fearful of God. The only relationship the unbeliever has with Creator God is the relationship between the condemned and the Judge. In this case, the fear of God is really the fear of God's judgment and recognition that God is the One who pronounces the sinner's condemnation. Remember that God does not have to condemn the unbeliever because he or she already stands condemned in sin (see John 3:17-19).

The Christian, however, stands before a holy God as one who is forgiven and clean. Because of God's grace, He views us as saints. If you are a Christian, you may not feel very "saintly," but God has declared it to be so through His mercy. The word "saint" means "holy one," or "one who has been set apart." Christian, God has set you apart for His purposes, and He has forgiven you of all of your sin. When He sees you, He sees one who has been forgiven because of the sacrifice of Christ on the cross. The Christian's fear of the Lord comes in response to the awesomeness of God while at the same time it includes respect of God. Somehow, the believer must see the distance of God and the closeness of God at the same time. While God is so unlike us and therefore worthy of the utmost respect, and even fear, He also chooses to be close and is worthy of love and tenderness. While we must fall on our face before His holiness, we can also crawl up into His lap and enjoy His closeness.

Because God is the Sovereign of the universe, verse ten can be said with confidence: *"The LORD nullifies the counsel of the nations; He frustrates the plans of the peoples."* What does this mean? It points to the fact that God is a God of plans and purpose. He has a design for our world, and He is moving all things to their pre-determined end. Before the world began, God set some plans in motion that would ultimately end with Christ's Second Coming. History is not just about humanity and what mankind did in the past. History is HIS story. It is about how God is working in the lives of people to accomplish His purposes.

We get so caught up in our own story that we think we are the center of attention. We think we have the lead part, and God plays a supporting role. I live in Newnan, Georgia, and a number of movies have been made in this area. A few months ago, I had someone stop by our church and ask if the cast and crew for the second movie in *The Hunger Games* series could park in our lot. Some people around my city get little roles in movies when producers need crowd scenes.

Imagine for just a minute that I get picked to be in a crowd scene for some big movie. Let's say that I am in the back of a crowd as the camera pans over a scene, and that is the extent of my Hollywood career (I suppose I could say "Newnan" career). Wouldn't it be silly for me to throw a preview party and invite everyone to come watch my debut, as if I were the star of the movie? As a matter of fact, if you weren't watching real closely, you wouldn't even know I was in the movie. I am afraid that we treat God's story as if it is about us. We are only a small blip on the screen, while God has the starring role.

While nations think they are in charge, God really is. Leaders think they have all power, but actually "*the LORD nullifies the counsel of the nations.*" Presidents and kings can only do what God allows. God is sovereign over every nation; God is sovereign over the universe. A nation can only do what God allows. If a leader comes up with a plan that will not fit into God's story, God changes the plan so it fits into His script. This can bring us great comfort when it sometimes seems as if things are spinning out of control. We must remind ourselves often that God is in control!

We can be confident that nothing catches God by surprise and nothing thwarts God's plans. When a ruler, president, prime minister, or dignitary does something that seems to shake the spiritual underpinnings of the world, we must not fear. God has the final say. He may use the wicked acts of humanity to direct world events along the pre-determined path that ultimately brings Him glory because "*the counsel of the LORD stands forever, the plans of His heart from generation to generation.*"

Since history is really God's story, the nation who chooses to see her role as that of a supporting cast is the nation who is blessed: "*Blessed is the nation whose God is the LORD.*" If we, as a nation, want to be happy and at peace, we better surrender to God as the Lord. As we move further and further away from God, we can expect more sorrow and trouble. Our deliverance does not come because of a superior military or because of greater economic strength. The Psalmist said, "*The king is not saved by a mighty army; a warrior is not delivered by great strength.*" Our real victory and national blessings come in response to the favor of our Creator: "*Behold, the eye of the LORD is on those who fear Him, on those who hope for His lovingkindness.*"

Oh, that we would understand these truths. God cannot bless a nation whose hearts are not bent toward Him. God cannot bless a nation whose leaders direct the people away from Him. If we pass immoral laws, God cannot bless us. If we applaud immoral acts, God will not deliver us. May God give us an eternal perspective and help us to turn our hearts toward Him.

Further Thought...

- How can God be both close to us and far away at the same time? How should you respond to this truth?

- What does the word "Sovereign" mean? How does your life reflect the sovereignty of God?

- What do you think about God's command to "*fear*" Him?

- Think back to the founding of our nation. True history reflects upon the fact that our nation was founded by godly men and women who were seeking the Lord. One of the pilgrim's main objectives was evangelism and missions. Can you see how far we have moved away from the original purposes of our founding fathers?

- What are your thoughts about God's actions toward a country who has abandoned Him?

- What can you do in response to our nation as we seem to be embracing immorality?

PSALM 37 √
Defeating Worry

Do not fret because of evildoers, be not envious toward wrongdoers. 2 For they will wither quickly like the grass and fade like the green herb. 3 Trust in the LORD and do good; dwell in the land and cultivate faithfulness. 4 Delight yourself in the LORD; and He will give you the desires of your heart. 5 Commit your way to the LORD, trust also in Him, and He will do it. 6 He will bring forth your righteousness as the light and your judgment as the noonday. 7 Rest in the LORD and wait patiently for Him; do not fret because of him who prospers in his way, because of the man who carries out wicked schemes. 8 Cease from anger and forsake wrath; do not fret; it leads only to evildoing. 9 For evildoers will be cut off, but those who wait for the LORD, they will inherit the land.

Worrying is highly overrated, yet for many of us, it seems to be our favorite past time. While most Americans worry about something, we all find that worry does not usually bring about resolution to our issues.

Worrying can cause heart disease, cancer, migraines, and even diabetes. The Mayo Clinic estimates that more than eighty percent of their total caseload is directly related to worry. One medical doctor said that he believes that if people could learn to stop worrying, most diseases would be cured. Have you ever found worry to be helpful? While you might uncover one positive experience coming from worry, you will find at least 10,000 negative experiences. That's not a very good ratio.

While many of us choose worry, David is led by the Lord to begin this Psalm with these words: "*Do not fret.*" The word "*fret*" means "to become hot, angry, or excited." Many translators seem to agree on using the word "*fret*" as it points to anxiety filled worry. I had one elderly friend who used to call it "getting your knickers in a knot." At the time, I didn't know what knickers were, but I assumed I must have had them in a knot. Do you have that problem? God has a better way.

The thing the Psalmist must have been struggling with was fretting over the way he was treated by "*evildoers.*" The world is filled with evil people who constantly treat others wrong. This evil person could be a co-worker, a political leader, or someone who sits across from you in church. Yes, I said church. Satan comes to church more often than we realize.

The next several phrases and verses give us some practical responses to the evil in the world that helps us to overcome evildoers. What do you do when you are treated wrong by people or circumstances? The first answer is unfolded in verse three: "*Trust in the* LORD *and do good.*" In the midst of our dire circumstances, God tells us we are to trust in Him. We must acknowledge that we do not have the capacity to see the whole picture, but God does. Our view may look pretty dismal, but God is a master at using the bad to accomplish His good purposes.

George de Mestral's discovered how negative experiences can ultimately be good. He was a Swiss amateur-mountaineer and inventor who decided to take a hike with his dog. He had the familiar, yet irritating, experience of arriving home with little burrs stuck to his socks and pant legs, and his dog was covered with the little annoyances. Do you know what I'm talking about? We always called them hitchhikers, and they can be a real pain. It is usually some type of small seed that attaches to your socks so easily when you are hiking through a field, but then they are quite a challenge to get off. On one of these familiar hikes, Mestral pulled the little hitchhikers off of his socks and studied them under a microscope. After a close inspection, he got the idea of inventing Velcro. I have a sneaking suspicion that he kind of likes the little sock-suckers now.

Is it possible to see the evil things in the world as an opportunity for God to show up and do what only God can do? We are told to not only "*trust in the Lord,*" but we are also admonished to "*do good.*" I wonder if David was reflecting on our tendency to seek vengeance.

You know how that is. Someone treats you wrong on the highway, so there is something in you that thinks it is okay to get them back. We figure that since they acted like a jerk, we may as well join the party.

God says instead of retaliating, we should *"do good."* Do the right thing. Do the thing that most reflects the nature of Christ, Who abides in us. What does that mean? It means that when everyone else is tag-teaming up on you seeking to bring about your destruction, you choose to have an attitude that honors the Lord. You choose to do things that give witness to the Righteous God Who lives inside of you.

Abraham Lincoln was a great example of this perspective. It is reported that President Lincoln was once being criticized for acting kindly and respectful toward his opponents. One of his allies questioned, "Why do you try to make friends with them? You should try to destroy them." To this, Lincoln replied, "Am I not destroying my enemies when I make them my friends?"

Not only do we overcome evildoers by trusting in the Lord and doing good, but we should also *"dwell in the land and cultivate faithfulness."* I like the way the NASV translates this section. The word *"cultivate"* means "to feed," so the idea is that we are supposed to stay where we are (as opposed to running away from trouble) and do things that will help our faithfulness to God grow. I had a seminary professor once talk about the importance of "blooming where you are planted." I think that is kind of the idea. Instead of always looking for circum-stances or environments that are trouble free, embrace the trouble and allow the world to see God through your faithfulness and God-hon-oring attitudes.

You might need to spend some time thinking about specific things you can do to cultivate faithfulness in your life. It might mean not spending as much time with a person who has a negative attitude or chooses to gossip. It certainly would mean that we spend more time filling our minds with the truth of God.

The next part of the recipe for overcoming evildoers is found in verses four and five: *"Delight yourself in the LORD; and He will give you the desires of your heart. Commit your way to the LORD, trust also in Him, and He will do it."* I love these two verses. They can be marching orders for life, and they offer promises that will sustain you when all else seems to be lost. There are two commands in these two verses: *"Delight"* and *"Commit."* While the evildoers may delight in evil, God says we are to delight in the Lord. Do you delight in the Lord? To be delighted means to take great pleasure in something. It might happen to me when I come home and discover that my wonderful wife has prepared spaghetti or honeymoon casserole (a special meal we had at a bed & breakfast inn on our wedding night). The Hebrew word used in this verse means "to refresh oneself" or "to take one's pleasure in." Do you see what God is saying? As we struggle with what people may do to us, we must turn our attention to God and find great pleasure in our relationship with Him. Instead of being beaten down by people who mean to hurt us, we must be refreshed by the One Who has redeemed us.

The next command God gives us is to *"Commit your way to the LORD."* This doesn't just mean doing your thing and asking God to bless it, but rather it means doing the things that God *can* bless. When we commit our way to the Lord, it means that we are choosing the kind of actions and attitudes that reflect God's character and will. This could come in the form of someone saying, "God, I want to live my life in a way that honors You. I pledge my mind to think the thoughts of God, my heart to love the things of God, and my feet to go the way of God." When we choose to adjust our lives to the will and way of God, we find that God blesses our lives and truly gives us the desires of our hearts.

I don't think this passage necessarily means that when you delight in the Lord that He will give you a Mercedes Benz. I do think, however, that as you commit your way to God, He will so affect your life and your mind so as to cause even your desires to bend to His will. It could be a Mercedes, but it will also be a lot more. God wants *"to do far more abundantly beyond all that we ask or think"* (see Ephesians 3:20).

The end of verse five says, "*He will do it*," which probably leads some to ask what "*it*" might be. What is it that God is going to do when we commit our way to Him? While this certainly points back to the "*desires of our heart*," it also must point to the next verse: "*He will bring forth your righteousness as the light and your judgment as the noonday.*" God is saying that when we commit our way to Him, that is live in such a way as to reflect His will, His nature, and His way, that He is going to do something before the people around us (including the "*evildoers*") that puts us in stark contrast to the dark world in which we live. Our right choices and right character will be like a bright light. We will stand as if in a spotlight on a darkened stage, but God will be the One receiving the praise as the light in which we stand is none other than the glory of God.

The Psalmist points out one final ingredient to overcoming *evildoers*: "*Rest in the* LORD *and wait patiently for Him.*" Resting and waiting are probably two of the most difficult things for us to do. We all share the mentality of "don't just stand there; do something." I think God is saying, "Don't just do something, stand there." I do not mean to infer that God is saying we are to be lazy, because waiting before the Lord is far from passive. Resting in the Lord means that we do not worry over the circumstances of our lives, but rather we fully trust God.

Choosing not to worry is hard to do, because many of us have trouble with letting go of our circumstances and outcomes. It is almost as if we think God can't handle the world by Himself, and He needs our help. We would never admit that, but our actions give us away. Waiting means that we get on God's timetable and not our own. We become content with whatever God wants to do and whenever He wants to do it.

Waiting on God also means that if we do not see the results of our cultivated faithfulness for the rest of our lives on earth, that is okay. I think this is seen in our relationships with our children or grand-children many times. Grandparents rarely are allowed to see the power of their influence in the lives of their children or grandchildren, but nevertheless, many faithful Christians are bearing unbelievable fruit because of the faithful prayers and witness of a godly grandma.

We must learn that God's timing is always the right timing. God is never in a hurry, and God is never running late. He is always on time. Think about it. I do not think Jesus ever ran to do something. Even when His friend Lazarus was dying, Jesus didn't hurry to Bethany. God has a plan, and timing is a part of His strategy. We must learn to trust God AND His timing. Can you rest in the Lord and wait patiently for Him? When we trust, cultivate, delight, commit, rest, and wait, we will find God forming the most wonderful thing in and through our lives that makes His glory shine like the noonday sun in a darkened world.

Further Thought...

- Do you ever feel overwhelmed by the evil around you? Have you ever been abused by evildoers?
- Sometimes it is difficult to trust the Lord. Why do you think people have a difficult time with this?
- What are some ways you could "*cultivate faithfulness*" or bloom where you are planted?
- It is one thing to say you will be delighted in the Lord and another thing to actually do it. What would you need to do to find refreshment in God?
- Do you find it difficult to wait on God? Can you think of an example in your life when you did something on God's timetable, and not your own, and things worked out well?
- Why do you think it is important to wait "*patiently*" on the Lord?
- How might your life look differently if you trusted in the Lord?

PSALM 42 ✓
Feeling Forgotten

As the deer pants for the water brooks, so my soul pants for You, O God. 2 My soul thirsts for God, for the living God; when shall I come and appear before God? 3 My tears have been my food day and night, while they say to me all day long, "Where is your God?" 4 These things I remember and I pour out my soul within me. For I used to go along with the throng and lead them in procession to the house of God, with the voice of joy and thanksgiving, a multitude keeping festival. 5 Why are you in despair, O my soul? And why have you become disturbed within me? Hope in God, for I shall again praise Him for the help of His presence. 6 O my God, my soul is in despair within me; therefore, I remember You from the land of the Jordan and the peaks of Hermon, from Mount Mizar. 7 Deep calls to deep at the sound of Your waterfalls; all Your breakers and Your waves have rolled over me. 8 The LORD will command His lovingkindness in the daytime; and His song will be with me in the night, a prayer to the God of my life. 9 I will say to God my Rock, "Why have You forgotten me? Why do I go mourning because of the oppression of the enemy?" 10 As a shattering of my bones, my adversaries revile me, while they say to me all day long, "Where is your God?" 11 Why are you in despair, O my soul? And why have you become disturbed within me? Hope in God, for I shall yet praise Him, the help of my countenance and my God.

The backside of the desert – have you ever been there? There have been times I felt like I lived there. While a desert is a dry, arid place, the backside of the desert is seemingly several hundred miles further away from refreshment and hope. I am not referring to a literal desert. I'm thinking of a spiritual dryness we can sometimes experience that may lead us to wonder why things are happening or what happened to God. I can think of times in my life when I felt as if my spiritual life was as dry as an Arizona wasteland, and God's presence was far from me. I felt as if I had mounted my camel and ridden for days into the Sahara wilderness only to discover I had not carried enough supplies.

This time, however, it was not my lips that were parched, but rather my soul was dry and cracked because I had ceased enjoying the flowing refreshment of God's Spirit.

This kind of dry, spiritual experience seems to be the situation in the life of the man God used to write this Psalm. Though we do not know the human author's name, we know that he was a member of the Levitical family of singers (Sons of Korah), and God inspired him to write this Psalm as a word of instruction for future worshipers (Maskil – a song to be played for instruction or contemplation). It seems that this writer had been banished to a wilderness area, and many people think he was accompanying David when David had to flea Jerusalem during the rebellion of Absalom. The writer made reference to the wilderness of Mt. Hermon and Mt. Mizar. The question we must consider is this: "What do you do when you feel you are on the backside of the desert?"

The first thing we can glean from this Psalm is that thirsting for God is a good thing. It may not seem good at the moment, but ultimately, a parched, spiritual life can move us to a whole new reality of God's existence and care. The Psalmist described his arid condition: *"As the deer pants for the water brooks, so my soul pants for You, O God."* Do you sense the desperation in his voice and the longing in his heart? This desperation comes from a person who has enjoyed intimacy with God in the past but now discovers that God seems to be far away.

God uses times of desperation to lead us to realize our dependence upon Him. We have a tendency to move into times of self-sufficiency and a swelling of personal importance. We grow to think that we have arrived, and everyone must surely know of our great theological knowledge and uncanny spiritual perception.

It is also possible that instead of thinking ourselves to be great spiritual giants, we simply become satisfied with our mediocre existence. We become calloused to the fact that our heart is far from God and spiritual complacency has become acceptable. Regardless of the cause, God leads us to the backside of the desert so we will develop a great thirst for Him as we come to realize that unless God shows up, we are hopelessly lost.

God may use a personal tragedy to get our attention. He may simply tap into a growing discontent in our spirit that helps us to see that God has offered us so much more than the monotonous existence of our current circumstances. Acknowledging our strong desire and thirst for God's realized presence is a good place to be and probably the first step to spiritual refreshment.

It seems that the writer of this Psalm was experiencing some kind of torment from his enemies because he said, *"My tears have been my food day and night, while they say to me all day long, 'Where is your God?'"* Imagine being a person of great spiritual influence and consistent spiritual victories who has slipped into a place where God seems absent. Maybe things begin to happen that bring great pain and heartache, and the people around you are beginning to wonder about your spiritual condition.

Have you ever noticed that spiritual mediocrity prefers spiritual mediocrity? A person who is not walking with the Lord would rather everyone else be spiritually dry as well so their spiritual mediocrity seems to be a little more excusable because it is normal. It may be a relief to a person like this when he or she notes a spiritual giant is having personal heartache, and it seems like God has abandoned them. This may have been the case for this Psalmist. We know that in the past he had experienced a close relationship with God, but now, God seemed to be distant. It is encouraging to see that the writer did not allow the mediocre contentment of his contemporaries to pull him down into a status quo existence, but rather, he pursued God with even greater vigor.

Before we leave verse three, we must focus for a moment on the benefit of brokenness. The Psalmist cried day and night as he realized his spiritual condition. While we are quick to try to help someone stop crying, God may want us to experience the depths of despair. Many times, it is in the depths that we finally discover God has not abandoned us but rather God wants to teach us something about Himself (and maybe about ourselves as well).

We find throughout the Bible that many great, spiritual leaders found new strength and ministry effectiveness after going through a time of brokenness. Consider King David's mourning over the death of his child (see 2 Samuel 12) or Saul (who later became Paul) being struck blind while on the road to Damascus (see Acts 9). God uses brokenness to help us to become the men and women He wants us to be. Constant tears may not be bad if our crying ultimately leads us to renewal in Christ.

Verse four indicates that the Psalmist remembered the experiences of the past. When we find ourselves in a difficult spot, it would do us well to think back to the joy of the intimacy we once felt with God. Desert experiences can lead us to think there is no God, but with deep reflection, we can readily think of numerous experiences where we experienced God's love and presence. This walk down memory lane is not just for old time's sake, but rather it is to remind us that we can once again return to the warmth of God's embrace.

What should we think about? This Psalmist thought of times of worship when he found joy in expressing praise to God. In reflecting upon times of worship, we are reminded of the greatness of God. We are reminded of the qualities of God, and hopefully one of those qualities that will come to our minds is the omnipresence of God. God is everywhere! While we feel as if God is not with us, the Bible says *"He will never leave us or forsake us"* (see Hebrews 13:5). Reflecting upon worship will also remind us of the joy of being a part of the community of believers. Discouragement will not only lead us into despair, but it can also lead us into isolation. As we reflect upon the joy of community, we will find our hearts begin to warm and hope is rekindled in our spirits.

It seems that the Psalmist's brokenness and reflection moves him to direct his focus, once again, upon God. He says, *"Why are you in despair, O my soul? And why have you become disturbed within me? Hope in God, for I shall again praise Him for the help of His presence."* This verse has been helpful to me as it gives a little picture of the turmoil and inner debate that can go on inside the mind of a person. It also shows the progression that we must go through when we find ourselves in a spiritual wasteland. We must acknowledge our own despair and question its presence. We must declare that our hope is in God, and that regardless of our circumstances, we *"shall again praise Him."* This psalm comes from the lips of one who is in despair, but he has found the strength to declare his faith in Almighty God and his resolution to trust in God regardless of the circumstances.

Verse nine speaks to the tension of faith where the Psalmist feels in his heart that God is absent, but he knows in his mind that God is present: *"I will say to God my Rock, 'Why have You forgotten me?'"* Note that he wonders why it seems that God has forgotten him, but he calls God his *"Rock."* It reflects the dawning of a truth that underscores God's presence in our lives regardless of where we are and how we feel. Even when we feel abandoned, we are not. Even when other people around us declare God's absence, He is still there loving us, teaching us, and healing us.

Because I love the beauty of a waterfall and the refreshment of a mountain stream, I find great peace and pleasant reminders of my own experiences in verse seven: *"Deep calls to deep at the sound of Your waterfalls; all Your breakers and Your waves have rolled over me."* I have sat beside a pounding waterfall before and experienced the call of God's Spirit deep in my soul as He reminded me of His strength and sufficiency. Nature can be a megaphone declaring God's glory and a blaring announcement affirming His adequacy. As we reflect upon the beauty around us, we slowly begin to realize God's presence within us. The waves of His love and compassion really do seem to roll over us, and the desert that once seemed to suck the life from us has now become an oasis of God's abiding love.

We will find that even in the desert, *"the LORD will command His lovingkindness in the daytime; and His song will be with me in the night, a prayer to the God of my life."* His grace and mercy are a constant in our lives, and He places His song deep within our hearts. As we seek Him and declare our desperation for Him, we will find the joy of the Lord in our soul and the music of the Lord in our hearts. The words of despair are replaced with the songs of the Lord, and once again, we declare our hope is in God.

Further Thought...

- Have you ever been in a desert place? What was it like? Are you in one now?

- Are you really thirsty for God? It may be because you have not drunk from his provision in quite some time. What are some things that can lead you to become spiritually thirsty?

- If you are in despair, do you find it difficult to talk to God about it? Go ahead. Tell Him how you feel. Remember that the first step of getting out of the wilderness is to acknowledge your desperation for God.

- Can you think back to worship experiences in the past when God brought joy to your heart? Spend a few minutes reflecting upon the specifics of that experience and the feelings of love and joy you had in your heart.

- Does nature cause you to think of God's presence and love? Maybe it would encourage you to take a few minutes today to spend some time alone with God outside in a beautiful spot. Find a flowing stream, a blooming flower, or an unobstructed view of the sunrise and reflect upon the beauty and presence of God.

- In your reflections and praise of God, allow a song to flow from your heart. Sing to God of your love and faith. Allow one song to flow into another, and you will find that God's song will encourage your spirit.

- Consider verse eleven: "*I shall yet praise Him, the help of my countenance and my God.*" Will you pledge in your heart that regardless of your circumstances, you will share the resolve of the Psalmist?

PSALM 46
Experiencing God in the Midst of Trouble

God is our refuge and strength, a very present help in trouble. 2 Therefore we will not fear, though the earth should change and though the mountains slip into the heart of the sea; 3 Though its waters roar and foam, though the mountains quake at its swelling pride. Selah. 4 There is a river whose streams make glad the city of God, the holy dwelling places of the Most High. 5 God is in the midst of her, she will not be moved; God will help her when morning dawns. 6 The nations made an uproar, the kingdoms tottered; He raised His voice, the earth melted. 7 The LORD of hosts is with us; the God of Jacob is our stronghold. Selah. 8 Come, behold the works of the LORD, Who has wrought desolations in the earth. 9 He makes wars to cease to the end of the earth; He breaks the bow and cuts the spear in two; He burns the chariots with fire. 10 "Cease striving and know that I am God; I will be exalted among the nations; I will be exalted in the earth." 11 The LORD of hosts is with us; the God of Jacob is our stronghold.

"You're in big trouble." Those words still send a shiver down my spine even though the memory of them is decades old. They were typically employed by an older sibling when I did something irreprehensible while my mother was away. I remember the time I had the privilege of using them with my older brother. He accepted a gift of a large, white rat from our friend, Wally, and decided to hide the rodent for a few days while he worked up the nerve to tell my mother. Keeping the pink-eyed monster hidden over the weekend was not too difficult, but Monday morning posed another problem. My brother decided to hide the thing in a shoebox, with the lid held securely closed, and he slid the makeshift prison under my bed. He had to put it under my bed because we slept on bunk beds. Since he was the big brother, he got to sleep on the top bunk. Wouldn't you know, my mother decided to attempt to clean our room while we were at school. I'm not sure what possessed her to do this because she always insisted we clean our own room.

We wrongfully thought our little subterfuge was safe, and Harry the rat would remain a secret. Wrong! When we arrived home from school that fateful Monday afternoon, I raced to the room and looked under the bed. When my big brother lumbered in after me, I was able to utter those memorable words: "You're in big trouble." To this day, I do not know what happened to the rat. I do know that Dan was in BIG trouble.

Have you ever been in BIG trouble? What do you do when things are going to certainly go against you, and there seems to be no way out? Psalm forty-six was written in response to just such an occasion.

While we do not know the human writer of this Psalm, many theologians think someone wrote it in response to Sennacherib's invasion of Israel in 701 B.C. Sennacherib was the king of Assyria and the leader of the Assyrian army. He had already destroyed the northern kingdom of Israel and taken the Jews of the northern ten tribes off into captivity (Israel split into two kingdoms in 931 B.C. after Solomon died). The dreaded army was making its way south to Egypt and was taking city after city in horrific form.

As the Assyrian king moved toward Jerusalem, he sent a message to King Hezekiah telling the monarch that he didn't have a prayer, and it would be best if he go ahead and throw in the towel. The thing is, Hezekiah did have a prayer, and he offered it up to God as he spread Sennacherib's letter before the Lord (see 2 Kings 19:15-19). In the prayer, he told God that He (God) had a problem, and he asked God to deliver Israel from the hand of their enemy. Realize that Assyria thought that Israel did not have a chance against this formidable army, but Sennacherib had forgotten about the power of Almighty God.

During the night, God sent a plague on the Assyrian army, and one hundred eighty-five thousand soldiers died. The rest of the army woke up the following morning to find more soldiers dead than make up the population of the city in which I live, and the once formidable foe tucked their tail and returned home to Assyria.

In response to this great victory (assuming the Psalm was really written at that time), the Psalmists sang out this song of praise: "*God is our refuge and strength, a very present help in trouble.*" There was no doubt to the Israelites that God was the One who gave them the victory that day outside the walls of the regal city of Jerusalem. Regardless of the strength of Jerusalem's walls or the might of Israel's army, everyone knew that God was their refuge and strength. They were certainly facing impossible odds until God showed up as a "*very present help in trouble.*"

The Hebrew words for this passage point to a God Who is "willing to be found." He is not hiding in some unimaginable place, like my children do when we play Sardines in the Dark, but rather He stands beside us ready to assist us in our time of need. You could see this passage as relating to something that is troubling you, though I'm not sure the word "trouble" does the meaning of this text justice. It wasn't just a casual problem, but rather it was something that brought on serious distress, encouraged sleepless nights, and created a dread for tomorrow. Is there anything like that in your life? God is your refuge and strength.

Because of God's faithfulness, "*we will not fear, though the earth should change and though the mountains slip into the heart of the sea; though its waters roar and foam, though the mountains quake at its swelling pride.*" Wow. Look how the Psalmist described potential crisis. That sounds pretty scary. Even if your problems are the equivalent of a giant earthquake, you need not fear.

It is significant that this passage does not say that God delivers us *from* the trouble, but rather He delivers us *in* the trouble. He says "*we will not fear, though...*" Just because you are following Christ does not mean that you will no longer have troubles. Jesus actually said that "*in the world you have tribulation*" (John 16:33). In the midst of the trouble, you will find that God is dependable, and He will see you through. He will turn your chaos into order and your fear into confidence. With God as your Champion, every battle is a sure win.

The next section in this Psalm provides a beautiful and reassuring picture of God's constant presence. It is a contrasting statement when placed next to the turbulence described in the previous verses. This is not a raging, dangerous river, but rather it is a gentle, flowing stream. It is a picture of refreshment and enjoyment. I love to sit next to a beautiful, mountain stream. I have a picture of one on my computer I took while backpacking on the Appalachian Trail. When I have a particularly stressful day, I pause to stare at this picture, and I can almost hear the gentle gurgles of the cool mountain water flowing over the tumbled rocks.

In this Psalm, the picture is that of the calm that Jerusalem, the city of God, could experience because of God's presence and strength. You can almost hear the sighs of relief in the hearts of the Israelites when they awakened to find the Assyrian army retreating: *"God will help her when morning dawns."* I think we can also find the symbolism of the dark night in these words. Though the night is dark, morning is just around the corner. The Psalmist reflected on this in Psalm 30:5: *"Weeping may last for the night, but a shout of joy comes in the morning."* Satan loves to defeat us in the dark of our nights, but we must be reminded that joy is around the corner. God is always able to bring victory, even in our sorrow. We can say with great confidence, *"God is in the midst of her, she will not be moved."*

Verse seven is an interesting verse in light of the possible circumstances surrounding this Psalm: *"The LORD of hosts is with us; the God of Jacob is our stronghold."* Remember that Sennacherib returned to Assyria after 185,000 of his soldiers were killed by the Lord. Not all of his army died. How many do you suppose he had fighting for him? Here, the Psalmist reflects upon God as the *"LORD of hosts."* He is the Sovereign over a heavenly army that cannot be defeated. If we are surrounded by the enemy, God can surround the enemy. *"The Lord of hosts is with us!"* It doesn't really matter what size the army is that is opposing us. *"The Lord of hosts is with us!"*

Are you worried about your present circumstances? Are you stressed about potential outcomes you are facing? *"Come, behold the works of the LORD.*" Just take a break and feast your eyes upon the mighty works of God. He has leveled armies, made the lame to walk, fed five thousand people with a sack lunch, healed a blind man, and consoled a bereaved sister before raising her brother from the dead. "*Cease striving and know that I am God.*" I like how other translations render verse ten: "*Be still and know that I am God.*" Just stop. Stop complaining. Stop dreading. Stop fretting. Stop fearing. Be still and encounter the living God Who is more than able to surround you with His strength.

He says, "*I will be exalted among the nations, I will be exalted in the earth.*" Think about this for just a moment. As God accomplishes His purposes in the world, He will eventually be exalted in the earth. We do not have to wait until that time. We can exalt Him now. We can trust Him now as our Refuge and Strength. Look for God at work in your life, and give Him praise for being your Provider. Pause now and worship Him as your willing and available Helper when times are tough.

Further Thought...

- Have you ever faced a challenge that seemed impossibly difficult? How did you respond? *Cried, retreated inwardly 'til*

- Imagine being King Hezekiah. What would you say in your prayer to God about your circumstances?

- Do you have a beautiful image in your mind of a refreshing, flowing stream? How does that image help you to understand the work of God during times of turbulence in your life?

- Do you find it difficult to "*Be still?*" Why do you think God tells us to calm down and "*cease striving?*"

- What are some things you could do that would help you to "*know that He is God?*" *Read the word. Talk to Him. Listen for Him. Look for Him. Open my heart to Him.*

7-7-21

PSALM 51
Meeting a Gracious God with a Repentant Heart

Be gracious to me, O God, according to Your lovingkindness; according to the greatness of Your compassion, blot out my transgressions. 2 Wash me thoroughly from my iniquity and cleanse me from my sin. 3 For I know my transgressions, and my sin is ever before me. 4 Against You, You only, I have sinned and done what is evil in Your sight, so that You are justified when You speak and blameless when You judge. 5 Behold, I was brought forth in iniquity, and in sin my mother conceived me. 6 Behold, You desire truth in the innermost being, and in the hidden part You will make me know wisdom. 7 Purify me with hyssop, and I shall be clean; wash me, and I shall be whiter than snow. 8 Make me to hear joy and gladness, let the bones which You have broken rejoice. 9 Hide Your face from my sins and blot out all my iniquities. 10 Create in me a clean heart, O God, and renew a steadfast spirit within me. 11 Do not cast me away from Your presence and do not take Your Holy Spirit from me. 12 Restore to me the joy of Your salvation and sustain me with a willing spirit. 13 Then I will teach transgressors Your ways, and sinners will be converted to You. 14 Deliver me from bloodguiltiness, O God, the God of my salvation; Then my tongue will joyfully sing of Your righteousness. 15 O Lord, open my lips, that my mouth may declare Your praise. 16 For You do not delight in sacrifice, otherwise I would give it; you are not pleased with burnt offering. 17 The sacrifices of God are a broken spirit; a broken and a contrite heart, O God, You will not despise. 18 By Your favor do good to Zion; build the walls of Jerusalem. 19 Then You will delight in righteous sacrifices, in burnt offering and whole burnt offering; then young bulls will be offered on Your altar.

Have you ever felt like God was not fair? Maybe something happened in your life that brought great sorrow, and you wondered why God did not stop it from happening. Maybe someone received the promotion that really should have been yours. While life is full of experiences where we feel like we received the short end of the stick, can we really say that God is not fair? The better question might be do we really want Him to be fair? If God were fair, really fair, we would all go straight to hell – right now. We do not deserve anything because we are sinners.

The fact is, we do not want God to be fair. We want Him to be gracious. Had God been fair when King David committed sin with Bathsheba, a sin that included adultery, deception, and murder, the King would have been horribly punished for his sin and banished from God's sight for eternity. Think about the last time you wanted God to be fair with you. If we are honest with ourselves, the best we could really hope for in God's act of fairness would be a hot place in hell. In Psalm 51, King David was not asking God to be fair, but rather he was asking Him to be gracious. Note how he begins this prayer: *"Be gracious to me, O God, according to Your lovingkindness; according to the greatness of Your compassion blot out my transgressions."*

David's plea for grace was not based upon anything he had done to earn God's favor, but rather it was all based upon God's character of mercy and grace. He used the words *"gracious" "lovingkindness"* and *"compassion"* to refer to the aspect of God's nature that would lead Him to grant forgiveness for David's sin. If God were not gracious and merciful, we would all be hopeless; however, God's grace is full and His mercy is rich.

I love how the writer of Lamentations worded it (I have mentioned the reference earlier in this book): *"The LORD'S lovingkindnesses indeed never cease, for His compassions never fail. They are new every morning; great is Your faithfulness"* (see Lamentations 3:22-23). Remember that this book of the Bible is called "Lamentations" because there was great sorrow, or lamenting, in Israel due to their defeat and captivity. In the midst of this sorrow, the writer of the book of lament saw the mercy and grace of God.

David was counting on this aspect of God's nature for his forgiveness and restoration. You can almost hear the desperation in David's voice as he comes to the end of his pride and deceitfulness, falling on his face before a gracious, but holy, God. It was as if David was saying that if he did not receive the grace and mercy of God, he would be surely lost.

Look at the specific request on David's heart: "*blot out my transgressions.*" The word obviously means to "*wipe away,*" but it specifically means to thoroughly and completely wipe away. The word "*blot*" means to stamp with a dark mark or stain. It is easy for us to add a New Testament twist to this imagery by seeing the stain as being the blood of Jesus. We only experience forgiveness because of Jesus' death for us on the cross. When we pray this prayer, we are saying that we want our sin to be so covered by the blood of Jesus that no one, including God, will even recognize the sin as still being present. He follows this concept up with the words, "*Wash me thoroughly from my iniquity and cleanse me from my sin.*" He saw himself as being morally dirty and in need of a spiritual bath. He doesn't just want to be rinsed, but he wants to be thoroughly cleansed.

Notice the three words David used to describe his sin: "*transgressions,*" "*iniquity,*" and "*sin.*" It is interesting and significant that he used three different and descriptive words. The word "*transgression*" came from a Hebrew word that means to "revolt" or "rebel." It speaks of acting contrary to the will of the authority in your life. David saw God as his authority and realized his sin was a direct rebellion to God's will and way.

The word "*iniquity*" refers to something that is crooked or perverted. It could be used to describe a twisted attitude. David's actions were wrong and not the way things were supposed to be done. He saw his attitude as being twisted and possibly even arrogant. If you think about it, we must be arrogant when we think we are above God's commands.

The final word, "*sin,*" means to miss God's standard, or to miss the mark. God has a standard of living for His children, and David was far from it. These three words (*transgressions, iniquity,* and *sin*) describe our sins as well.

It is difficult to admit to ourselves this truth, but when we sin, we are in active rebellion to God and His authority in our lives. We often times excuse ourselves and even somehow deceive ourselves into feeling okay with our sin because, compared to others, we are okay. Others, however, are not the standard. God is. Our sin is a perversion of that which is right. Sin is a twisted attitude of arrogance that lowers the standard to something we might accept, but something that is far from the mark of God's holiness.

Verse four presents an interesting perspective in regard to repentance: "*Against You, You only, I have sinned and done what is evil in Your sight, so that You are justified when You speak and blameless when You judge.*" I am confident that David initially recognized his sin as being against Bathsheba and Uriah (her husband). It would be incomprehensible to think that David would consider coerced adultery and murder not to be a sin against these two people who were impacted. It does seem, however, that David saw his sin against God to be so significant, that his sin against people was not as notable. While it is difficult to grasp his choice of wording, "*Against You, You only, I have sinned,*" his point is well made. Our sin, while it can certainly be against others, is mainly against God. God is more offended with our sin than anyone else, even the people against whom we sin. This means that God is more offended with adultery than the innocent spouse. God is more offended than the murder victim. God is more offended when we lie than the one to whom we have lied. Sin is very offensive to God, and even more so than to anyone else, because God is the only One Who is eternally holy. We are made holy by God's choice and grace (holy means "set apart"), but God is holy by nature. He is set apart and unique to all other creation. All sin is a personal affront to our holy God.

When I sin against you, you are offended, but so is God. When I sin against another friend, you are not really offended, but God still is. It is time for us to stop minimizing our sin and recognize it to be an egregious act against a perfect, righteous God. I do not believe we can be thoroughly broken over our sin unless we can understand how seriously offensive we are to our holy God. Understanding this also maximizes our grasp of God's grace. We realize how much more amazing is God's lovingkindness when we fully perceive how horrific is our sin.

What is it that God really wants? It is more than just making sure we outwardly check off certain actions, which we would define as to be obedient. Verse six says, *"Behold, You desire truth in the innermost being, and in the hidden part You will make me know wisdom."* God is saying through David that He wants us to be on the inside what we appear to be on the outside. Even our deep, down motives and attitudes should be in accord with God's truth. Are you really the same on the inside as you are on the outside? I once heard a story about a little, defiant boy who was told numerous times by his mother to sit down. For some reason, he felt that he must stand up, but he finally complied. As he lowered himself into his seat, he said, "I may be sitting down on the outside, but I'm standing up on the inside." While it sounds to me like the child needs to be disciplined, it also reveals an uncomfortable picture of many of us. We may act a certain way on the outside, in order to keep up appearances, but God looks at the heart. He knows us inside and out.

What God really wants is that our motives and moral interior stand in agreement with God's truth and our outward actions. In other words, when we are all alone, we act the same as we would when we are in a crowd of people we most want to impress. When we do not do this, we are like the religious hypocrites of the New Testament. Have you ever acted hypocritically? It breaks God's heart. The only time Jesus ever really publically rebuked someone was when that someone was a religious person (especially a leader) who was play acting a religious role when deep down in his innermost being, his heart was far from God.

Once David was confronted by the prophet Nathan (see 2 Samuel 12), he became broken over his sin. This brokenness was severe, and ultimately ended in the death of his child. While we often try to avoid brokenness, we will find that brokenness is really the only path toward wholeness or holiness.

Remember the words of Jesus in Matthew 5:4: *"Blessed are those who mourn, for they shall be comforted."* Mourning over our sin and offensiveness to God is a necessary part of repentance. We must not just feel sorry that we were caught, if that is indeed the issue, but we must be sorry we ever went against God's authority in the first place.

In the midst of our brokenness, we can pray, *"Make me to hear joy and gladness, let the bones which You have broken rejoice."* We need to consider deeply the place of brokenness in repentance. I think I am right to say that if there is no brokenness over sin, there is no repentance from sin. It is for this reason that some people have to fall hard before they ever look up to God for help.

So, how do we respond to this truth? As crazy as it may seem, we should desire brokenness for ourselves and for our friends and family around us. Consider the words of verse seventeen: *"The sacrifices of God are a broken spirit; a broken and a contrite heart, O God, You will not despise."* I do not believe this means to wallow in our sin, and it may not even mean to weep for extended periods over our sin. Satan loves to use a "worm theology" to keep us from seeing ourselves as children of God. This kind of thinking means that we see ourselves as worthless and devalued before God. While we must be broken over our sin, we also must be open to God's grace. I mean instantly open. Even though there is deep sorrow in our hearts when we go our own way, there can also be instantaneous repentance and prompt restoration. While restoration can be swift, repentance is often times a process. We are so good at making ourselves feel good about our actions that we can easily paint our sin to be acceptable in our own eyes. It is not acceptable in God's eyes, and it may take some work for us to come to the place where we realize just how wrong our sin really is. We must understand that not only is sin contrary to the way things are supposed to be, but our sin is the very thing that put Jesus on a cruel cross to die a horrific death.

Only God can create in us a "*clean heart*" and renew in us a "*steadfast spirit*." The word "*steadfast*" literally means, "right," "constant," or "firm." The idea is that David is asking God to give him an inner motive and desire to never be moved to sin like this again. He also asked God not to remove His Holy Spirit from him. We know that since Pentecost, God's Spirit lives within us and will therefore never leave us; however, we can lose the realized presence of God in our lives, and God's Spirit may cease using us meaningfully as a result of our unconfessed sin. Sin can block the flow of God's power and realized presence in our lives making us ineffectual in our work with God and unproductive in our fruit for God.

One of the results of this kind of repentance and renewal is revealed in verse thirteen: "*Then I will teach transgressors Your ways, and sinners will be converted to You.*" This means that in response to God's redeeming work in our lives, we will want to reach out to others and help them come to know Christ personally. We will become friends and encouragers of the wayward and teach them of the grace of God that we have experienced. We will become evangelists as we share with others the wonderful news of God's love and forgiveness. While Satan intended to use our disobedience for his agenda, God somehow even takes sin followed by repentance and turns it around for Kingdom purposes.

This passage contains another phrase that gives a result of our repentance: "*Then You will delight...*" While the text speaks of God delighting in our sacrifices, etc., I want to focus on the fact that when we get right with God, God is able to once again find delight in us. The fruit of repentance, according to this passage, is not only healing and renewal and fruitful ministry, but it is also a joy-filled relationship with our heavenly Father.

Further Thought...

- Have you ever really felt broken and desperate because of sin? What did you do about it?

- Go back and review the three different words King David used for sin (transgressions, iniquity, & sin). What is the significance of each of those words? Can you think of times you committed sin that would fall into one of those categories?

- According to this Psalm, what do you think is the beginning point of repentance?

- What difference does it make to you when you consider that all sin is a personal affront to God?

- Make a list of some of the benefits of brokenness and repentance before God.

- Do you think this Psalm provides a good model for repentance and confession of sin? Is there any unconfessed sin in your life right now? Why not go ahead and pray the Psalm back to God as your prayer of confession and repentance?

PSALM 90 ✓

Counting Your Days

Lord, You have been our dwelling place in all generations. 2 *Before the mountains were born or You gave birth to the earth and the world, even from everlasting to everlasting, You are God.* 3 *You turn man back into dust and say, "Return, O children of men." 4 For a thousand years in Your sight are like yesterday when it passes by, or as a watch in the night. 5 You have swept them away like a flood, they fall asleep; in the morning they are like grass which sprouts anew. 6 In the morning it flourishes and sprouts anew; toward evening it fades and withers away. 7 For we have been consumed by Your anger and by Your wrath we have been dismayed. 8 You have placed our iniquities before You, our secret sins in the light of Your presence. 9 For all our days have declined in Your fury; we have finished our years like a sigh. 10 As for the days of our life, they contain seventy years, or if due to strength, eighty years, yet their pride is but labor and sorrow; for soon it is gone and we fly away. 11 Who understands the power of Your anger and Your fury, according to the fear that is due You? 12 So teach us to number our days, that we may present to You a heart of wisdom.*

I woke up this morning with a little dread. I shouldn't dread another day, but rather I should see it as a gift from the Lord; after all, the Psalmist said *"This is the day which the LORD has made; let us rejoice and be glad in it"* (Psalm 118:24). I could have dreaded it because there is a 100% chance of rain today, there's a flash flood warning out, and I'm exhausted from two weeks of fulfilling the challenges of a rigorous schedule. As I got dressed early this morning in the gloom of my own thoughts, I tried to convince myself that my feelings of despondency came from the fact that I was going to get my car tags today. I find little pleasure in paying taxes in any form, though I am grateful for good roads and all the other things that tax money may provide.

I must be honest. I think I have the dreads because today is my birthday. There was a time when I faced birthdays with excitement and anticipation, but those days ceased somewhere in my twenties or thirties. Birthdays became neutral experiences in my late thirties and early forties. As the half-century mark approached, the anticipated day began to be filled with a little melancholy. I know what some of you are thinking. If you are older than me, you might be thinking, "You're just a youngster. You haven't seen anything yet." Maybe so, but I have seen today and the last years of my life. Some of you are younger, and you're thinking, "What a baby. At least you're not dead." As I've sat down to work on the next chapter, wouldn't you know but it happened to be Psalm 90: "*So teach us to number our days, that we may present to You a heart of wisdom.*"

I'm starting with the final verse of today's selection because it is a culminating thought. Moses wrote this Psalm, and God inspired him to begin verse twelve with the word "*So.*" In response to everything God said through the first eleven verses, Moses was led to conclude that we need God to "*teach us to number our days.*" God is challenging us to do more than just work on our ability to count. I can count as good as the next person, but there are times I am not doing a good job at numbering my days. I think I am not the only one with this problem. Evidently, it's a problem with all of humanity because Moses asked God to "*teach*" us. If we already knew how to value the importance of a day and understand life's brevity, we would not need education on this topic.

We need help with this so that we can live each day by giving ourselves to God as a gift, with a "*heart of wisdom.*" We all know how easy it is to live a reactive life instead of an anticipatory life. Do you react or anticipate? Embracing our moments with godly wisdom will help us to not only maximize our opportunities, but it will also help us understand our roles as stewards. If you think about it, today is not mine. We may feel like we should be pampered on our birthday, receiving special privileges, gifts, or grace; however, your birthday is not really *your* special day. All 365 days of this year in my life belong to the Lord. I am just the steward of each of them. I need to be able to charge into each day with the wisdom necessary to live the moment in such a way as to honor the Lord, love my neighbor as myself, and bear eternal fruit that will last and bring glory to God.

As I mentioned earlier, this Psalm is quite ancient, indeed, as it was written by Moses, the great deliverer of Israel. It is not my intent in this writing to solve the dilemma as to when the Exodus from Egypt happened, so let's just assume it happened around 1450 B.C. If that is the correct date, Moses would have died around 1370 B.C. It appears that Moses was led by God to write this chapter toward the end of his life, and he was reflecting on his understanding of God and God's work in his life (Could he have written it on *his* birthday?).

Remember that Moses spent the last forty years of his life wandering in the wilderness with the Israelites. This thought makes Moses' opening statement even more significant: "*Lord, You have been our dwelling place in all generations.*" As a nomadic people, the Israelites moved locations often. During the wandering phase of their history, they never had a place to call home. Moses realized that it did not matter that they had no permanent home because God was their "*dwelling place.*" Maybe as we gain a heart of wisdom, we too will conclude that regardless of the physical location of our home, God is actually our dwelling place.

For Moses, and for us, God was a place of provision and protection. He represented security, comfort, and love. It does not really matter what particular street address we may occupy; we find our true home with God. Could it be that over 3000 years before Jesus said, "*I am going to prepare a place for you*" (see John 14:2), Moses was led to understand that we are never at home until we are at home with our Creator?

Verses two through six offer a contrast between man and God. He begins this discussion in verse two with a statement of God's eternal existence and creative responsibility for the world: "*Before the mountains were born or You gave birth to the earth and the world, even from everlasting to everlasting, You are God.*" If we are going to number our days with wisdom, it is paramount that we understand that God is the One Who

gave us our days. In coming to this understanding, we realize our place
and God's sovereignty. While some statements in the Bible carry equal
significance, there is not one more important than Moses' declaration:
"*from everlasting to everlasting, You are God.*" We need to be reminded of
this often. God is eternal, and He is in charge.

We should even take a step further by reflecting upon God's
eternal nature and sovereign rule as compared to our temporary status
and subordinate role. Maybe we should sit on the side of our beds
every morning and make this declaration: "You are God, and I am
not." It is so easy to forget this. We often think that we know better
than God, and maybe He should have come to us for advice before He
acted. Before He formed the mountains (and us for that matter), He
existed. He is eternal; He is Creator; He is large; and He is in charge.

Not only do we see God's eternal existence underscored, but we
are also reminded of His holy nature. While God is holy and perfect,
we are not: "*You have placed our iniquities before You, our secret sins in the light
of Your presence.*" Even my "*secret*" sins are brought under God's scrutiny
in His overwhelming light. Were it not for God's probing light, we
would not even know of the secret sins that are buried deep within our
own hearts.

While God's light reveals our sin, it also reveals the way we should
go. Jesus addressed this benefit in John 3:21, "*But he who practices the
truth comes to the Light, so that his deeds may be manifested as having been
wrought in God.*" It's quite interesting to think that a holy God wants a
relationship with unrighteous humanity. Sin lies deep within our lives
that has been so covered over by years of neglect and a lifetime of self-
deception, and God is patiently working in our hearts to help us see
the thoughts, actions, and motives for which Christ had to die.

God is not only patient, but also quite compassionate. I am grateful
that God is loving toward me and very long-suffering. I must also
acknowledge that God does hate my sin. Verse seven establishes God's
holy reaction to our sin: "*For we have been consumed by Your anger and by
Your wrath we have been dismayed.*" It is a lot more enjoyable to sing *Jesus*

Loves Me than to reflect upon being *"consumed"* by God's *"anger."* Does God really get angry? Is He really a God of wrath?

I once sat across from a friend of mine who was a homosexual, and he justified his sinful lifestyle by saying that "God is love." To that I replied, "True, but God is also wrath." Looking back on that moment, it was easy for me to see God's wrath toward my friend's homosexuality, but it was more difficult for me to picture God's wrath toward my lust or dishonesty. I try to remind myself often that Jesus had to die for both of us because we are both sinners consumed by God's wrath.

There are consequences for our sin. For those who refuse God's grace and forgiveness, sadly the consequence is eternal separation from God. The unbeliever is fully *"consumed"* as he or she experiences the full expression of God's wrath. It is only because of God's grace and the redemption that we have in Christ that Christians are spared from God's wrath. Romans 5:9 says, *"Much more then, having now been justified by His blood, we shall be saved from the wrath of God through Him."* Thank God for our justification in Jesus Christ!

Regardless of this eternal deliverance, it is true that we still finish our life *"like a sigh."* Life can be tedious and tiring. We will eventually finish this life feeling the full consequence of broken humanity in death. While believers are spared from hell, we are not spared from the painful crossing into eternity. I realize that some people die in their sleep, but I think it is safe to say that leaving this earthly body is not really an easy chore. God created us for life and peace, but sin changed everything. We do not know how long we will live, but the conclusion of our days on earth will come. We might have seventy years or eighty years; Moses had around 120 years. The length of our time does not really matter because every day is not only a gift from God but also belongs to God.

It's still raining, and it's still my birthday. This Psalm presents a ray of sunshine on a dreary day, and it presents some much-needed perspective. The quality of my day depends upon my perspective of ownership. If this day belongs to the Lord, which it does, then I must embrace it and seize it while making the most of the opportunities offered. Our challenge is to recognize life as a stewardship and to number our days carefully and strategically so we can live each day in such a way that our actions reflect a heart of God-given wisdom. This will bring us our greatest joy and give God the greatest glory.

8-8-20

Further Thought...

- Do you face birthdays with dread or joy? If they are not really pleasant days, how could you change your perspective?

- Think for just a moment about God's eternal existence and sovereign rule. Read verse two again: *"Before the mountains were born or You gave birth to the earth and the world, even from everlasting to everlasting, You are God."* What difference does God's eternality make as you consider your life?

- Do you find it easier to recognize sin in other people instead of in yourself? Why do you think that is true?

- Have you turned from your sin and trusted Jesus as your Savior? How does it make you feel to think of God as a God of wrath? How does it make you feel to know that if you are a Christian, you have escaped the eternal wrath of God?

- Have you ever considered yourself as a steward of the seconds, minutes, hours, and days of your life? How differently might you live the next two hours of your life if you consider the fact that these 120 minutes belong to the Lord, not you? How might your life decisions be impacted by this understanding?

- Have you ever made a "bucket list?" A bucket list is a list of things you want to do before you "kick the bucket" or die. Do you think your bucket list should reflect God's ownership of your life? Why not prayerfully create a revised bucket list that expresses your role as a steward of the life God has loaned to you?

PSALM 91

Safe and Secure

He who dwells in the shelter of the Most High will abide in the shadow of the Almighty. 2 I will say to the LORD, "My refuge and my fortress, my God, in whom I trust!" 3 For it is He who delivers you from the snare of the trapper and from the deadly pestilence. 4 He will cover you with His pinions, and under His wings you may seek refuge; His faithfulness is a shield and bulwark. 5 You will not be afraid of the terror by night, or of the arrow that flies by day; 6 of the pestilence that stalks in darkness, or of the destruction that lays waste at noon. 7 A thousand may fall at your side and ten thousand at your right hand, but it shall not approach you. 8 You will only look on with your eyes and see the recompense of the wicked. 9 For you have made the LORD, my refuge, even the Most High, your dwelling place. 10 No evil will befall you, nor will any plague come near your tent. 11 For He will give His angels charge concerning you, to guard you in all your ways. 12 They will bear you up in their hands, that you do not strike your foot against a stone. 13 You will tread upon the lion and cobra, the young lion and the serpent you will trample down. 14 "Because he has loved Me, therefore I will deliver him; I will set him securely on high, because he has known My name. 15 "He will call upon Me, and I will answer him; I will be with him in trouble; I will rescue him and honor him. 16 "With a long life I will satisfy him and let him see My salvation."

Wouldn't it be amazing to be a super hero? It would be awesome to fly faster than a speeding bullet or leap from tall buildings and swing down the street on the webs shooting from your wrists. One thing I like about super heroes is that they always seem to get out of trouble, and they always win, in the end. Though we cannot really be a super hero, we can be someone like Lois Lane. Being Superman's heart throb had some real advantages. Whenever Lois would get into trouble, Superman always seemed to show up at just the right time. While the prospects of being Ms. Lane is a little difficult for me to grasp, I really like the idea of living daily in the protection of someone who always wins in the end.

After years of struggle, the Psalmist who wrote Psalm 91 came to understand that he (or she) was God's heart throb. Though we do not know which human writer God used for this chapter, we do know that this person found great security in his relationship with his Creator. Many scholars connect Psalm 91 to Psalm 90 and attribute the writing to Moses. If Moses did write it, we can certainly connect to some of the struggles and threats he faced in his life. He started with a strong statement of confidence in God: "*He who dwells in the shelter of the Most High will abide in the shadow of the Almighty.*" This verse contains a conditional promise: if you dwell in God's shelter, you will stay in His shadow. Let's think about the significance of this for just a moment.

The result statement of this verse is that we have the opportunity to "*abide in the shadow of the Almighty.*" When I think about this as an option for life, I like the idea. The word "*abide*" carries with it an idea of permanence. The Hebrew word means "to spend the night," and it could even carry with it the concept of moving in permanently.

I have had experiences in my life where abiding permanently would not have been a good idea. For example, the other day, I felt as if I was abiding in the traffic jam in downtown Atlanta. I once had a college class that seemed as if it would never end, and I have had the unfortunate experience of abiding within the sound of someone's voice who prattled on incessantly about something that made no difference in my life, or anyone else's for that matter. In this case, however, the Psalmist is saying that we have the opportunity to camp out in the shadow of Almighty God. The idea is that we can be so close to God that we are standing in His shadow. I can't think of a place I would rather be. I cannot imagine being any safer and finding any greater security than being in close proximity to the God of the universe. I have this picture in my mind of one of my children, as a preschooler, holding onto my leg in order to find greater comfort from my presence. God says we can live just that close to Him.

It is important to note the names the Psalmist attributed to God in these first two verses. There are four different names used for God that give us insight into His nature and character. The first one, *Most High*, speaks of God's place when compared to every other creature. It is His place of prominence and preeminence. There is no one higher than God; and therefore, there is no one worthy of our unconditional obedience, service, and worship.

The second name of God, *Almighty*, is the Hebrew word *Shaddai*, and it points to the fact that God is all powerful. There is nothing too difficult for Him to do. This means He is better than Superman, because even Superman has his limitations: kryptonite. God has no limitations. He is *El Shaddai* – God Almighty.

The third name, Lord, is the personal name God chose for Himself when He introduced Himself to Moses at the burning bush. It means, "*I Am*," and when it is used in Scripture, it points back to God's personal involvement in the lives of His people, His present reality in the midst of every circumstance, and His desire for intimacy as He relates to humanity.

The final name, *God*, is more of a title or designation, but it is made personal with the pronoun "*my*." He inserts this pronoun three times in rapid fire succession to emphasize God's personal availability and sufficiency. The Psalmist said that God is "*my refuge, my fortress*" and "*my God*." This is quite significant in that no one who practiced pagan worship could even come close to describing his or her relationship with a pagan deity with such intimate terms. God is communicating through this song of worship that He is indeed our security and strength, regardless of what enemy we may be facing.

Verses three and four tell us two things God will do on our behalf. He will "*deliver*" us and "*cover*" us when we are being threatened. It is interesting that He is comparing our enemy to a trapper. Is it not true that Satan is working to ensnare us in his traps and deceive us with his tricks? The idea of being delivered from a trap could provide us with the picture of walking along in the forest and having God snatch us up just before we accidentally spring a trap that would surely snap with our next step. The other picture is one where we have already stepped into the trap and found ourselves painfully ensnared. God lovingly comes, removes the trap from our bleeding leg, and carries us home to safety where He no doubt tends to our wounds. There are times that we slip into the traps of our enemy, and even then, God is our Deliverer.

There are so many wonderful words used in this Psalm to describe what God offers to those who seek Him: shelter, refuge, fortress, and deliverance. He uses the imagery of hiding under God's wings of protection as well as finding God to be for us a shield and even a bulwark, or strong, outer wall of a fort. Can you see emphasized over and over in this Psalm statements of God's faithfulness and adequacy as we face the battles and uncertainties of life? It is easy for us to be overwhelmed by the struggles of life, but God is reminding us in this Psalm that He is able to deal with whatever comes our way. If we want real shelter, we must go to Him. If we want real protection, we must run to Him and place our confidence in Him.

So, what happens when you run to God for protection and preservation? "*You will not be afraid.*" Fear is so crippling and debilitating, but God says we can conquer fear when we place our faith in Him. The Scripture says we will not be afraid of "*the terror by night, or of the arrow that flies by day.*" I am not sure which one of those scenarios is worse. Have you ever really been afraid in the night? Have you ever heard someone in your home after being awakened during the night? I have not, but I can imagine that would be pretty frightening. It seems to me that the Psalmist is describing a sneak attack by our enemy at night and an all-out assault during the day. There is an inference made in verse five that these things *will* happen. While, hopefully, no one will ever break into your house, Satan will attack you when you least expect it. He will come at you with a full, frontal assault. That assault may come in the form of sickness or in being hurt deeply by someone you love. It might happen through a moral temptation or by a personal failure.

Regardless of how it happens, we must be prepared and learn how to run back to the safety and security of God's shadow.

Verses seven through ten offer to us incredible statements of the over-arching sweep of God's protection, but we must consider what God means with these statements. The last verse of this section is sort of a summary statement and presents to us a concept that is difficult to understand: *"No evil will befall you, nor will any plague come near your tent."* I read this verse, and I can't help but say, "Really?" I've known some godly people who encountered evil.

My family and I just watched one of my favorite movies, though it is one that requires a box of Kleenex nearby: *The End of the Spear.* If you have never seen it, I encourage you to do so as soon as possible. It tells "the rest of the story" of a horrible tragedy that took place in 1956. By that, I mean that it begins by telling a story that was quite familiar to me because I had heard about it all my life. Missionaries Jim Elliot, Nate Saint, Ed McCully, Roger Youderian, and Pete Fleming were murdered by the Huaorani Indians in Ecuador while attempting to reach this savage tribe with the life-changing gospel of Jesus. If you watch the first part of the movie, you will be stunned by the savage murder of these men who were there to tell an unreached tribe of people about Jesus.

If you stopped the movie at the murders of the missionaries, you would feel hollow and would possibly question the love and power of God. It is startling to see the men put to death for their faith. Why didn't God stop the massacre from happening? I am certain God could have stopped it, but He chose not to do so. Why? I am convinced that God was fully aware of what was going on, but He was also aware of what would happen if the men were killed. After the bodies were discovered, some of the wives of these men eventually went into the jungle to reach out to these savage people. After some amazing events, the Huaorani people were eventually reached for Christ. This would not have happened had it not been for the death of the five men.

From our perspective, five men being brutally killed seems like a huge price to pay. Think of it from God's eternal perspective. The span of a person's life is quite short to God. In trying to understand God's perspective, consider the contrast between a gnat and a human being. While a gnat lives for only four months, I'm planning on dying at ninety-six-years-old while climbing Mt. Katahdin in Maine. If I live that long, I will live 288 times longer than a gnat. I've shortened the lifespan of a number of gnats with the swat of my hand, so I'm sure I have affected the statistics a little.

Think about how God relates to us. The 1:288 ratio does not even come close to our comparison to God, which is time:eternity. In comparison, a gnat's life would seem quite long. While it seems like bad things are so horrible to us, from God's perspective, they are really not as devastating. Even if we have to live our entire life in suffering, that is really nothing compared to eternity. Suffering and murder happen because we live in a broken world, but God works with the broken to accomplish the eternal. I think that God chose to bring the five missionaries on home to heaven because He knew that in doing so, many more people would be impacted for eternity, and these five faithful men were able to come home sooner than they expected.

So, when God says, *"No evil will befall you,"* we must somehow allow ourselves to view evil from God's perspective. The verse cannot mean that if you are serving the Lord, nothing bad will ever happen to you, but when the bad does come our way, God will ultimately triumph. I like the way Matthew Henry addressed this verse nearly 400 years ago: "Though trouble or affliction befall thee, yet there shall be no real evil in it, for it shall come from the love of God and shall be sanctified; and it shall come, not for thy hurt, but for thy good." I think if you could ask one of the five missionaries who were killed if they would call what happened to them "evil," I believe they would say, "No. It was only good that happened that day." Good triumphed that day in the jungle because a tribe of people, who had never heard the gospel, was won for Christ. We must embrace life as we live it but view it as God sees it.

Note verses eleven and twelve: *"For He will give His angels charge concerning you, to guard you in all your ways. They will bear you up in their hands, that you do not strike your foot against a stone."* Do those verses sound familiar to you? It was this passage that Satan referenced when he was tempting Jesus in the wilderness (Matthew 4:6). This is a marvelous passage that hints to the spiritual battles that take place daily in the lives of God's children. While there is no way for us to fully understand the spiritual warfare going on around us, we can be confident that God's angels have charge over us. I shudder to think what could happen in my life were it not for an all-powerful God and His ministering angels working on my behalf to help me defeat the evil one daily in my life. Hebrews 1:14 also addresses the ministry of angels in our lives: *"Are they not all ministering spirits, sent out to render service for the sake of those who will inherit salvation?"* We should thank God for His work and the service of His *"ministering spirits"* who work to accomplish God's purpose in our lives.

Verse fifteen is probably a good summary verse for this chapter that would be an excellent verse to commit to memory: *"He will call upon Me, and I will answer him; I will be with him in trouble; I will rescue him and honor him."* When we call upon God, He will answer us and will be with us in trouble. God even says that He will honor us. Imagine that; the God of the universe will honor me when I walk in His ways and seek His face. When trouble comes, seek God and His will. Allow Him to work in the circumstance to bring you good and Himself glory. It is then that we will enjoy the life God gives to us and enjoy the salvation that comes as we surrender to Him.

Further Thought...

- Review the names of God in the first two verses. What is the significance of each name to you?

- What does it mean to you to dwell in the shelter of the Most High and abide in the shadow of the Almighty?

- Since God is your fortress, how should you respond?

- Have you ever experienced real evil in your life? Did it make you feel abandoned by God? How do you think you should respond the next time something bad takes place in your life?

- How do you feel about angels watching over you? Is there anything you think you should do in response to their presence?

8-24-00

PSALM 95

A Call to Worship

O come, let us sing for joy to the LORD, *let us shout joyfully to the Rock of our salvation. 2 Let us come before His presence with thanksgiving, let us shout joyfully to Him with psalms. 3 For the* LORD *is a great God and a great King above all gods, 4 in Whose hand are the depths of the earth, the peaks of the mountains are His also. 5 The sea is His, for it was He who made it, and His hands formed the dry land. 6 Come, let us worship and bow down, let us kneel before the* LORD *our Maker. 7 For He is our God, and we are the people of His pasture and the sheep of His hand. Today, if you would hear His voice, 8 do not harden your hearts, as at Meribah, as in the day of Massah in the wilderness, 9 "When your fathers tested Me, they tried Me, though they had seen My work. 10 "For forty years I loathed that generation, and said they are a people who err in their heart, and they do not know My ways. 11 "Therefore I swore in My anger, truly they shall not enter into My rest."*

Worship is the believer's first priority. Worship is first because God is first. In evangelical churches, we have a tendency to elevate evangelism as the most important thing. Evangelism is actually a means to an end. The end is always God. Through evangelism, we are reaching more people so they can give worship to God. God is so worthy of worship that we must lead as many people as possible to faith in Christ so they can become a part of the great, worshipping family of God.

In our churches, regardless of the style and preference of music, we have typically made worship about us instead of about God. We do not realize it, but when we are the center of worship, we have robbed God of the glory that is rightly His. Warren Wiersbe summed it up well in *Real Worship – Playground, Battleground, or Holy Ground:* "We worship God because He is worthy and not because we, as worshipers, get something out of it. If we look upon worship only as a means of getting something from God, rather than giving something to God, then we make God our servant instead of our Lord, and the elements of worship become a cheap formula for selfish gratification." We are often so focused on *how* we will worship and what *we* will get out of it that we fail to understand the real issue is *Whom* we will worship and what we can *give* through worship.

King David is usually considered the human writer of Psalm 95 because the Greek translation of the Old Testament (the Septuagint) includes his name in the title, but the original Hebrew text does not attribute the Psalm to him. The whole song is a call, or command, to set aside all the things that do not matter and to come into God's throne room and give Him worship: "*O come, let us sing for joy to the* LORD, *let us shout joyfully to the Rock of our salvation.*"

In the first verse, we quickly see a conflict with reality in most congregations across our country. He begins with a call to sing. While human beings are made to sing and God commands us to sing, most church goers do not sing when they gather for worship on a Sunday morning. Why is that? I have considered two possible reasons. Either, they do not have anything to sing about – which means they are not believers, or worship has become a concert instead of a gathering of believers who have come to declare God's worth. If it is a concert, then we gather to enjoy the professionals who are singing on the stage. It is almost as if there is a disclaimer announced before the service begins: "The musicians singing on stage are trained professionals who have spent years in perfecting the gift of song. Without proper training, singing can be painful to the person beside you and disappointing to the neophyte who attempts to engage." Since the normal church attender is not a "professional," and since the last thing he or she wants to do is to create pain in someone else, many just sit back for the show and forget that they are part of the show for an audience of One: God.

The Psalmist then says, "*Sing for joy.*" Actually, within this first verse, the idea of *joy* is emphasized twice. The Christian can sing *for* joy as well as sing *from* joy. Sadly, a lot of churches are full of unhappy people who have forgotten what it is like to be joyful. It is quite easy to lose our joy because we live in a world that specializes in trying to steal anything in us that remotely reflects God's nature. I believe a lot of the miserable people who show up for worship on Sunday could possibly find the joy of the Lord if they would choose to engage in worship. God has uniquely created singing so that the one who engages is the one who benefits the most. It is quite interesting. God has commanded us to sing, and scientists have learned that singing is very good for us. We sing *from* joy because our salvation has produced within us a reservoir of joy that can never run dry.

This first verse also tells us that we are to *shout*. I have not had much experience in worshiping in shouting churches. Most of the churches of which I have been a part have been quiet, cerebral congregations. Without much effort, one could probably hear the heartbeat of the worshiper sitting three rows back. For people like me, we must figure out how we are going to obey this command: "*shout joyfully to the Rock of our salvation.*" Let's not be so quick as to relegate the shouting part of our worship to our more expressive Charismatic brothers and sisters. Most people do a pretty good job of shouting at ballgames or when something really good happens to them. I have to admit that while many people shout at appropriate times, I even find that most of my sports celebrations have not risen above about seventy-five decibels, if that. There are times I seem to be shouting more loudly on the inside than I am on the outside; however, I do remember a few times in sports history that I have lost myself with such a loud expression of joy that I surprised even myself. What brought that on? I think it came with a realization of such an accomplishment that I felt an explosion of joy and relief deep in my spirit. We can, and should, experience the same kind of relief and joy when we worship Almighty God Who has redeemed us from our sin.

Maybe some of the problem is that we have forgotten that God said we are to "*come before His presence with thanksgiving.*" If we are overwhelmed and overjoyed with thanksgiving, it may be a lot easier to lose ourselves in worship and not think too much about the people who are around us.

If we are going to come before the Lord with joyful singing, it might help us to spend some time before worship reflecting upon the incredible blessings of God. It is so easy to take these blessings for granted that worship elicits more of a yawn of boredom than a shout of joy. These reflections will lead us to remember that God is a "*great God*" and a "*great King.*" If our focus is more on ourselves and whether or not we are going to get anything out of worship, our eyes are upon the wrong person. Worship is not about us. It is about God Who holds the earth in His hands and Who made the seas and the mountains.

In acknowledgment of God as our Creator, the Psalmist issued another call to worship in verse six: "*Come, let us worship and bow down, let us kneel before the* LORD *our Maker.*" In the first part of the Psalm, we are admonished to worship God with our voices (singing and shouting), while in the second part of the Psalm, we are challenged to worship God with our bodies.

Verse six contains the picture of one entering a throne room and kneeling in reverence before the King. While worship is loud celebrating and shouting, it is also reverential kneeling and bowing. We use our bodies to express our hearts. Verse seven expresses the reason we bow before God: "*For He is our God, and we are the people of His pasture and the sheep of His hand.*" We must not forget this. We are but mere sheep, the people of His pasture; He is God, the Shepherd. We kneel and bow before Him because He alone is God, our Sovereign and King. This verse serves as a transition to the second half of the Psalm.

As the Psalmist called us to worship through the words of the first half of this Psalm, he knew that worship would cause our hearts to soften and our ears to be open to the wooing and pleading voice of our Creator. The second part of verse seven marks a significant transition in thought: "*Today, if you would hear His voice, do not harden your hearts.*" One great danger of any human being, including Christians, is the potential to develop a hard heart. When God inspired the writer to use the word "*heart*" in this passage, He of course was not speaking of the pumping organ in the center of our chest; but rather, He was talking about our inner being that includes our mind, will, and emotions. Even as we were commanded to sing and shout in the first part of the Psalm, in the second part we are commanded to have a soft, pliable heart. What does that really mean?

In order to fully understand this command, we must look at the illustration provided in this section. We are warned not to harden our hearts as the Children of Israel did *"at Meribah, as in the day of Massah in the wilderness."* The full story of Israel's actions is recorded in Exodus 17:1-7, and you can quickly see this was a story of selfishness, complaining, and contempt. God had done amazing, miraculous things in order to deliver the Israelites from bondage to the Egyptians, but once they crossed the Red Sea and were delivered from the Egyptian army, the Jews ran out of water. If you processed things for a moment, you might be led to think that if God could bring about all the plagues on Egypt, lead Pharaoh to change his mind and let the Israelites go, part the Red Sea so the Jews could walk across on dry ground, and drown the Egyptian army in the water as the seas crashed back down upon them, then God should be able to handle the thirst of a couple of million people. Though the Israelites should have had faith to believe, they did not.

Before we get too down on these poor Jews, let's think back to our own lives. Has there ever been a time when you doubted God's provision? Can you think of a time when you started to grumble or worry instead of rejoice and have faith? Instead of thumping the Children of Israel into the Red Sea, which God could have done, God told Moses to strike a rock, and a massive stream flowed forth. Moses named the place *"Massah,"* which means "to test," and *"Meribah,"* which means "to quarrel." Isn't that interesting? If I were Moses, I would have named it "Flowing Waters" or "God, Our Provider," but instead, Moses focused on the lack of the faith of the people - so much for the power of positive thinking.

Sometimes we need a reminder of our sin and rebellion and candy-coating the truth does nothing for future generations. Moses wanted future generations to see the results of a heart that had become hardened and self-centered, and he wanted the Israelites to be reminded that obstinacy tests God. This site is mentioned later in the Bible as a site of the rebellious rejection of God. For us to complain and gripe against God is to reject Him as our Provider and ignore Him as our Sovereign.

A hard heart refers to the unpliable nature of a human being whereby we place ourselves in the position that belongs only to God. We think we do not need to obey God's commands, submit to God's authority, listen to God's Word, or follow God's leadership. A hard-hearted person is acting like a rebellious teenager who thinks that no one has the right to tell him what to do. The sad thing is that the longer we go with a hard heart, the more difficult repentance becomes. Whereas at first we might hear the still small voice of a loving, compassionate God, we will later not be able to hear God's voice at all, if we continue to ignore His calls.

The opposite of having a hard heart is having a soft heart. This would be a life that is pliable to the Master's touch. It would be a person who is responsive to God's leadership and sensitive to God's voice. Repentance would flow easily and quickly from this kind of heart, because this person daily acknowledges his or her dependence upon God and willingness to trust God completely in all things.

The last sentence is disturbing to those of us who like to think of God as being like a loving, beneficent grandfather: *"Therefore I swore in My anger, truly they shall not enter into My rest."* Does the Bible really say that God was angry? You better believe it does. Does God get angry when I sin or when you sin? I would imagine so. Not all anger is sin, but we must realize that our intentional sin is an affront to God's holiness, disrespect toward God's nature, and abuse of God's grace.

This verse points to the consequences of our sin: *"they shall not enter into My rest."* We could quickly say this verse was pointing to the fact that because of Israel's disobedience, they would not be allowed to enter the Promised Land. That is true, but is that all it means? I don't think so. There is an eternal message here. When people ignore God's call to repentance and faith in Christ, hell becomes their destiny, not heaven. Heaven would be God's rest, and people who refuse Christ's offer of forgiveness and submission to His lordship, rest is not in their futures (see Matthew 13:36-43).

There is another message in this passage for Christians. God offers to His children rest, or "peace that passes understanding" (see Philippians 4:6-7). When we choose to go our own way and refuse to trust God, we are setting ourselves up for frustration and stress. When we trust God and surrender daily to His authority and leadership in our lives, we will find a peace and a joy we've never known possible. When I was a child, I memorized Isaiah 26:3 in the King James Version, and I have always found it to bring comfort and encouragement: *"Thou wilt keep him in perfect peace, whose mind is stayed on Thee: because he trusteth in Thee."*

Look again at the two sections of this Psalm. First, there is a call to worship where we rightly understand God's place as our Sovereign, and then there is repentance from hard-heartedness and lack of faith in God. Is it possible that true repentance is missing in the lives of some people because true worship is also not experienced? One of the underlying messages of the Psalms is a constant call to encounter God in worship. A. W. Tozier opined that this kind of gut-wrenching, life-altering worship is missing from the modern church today: "Worship is the missing jewel in modern evangelicalism. We're organized, we work, and we have our agencies. We have almost everything, but there's one thing that the churches, even the gospel churches, do not have: that is the ability to worship. We are not cultivating the art of worship. It's the one shining gem that is lost to the modern church, and I believe that we ought to search for this until we find it" (from *Worship, the Missing Jewel*).

Further Thought...

- Do you believe that worship is the believer's first priority? Is there a conflict with this thought in your own mind with some other discipline or act of obedience that ought to come first?

- Why do you think people today are so focused on what they *get* out of worship? Have you personally been more oriented to this kind of thinking? What can people do to change their perspective?

- Do you sing? Are you a shouter? What do you think about God's commands to sing and shout?

- What do you think causes a hard heart? What are the results of a hard heart?

- How does someone overcome having a hard heart?

- Have you ever had a hard heart? Is your heart hard and calloused now? What are some things you can incorporate into your life to keep your heart pliable and responsive to God?

PSALM 99

Responding to the Greatness of God

The LORD reigns, let the peoples tremble; He is enthroned above the cherubim, let the earth shake! 2 The LORD is great in Zion, and He is exalted above all the peoples. 3 Let them praise Your great and awesome name; holy is He. 4 The strength of the King loves justice; You have established equity; You have executed justice and righteousness in Jacob. 5 Exalt the LORD our God and worship at His footstool; holy is He. 6 Moses and Aaron were among His priests, and Samuel was among those who called on His name; they called upon the LORD and He answered them. 7 He spoke to them in the pillar of cloud; they kept His testimonies and the statute that He gave them. 8 O LORD our God, You answered them; You were a forgiving God to them, and yet an avenger of their evil deeds. 9 Exalt the LORD our God and worship at His holy hill, for holy is the LORD our God.

"I am the great and terrible Oz…" After auditioning for the part in tenth grade, I became the great and terrible Oz in the play, *The Wizard of Oz*. I do not remember many of my lines, but I remember my opening statement to the heartless Tin Man, the brainless Scarecrow, the cowardly Lion, and the displaced Dorothy: "I am the great and terrible Oz." I was not really so great, and I was not that terrible, but the four creatures who stood before my fearsome façade trembled in my presence, especially the lion. Toto was not fazed by my fierceness; however, and the little, yappy piranha dog had the nerve to expose me as I tried to hide behind the curtain. Full disclosure for the tiny and not so terrible Oz was a near mortal blow to my esteem, but I managed to recover.

My experience in the play was not only a great learning experience for a budding thespian, but it also led our group to talk about the tendency people have to hide behind false pretenses and trumped up images to become someone they are really not. No one needed to tremble before me because I was a little guy with no real power at all.

On the other hand, God presents no false pretenses or trumped up images. While we prefer the image of sitting in God's lap enjoying His laughter, there is another image of God presented in the Bible that is a little more difficult for us to accept. The Psalmist addressed it in the opening words of this Psalm: *"The LORD reigns, let the peoples tremble."* Does God really want the people to tremble? Oz did, but he had issues and probably needed a therapist. Maybe it is not so much of a *want* from God but rather a *result* of being God. Whenever we come face to face with the awesomeness of Almighty God Who reigns as King of kings and Lord of lords, trembling is a common affect upon people as they gaze upon His glory.

The problem we have is that we prefer not to think of God in this light. We like the grace side of God that promotes His accessibility, gentleness, and love. We tend to shy away from the *"touch this mountain and you shall surely die"* passages. We prefer the up-close God of warmth and compassion and not the far-removed God that promotes fear and trembling. Nevertheless, God is a mighty God, which leads us to become a trembling people.

So, maybe you haven't trembled in a while. Why not? I would never want to present an image of God that does not invite us into a personal relationship where we will be enveloped by love and grace, but there is another aspect of God which we must not forget. If our focus has been on the gentle, accessible side of God, we may have somehow been able to ignore the part of Him that should create such awe and respect in us that we may shudder a bit as we realize His majesty.

One reason we may have a tremble-free relationship with the Almighty is that our relationship is so distant that we no longer fear God. I remember an experience I had years ago while scuba diving that led me to tremble for quite some time. My friend and I were diving in the waters of the Gulf of Mexico, and we suddenly realized we were being sized up for dinner. From the way things were looking, I think my friend was to be dinner, and I was to be dessert. The Black Tip shark swam in from the deeper water and began circling us as we hung motionless in the water. I noticed its perpetual frown and even got a glimpse of its small, sharp teeth on a nearby pass. When the creature began moving toward my friend's leg, I made a noise underwater. Because I am a man, I will not call it a scream but rather a guttural expression. Whether or not sharks hear noises like that, I do not know, but the thing made a quick U-turn and began to circle us. As it came toward us again, I swatted at it with my fin, and it darted off in a different direction.

While the experience seemed to last for an eternity, I will leave the telling of it to a few sentences. Obviously, the shark either decided we were not good enough for dinner or it was really more curious than hungry. It eventually swam back for deeper water, and we swam back toward our world: dry land. When we came to a sand bar, the two of us stood in chest deep water, and I for one was trembling so significantly I could not speak.

Here's the interesting thing. While that event chilled me to the bone at the time, I haven't trembled over the experience for many years. I have seen a number of sharks since then, and I haven't lost my nerve yet. The further I get away from the experience, the less emotional I have become about it. I believe the principle is the same in our relationship with God. Maybe we spend less time trembling because we spend less time in His presence. To know God is to know Him not only as Savior and Friend, but also as Holy and Awesome: "the Great and Terrible God."

When we pause to gaze upon Him "*enthroned above the cherubim,*" it is very appropriate to do a little shaking. The cherubim were angels who were given specific tasks of ministry. For example, God placed cherubim in the Garden of Eden to protect the tree of the knowledge of good and evil. This passage says that God sits enthroned above these angels.

One problem is that we forget that "*He is exalted above all the peoples.*" We would never say God is not exalted, but we live like He is at least not exalted above us. Many times, we place ourselves above

God by making decisions that are contrary to His will or living as if we are more comfortable with time instead of eternity. When the Psalmist said "*above all the peoples*," that includes us. He is exalted above us. He is the great and awesome God.

Our natural reaction should be "*praise*" because His name is "*great and awesome*" and "*holy is He*." The words "*great and awesome*" mean "producing dread." If there is open, blatant sin in our lives, dread at God's presence should be a natural response. A time is coming when those will stand before God who have not been forgiven for their sin through faith in Christ. It will be a day of great dread indeed. For us as Christians, our awe comes from recognition of His glory and His "otherness." If there is discomfort in His presence for the repentant believer, it comes because our focus is upon our unworthiness and not because God wants us to run in fear. While God wants us to know of His compassion and nearness, we must never forget His awesomeness and holiness.

Isn't it interesting that the Psalmist said God's *name* is great? Why didn't he just say that God is great? In our twenty-first century mind-set, a name is simply a moniker given to us at birth that distinguishes us from other human beings. Sometimes, that can be confusing, even if your name is Tim Riordan (which I assume it's not). Would you believe that there are other Tim Riordans living within close proximity to my home? It's not like my last name is common, like Smith or Jones. Years ago, I received some phone calls for another Tim Riordan. I couldn't believe there was another guy living so closely to me wearing my name. I hope he was wearing it well. While I received his calls, I was kind of hoping he was receiving my bills.

In the Bible days, a name was not so much a label as it was a description of one's character, nature, or position. Do you remember how God changed Abram's name to Abraham? While Abram means "exalted father," Abraham means "father of a multitude." God's name is "*great and awesome*" because His nature and being is glorious and majestic. It is not the label, God or Jehovah that is great, but rather it is the character the label represents that is great.

There is an emphasis in this passage upon the holiness and justice of God. You can put the character and nature of God into two different categories. There is the one category that contains descriptions of God like gracious, kind, compassionate, and merciful. Then there is the category containing holy, just, righteous, and wrathful. You may find it interesting that the most often used word to describe God's nature in the Bible is the word "holy." Holy means "set apart." God is set apart unto Himself. There is no category into which God can fit. He is His own category. He is perfect while we are imperfect. He is righteous while we are sinful. He is huge while we are small. He is holy – set apart – while our holiness only comes in Christ. When we become Christians, God sets us apart for His purposes thereby making us holy.

God's holiness is also seen in that He "*loves* justice" and has "*established equity*." I do like how the Holman Christian Standard Bible translates verse four: "*The mighty King loves justice. You have established fairness; You have administered justice and righteousness in Jacob.*" Spend a few moments thinking about the consequences of a God who loves justice. It is interesting to read through the Bible noting how often God calls us to reach out to the widow and defend the orphan. God is touched when people are treated wrongly. Whenever we stand up for those who are mistreated, we are standing on God's side. We could build a case against abortion from just this perspective. Is it just to take the life of an unborn baby? Does abortion represent equity, or fairness? I do not believe so. I would imagine the child did not feel he or she was treated fairly as whatever process the abortionist used to snuff out the child's life was implemented.

When the poor are mistreated, the Church should stand up and insist that justice prevail. When someone is abused, we must share God's heart of compassion followed by action and seek to do something about it. Whenever we love justice and establish equity through our actions, we are responding to the holiness of God.

God's holiness also calls us to worship: "*Exalt the LORD our God and worship at His footstool; Holy is He.*" We exalt, or praise, God and lay

prostrate at His feet because He, alone, is holy. The word that is translated as *"worship"* actually means "bow down." We are commanded to
bow down at God's footstool, which would suggest bowing before
God's feet. This physical action is an expression of inward humility.
While we hold God up highly, we recognize our lowly place. When was
the last time you bowed down? I know we typically bow our heads
when we pray, but maybe our personal worship could be enhanced
sometime if we would simply lay before the Lord in an act of total
humility.

In verse six, the Psalmist used Moses, Aaron, and Samuel as illus-
trations of people who encountered God through acts of worship and
submission. These men called upon the Lord, and God heard them
and responded to them. Why did God respond to the prayers of these
men? Verse seven says because *"they kept His testimonies and the statute
that He gave them."* Is this saying that answered prayer is conditional
upon our obedience? That is exactly right. As we submit to God's will
and way, we find that we encounter God more vividly in our prayer
life.

Jesus expressed this truth clearly in John 15:7: *"If you abide in Me,
and My words abide in you, ask whatever you wish, and it will be done for you."*
The Church in America today is a weak Church experiencing
powerlessness in prayer. Why is that? I believe it is in part because we
are also a disobedient Church. Instead of living according to God's
ways, we live according to our own ways. Our prayer lives are more
oriented to our own will instead of God's will. The call to prayer, then,
is also a call to obedience. It is a call to Lordship as we surrender daily
to the will and ways of Jesus Christ. We *"exalt the LORD our God and
worship at His holy hill"* for He is holy, and when we stand rightly before
God in willful submission and obedience, we will hear from Him, and
He will change our world.

Further Thought...

- Have you ever trembled before God? Does trembling seem a little opposite of everything else you have been told you should do in your relationship with God?

- What do you think is a proper attitude toward Christians trembling? Does your perspective contain a correct understanding of grace, mercy, justice, and holiness?

- What does it mean for you to think of God's name as great and awesome?

- Can you think of any examples in the Bible where God acted in justice and fairness? Can you think of any examples in your life where you personally witnessed someone being treated unfairly? Did you do anything about it?

- Do you see the tension that exists between justice and mercy? How can Christians be involved in social causes that will express both God's justice and His grace?

- Why not close this chapter by lying on the floor before the Lord in personal humility and worship?

PSALM 103:1-14

The Song of the Redeemed

Bless the LORD, O my soul, and all that is within me, bless His holy name. 2 Bless the LORD, O my soul, and forget none of His benefits; 3 Who pardons all your iniquities, Who heals all your diseases; 4 Who redeems your life from the pit, Who crowns you with lovingkindness and compassion; 5 Who satisfies your years with good things, so that your youth is renewed like the eagle. 6 The LORD performs righteous deeds and judgments for all who are oppressed. 7 He made known His ways to Moses, His acts to the sons of Israel. 8 The LORD is compassionate and gracious, slow to anger and abounding in lovingkindness. 9 He will not always strive with us, nor will He keep His anger forever. 10 He has not dealt with us according to our sins, nor rewarded us according to our iniquities. 11 For as high as the heavens are above the earth, so great is His lovingkindness toward those who fear Him. 12 As far as the east is from the west, so far has He removed our transgressions from us. 13 Just as a father has compassion on his children, so the LORD has compassion on those who fear Him. 14 For He Himself knows our frame; He is mindful that we are but dust.

I committed a big sin. At least in my mind, it was the biggest sin I had ever committed in my life, and at the ripe, old age of fourteen, I was steeped in guilt and shame. I was actually a very good kid, and my parents trusted me completely, but then with a few acts of deceit, I broke their trust. I was so ashamed that I could not look at them for days. I felt such a load of guilt that I was not sure how I could function normally. I repented of my sin daily. I mentioned my acts of deceitfulness numerous times in passionate prayer as I pleaded for God's forgiveness, but for some reason, I didn't feel forgiven. I mentally beat myself up, and while I was down, Satan took a few shots at me as well. Even though my family had forgiven me, I could not forgive myself. Even though that sin was paid for at the cross, I could not seem to accept God's forgiveness.

After begging for forgiveness for about eight months, God spoke clearly to me through Psalm 103. While God seemed to address me face to face about my sin later in the Psalm, the early verses set up the comfort that I would experience by the time I got down to verse twelve.

The early Bible editors attributed this Psalm to King David, though his name is not included in the original text. Since this early attribution, some have questioned Davidic authorship. Regardless of whom God used to write it, this Psalm overflows from the grateful heart of an individual who had experienced God's grace and mercy.

The joyful spirit is readily seen in the opening words: *"Bless the* LORD, *O my soul, and all that is within me, bless His holy name."* I have written in previous chapters about the word *"bless."* In this context, it is used in a verbal form and indicates more than praise. It means to "praise with affection and gratitude." One can praise God by acknowledging His character and attributes, but the Psalmist is praising God while expressing his love and thanksgiving for the mercy of God. I can almost imagine the words bursting forth from the heart of a person who found it difficult to be contained as he exalted, *"All that is within me, bless His holy name."* Can you imagine everything that is within you blessing the Lord? I want all that is in me to bless the Lord, but honestly, if everything in me is going to bless the Lord, I might need to change some of the "everything" that is within me.

I believe the Psalmist is referring to his mind, his will, his emotions, his attitude, and his actions. I think he is pointing to his successes and his failures, his brokenness and his healing. He resolved that he wanted every part of his being to be like a trumpet blasting out the praises and glory of God.

The second verse begins moving us to see what might have created such an overflow of praise and worship. This verse sets up the next several verses as the writer begins to delineate some of the blessings of the Almighty: *"Bless the* LORD, *O my soul, and forget none of His benefits."* He commands us, almost as if he is reminding himself, to remember all of the benefits of God. God has done so much for us, and we all have

the tendency to take the *"benefits"* of God for granted. The Psalmist
said that we must remember everything God has given us. It would do
us well to periodically recite some of the blessings of God. Maybe we
should write them down and review them often. We should make this
a part of our regular family worship and our personal devotional life.
We are prone to forget what God has done, but we must not!

The first *"benefit"* is the fact that God *"pardons all your iniquities."*
This is huge. Right up front, the Psalmist speaks of God's grace and
mercy. While we may be overwhelmed by our sin and seemingly unable
to get passed it, God says He pardons us. A lot of the English translations use the word "forgives" while the New American Standard
translators chose the word "pardon." This word carries with it the idea
of being released from legal penalties we incur because of our sin.
"*Pardon*" forces us to think of the penalty of our sin, and the only way
we could be excused from a full payment was an act of mercy. The
penalty is death. Romans 6:23 clearly states, *"The wages of sin is death."*
The full payment of sin required death, but God said He *"pardons all
[our] iniquities."*

While several Hebrew words can be translated as sin, the word for
iniquities means twisted or perverted. It is saying that God will pardon
everything we do that is contrary to the right way or *His way.* We are all
full of iniquity. We do things every day both intentionally and
unintentionally that are twisted. While these actions twist our lives,
they also twist God's heart. He loves us and personally feels every act
of sin committed by every human being that has ever lived. While you
may be offended when someone sins against you, you are not touched
nearly as significantly when someone sins against me. Think about it.
Every sin ever committed is a sin against God.

Note the little three-letter word in that short phrase: *"all."* Does
that really mean that God offers us forgiveness for every single sin we
commit? We need to stop on this tiny word for a moment because
there is a huge battle being waged every day where the evil one is trying
to erase that word from our minds. If Satan can get us to believe that

all of our sin is not pardoned, then he has us right where he wants us: living in guilt and shame. Our enemy can debilitate us by causing us to believe that we have committed a sin so big that it must fall outside of the boundaries of God's forgiveness. The boundaries of God's forgiveness are drawn with the blood from Immanuel's veins, and every sin ever committed can be covered when it is accompanied by brokenness and repentance.

Many years ago when I read this little word, *"all,"* hope stirred within my heart. I later looked back at this verse and thought of it in light of Calvary. Jesus died for my sin over 2000 years ago. When I became a Christian at the age of seven, all of my sin was covered by the blood of Jesus Christ. When the blood was applied to my life as a little boy, that application had a lifetime affect that covered every sin I would ever commit. At the moment I repented of my sin and trusted Jesus as my Savior, my sin-debt was wiped clean, and that cleansing had an eternal impact. Jesus didn't just die for my sins, but He died for my sin. There is a big difference.

If I had to confess every sin to God before it was forgiven, I would spend eternity in hell. There is sin in my life that I haven't figured out is there, yet. Christians die every day with unconfessed sin in their lives. While I believe strongly that we must confess our sin to God, we are not confessing so that God *will* forgive us our sin. If you are a Christian, your sin *was* forgiven the very moment you bent your heart toward God, repented of your sins, and trusted Him as your Savior. Christian, when you confess your sin, you are not begging for God's forgiveness as if He might not forgive you this time. The Psalmist was inspired by God to tell us 1000 years before Christ died on a cross that our gracious heavenly Father *"pardons all [our] iniquities."*

Let's not take this pardon for granted or even misunderstand the basis of our forgiveness. All of humanity is not generally forgiven. The Bible says that sin must be punished. The joy of Christianity is that Jesus took the punishment in our place on a cruel cross. This is why the Psalmist said that we must not forget any of the benefits of God, and the number one benefit we must not forget is the benefit of forgiveness. Sin is a horrible thing, and that is why our forgiveness required the horrific death of the sinless Son of God on a cross. He died there to pay for your sin and for mine. Forgiveness comes when we turn from our sin and trust Jesus as our Savior.

Now, look at the rest of the list of benefits we have because of God's grace. He *"heals all our diseases."* Do you believe that? You may be saying, "Now wait just one minute. My _____ died (insert the relationship of someone close to you who has passed away), and God didn't heal her or him." Sometimes God does heal our sicknesses on earth, but other times, He heals them through death. You may say that is a cop out, but I do not think so. We are so tied to this life that we cannot view healing from an eternal perspective. Heaven is such a wonderful place that we should not begrudge God for taking us there. The Bible indicates that disease and death are a result of The Fall when Adam and Eve sinned in the garden and death was passed upon all mankind. While sin brought death, Jesus Christ brought life. I do not want to belittle God's healing ministry on earth, because sometimes God heals people for His glory and for a testimony of His power. Sometimes, death is simply a part of God's plan, and we must by faith accept that God is working out His purposes in ways we cannot understand.

God *"redeems your life from the pit"* and He *"crowns you with lovingkindness and compassion."* Don't run past this thought too quickly. God is full of lovingkindness and compassion. God loves us so much and reaches out to us daily with grace and mercy. He *"satisfies your years with good things, so that your youth is renewed like the eagle."* Did you catch that? He wants us to be satisfied with this life. Isn't that interesting? He has provided us eternal life, but He also wants us to enjoy the life we have in the meantime. He blesses us with good things, and He renews us daily through His power. Let's not confuse the concept of *"good things."* These words can point to something as beautiful as a morning sunrise or a blooming rose in the spring. It may be the joy from the laughter of your baby or the thrill of your preschooler telling you of her love. It can include the bliss of married love and the satisfaction of a job well done. Life is full of good things. Don't miss them while you are searching for something else that will not satisfy.

Verses six through ten contain various statements of grace that are not only beautiful but also bring great relief. We have already looked at God's compassion and grace. Note that He is *"slow to anger."* Aren't you glad of that? I wish I could say that my sin stopped at age fourteen, but that would be far from the truth. God has been so gracious toward me and *"slow to anger."* I have not deserved His mercy, but He is *"abounding in lovingkindness."* It says that God *"will not always strive with us, nor will He keep His anger forever."* Does God really *"strive"* with us? This term is an interesting word. Not only can this Hebrew word be translated as strive, but also accuse, or contend. It can be seen as a legal term to describe judgment that is passed upon the condemned. We can look at this concept from a New Testament perspective and realize that because of the blood of Jesus, God does not take believers to the final end of His judgment. Jesus has taken the judgment upon the cross, so we can experience God's grace in our lives. Because God is gracious, He does not accuse us nor hold onto His anger. While our sin results in God's anger for a season, He does not unleash eternal judgment upon believers because we have been forgiven. I am so grateful that *"He has not dealt with us according to our sins."* I am a living, breathing testimony of the mercy of God, and so are you.

It was verses eleven and twelve that God used many years ago to set me free from self-imposed bondage and the lies of my enemy: *"For as high as the heavens are above the earth, so great is His lovingkindness toward those who fear Him. As far as the east is from the west, so far has He removed our transgressions from us."* Think for just a moment about the first illustration. How high are the heavens above the earth? It is immeasurable. The heavens above the earth never have an end. Neither does God's lovingkindness. When I was reading this verse on the front porch of a Christian camp in north Georgia, I acknowledged to myself that I certainly respected, feared, and stood in awe of God. Since that was the case, I had to acknowledge that the Bible said God's lovingkindness toward me could not be measured. It did not matter how bad my sin appeared to me and how ashamed of my failure I was at the time, God's mercy was flowing toward me like an unrestrained mountain stream after a strong spring rain.

Look at the next comparison: "*As far as the east is from the west.*" Stop there for just a moment. How far is the east from the west? If you were to begin measuring this distance, you would start at a given point and look for the end of the east. There is no end. Imagine using the geometric concept of a ray (a point on one end with an arrow on the other). The arrow would continue on for infinity looking for the end of the east and the end of the west. It can't be measured. Once again God used an illustration of His limitless grace by offering a measurement without boundaries. God removed my transgression from me as far as the east is from the west.

"*Transgression*" means "crime or offense." It carries with it the concept of "rebellion." God spoke to my heart that day in a big, wooden rocking chair. He reminded me that my sin that had brought such shame to my heart had been nailed to the cross 2000 years earlier. When I accepted his forgiveness and became a Christian at the age of seven, that sin was covered by the blood of Jesus. Every time I confessed that sin to God and begged for His forgiveness, I believe God was saying with compassion, "I distinctly remember forgiving that sin and removing it from you as far as the east is from the west." I realized at that moment that Satan was crippling me by doubt and shame while God was offering me grace and renewal. I stood at a crossroad that day. Would I believe God and His Word or would I listen to the accusations of the one who hates me vehemently? I placed my faith in God's Truth that day and left the large front porch of that retreat center with a song in my heart that I hadn't sung for eight months. It was the song of the redeemed.

Further Thought…

- Have you ever made a list of the benefits of God? Take a moment to create a list of at least twenty-five blessings you have from your Creator.

- Was forgiveness at the top of the list? Have you ever considered the fact that every sin that has ever been committed by any human being throughout all of history is a personal affront to our holy God? Why do you think God is personally offended by every sin? What could be the theological basis for this offense?

- What are some things in your life that have brought intense satisfaction? Have you ever spent a lot of time pursuing something that in the end did not satisfy? What was it? Did your vain pursuits teach you any important lessons?

- Have you ever committed a sin that you felt like God couldn't forgive? Has Satan ever heaped shame upon you and led you to think that you are worthless? Remember that while Satan shames, God convicts. There is a big difference. How would you describe the difference between those two concepts?

- Think for a minute about the power of God's Word. What should you do whenever you feel ashamed of your sin and be tempted to beg for God's forgiveness for the second or third or fourth time?

- In addition to confessing our sin, we should also thank God for the forgiveness that is ours in Christ. Take a moment and thank God for the cross and for His mercy that has been offered to us through Jesus.

PSALM 116

A God Who Stoops

I love the LORD, because He hears my voice and my supplications. 2 Because He has inclined His ear to me, therefore I shall call upon Him as long as I live. 3 The cords of death encompassed me and the terrors of Sheol came upon me; I found distress and sorrow. 4 Then I called upon the name of the LORD: "O LORD, I beseech You, save my life!" 5 Gracious is the LORD, and righteous; Yes, our God is compassionate. 6 The LORD preserves the simple; I was brought low, and He saved me. 7 Return to your rest, O my soul, for the LORD has dealt bountifully with you. 8 For You have rescued my soul from death, my eyes from tears, my feet from stumbling. 9 I shall walk before the LORD in the land of the living. 10 I believed when I said, "I am greatly afflicted." 11 I said in my alarm, "All men are liars." 12 What shall I render to the LORD for all His benefits toward me? 13 I shall lift up the cup of salvation and call upon the name of the LORD. 14 I shall pay my vows to the LORD, oh may it be in the presence of all His people. 15 Precious in the sight of the LORD is the death of His godly ones. 16 O LORD, surely I am Your servant, I am Your servant, the son of Your handmaid, You have loosed my bonds. 17 To You I shall offer a sacrifice of thanksgiving, and call upon the name of the LORD. 18 I shall pay my vows to the LORD, oh may it be in the presence of all His people, 19 in the courts of the LORD'S house, in the midst of you, O Jerusalem. Praise the LORD!

"He thinks he's all that." When I heard a young person say that a few years ago, I knew exactly what she meant, even though the phrase was new to me. I've known people my whole life who thought they were "all that." When I was in high school, I played football, and when I was in college, I was a part of the school of music. Both of these environments seemed to spawn people who were really hung up on themselves. On top of that, I've been a part of churches my whole life, and it seems like every local congregation has a tendency to birth its share of spiritual elitists. There were people in each group who could have at least qualified, in my opinion, to be "all that." There were many, however, who had none of "that" but thought they did. Have you ever known anyone like that? Can you think of someone in your past who did seem to excel above the normal mediocrity and would qualify for the "all that" group?

I remember a few years ago inviting one of my favorite contemporary singers to come to my church: Charles Billingsly. To start with, I almost did not do it because I felt like he was so "big time" that he would never come. Surprisingly, he accepted the invitation, and the night he came, you would have thought he was singing before thousands of people instead of two or three hundred. Not only did he pour his heart out in ministry, but he treated me and the rest of my congregation as equals. Now, don't get me wrong. I know that we are equals, but there is something about being in the presence of a celebrity that makes us feel like mere mortals and the celebrity appears to be a god. Charles was "all that," but he didn't seem to know it. On top of that, he made me feel special, even though I am a simple mortal.

God is "all that." One thing I love about God is that stooping is a part of His nature. While we do not deserve to have the attention of the Almighty, He is focused upon us with laser-like intensity and compassion. We saw from a previous Psalm that we are the "apple of His eye" (see Psalm 17:8) and only a little lower than God (see Psalm 8:5).

The writer of Psalm 116 was enamored with the fact that God *"inclined His ear"* to him. This gives me a picture of God stooping to look into the eyes of His child very much like we might stoop to gaze into the face and give our attention to a young preschooler. When a young child looks up at us to communicate something, we do not have to stoop in order to hear her, but we do it anyway to communicate love and undivided attention. God does the same thing with us. He stoops, and He listens.

We do not know who God used to write this Psalm, but we do know that it came in response to God's deliverance over death. Some have thought it to be written after the Israelites returned from exile to

Babylon, while others think it was written by Hezekiah after God spared his life (see Isaiah 38). Regardless of who the human author may have been, God inspired it so that we would understand some things about His nature: He is a God who stoops.

He started the Psalm by saying, "*I love the LORD, because He hears my voice and my supplications.*" Think for just a moment about how radical this statement would have been during the Old Testament period. The Jews lived in a world filled with pagan idolatry, and every nation around Israel worshiped numerous gods. None of these gods, however, heard the voices of the supplicants or were aware of their libations. This writer, however, loved God because He does in fact listen. Note how the editors use all capitals for "*the LORD*" once again emphasizing the Hebrew word used is Yahweh. This is significant in that this Psalmist was saying that he loves the God who gave us His name and Whose name means "I am always present." This God Who is present is also the God Who gives us His undivided attention.

Notice that God not only hears our voices, but He also hears our "*supplications.*" We all know what it is like to hear someone's voice without really hearing what they are saying. As I am writing this section, I am sitting in a public setting with numerous conversations going on around me. Now, these people are not sitting right beside me, but if I were to focus on their conversations, I would be able to hear with detail what they are saying. I have chosen instead to tune them out and to focus on writing about Psalm 116. The voices in the background are simply room noise. I am so grateful that my voice is not just room noise to God.

He hears "*my voice*" AND "*my supplication.*" The word "*supplication*" means "pleading." The Psalmist is indicating that he was in a desperate spot and was pleading for God's mercy and intervention. God heard him and responded. If this was written by Hezekiah, we know that God's response brought healing from leprosy or perhaps deliverance from Sennacherib. If it were written by David, then one can assume the deliverance rescued him from the hand of Saul or of Absalom. We can reflect upon times in our own lives when God has stepped in and delivered us from sure peril. It could be a deliverance from a threat of death, or it could be that He rescued us from another type of calamity. God listens to our cries of desperation as we fully cast our cares upon Him.

Verse five is a declaration of praise in response to God's actions: *"Gracious is the LORD, and righteous; Yes, our God is compassionate."* Look for a moment at the three qualities attributed to God. He is indeed *"gracious."* The use of this word in the Old Testament, describing God's kindness or mercy, is only used of God. While I am sure there were some people who were gracious, this particular Hebrew word is special and uniquely used for Holy God.

Not only is God uniquely kind and merciful, but He is also *"righteous."* God is not the only one in the Old Testament Who is thought to be righteous. Consider Noah (see Genesis 7:1), David (see 1 Samuel 24:17), and Job (see Job 34:5). God's righteousness, however, is different than every other human being who displays good conduct. While Noah, David, and Job followed a standard of righteousness, God is the standard. God alone is completely right and just. To say that God is righteous or just is to indicate that everything about God is right. This means that when God acts, He does so rightly. There are times we are tempted to question God's acts, as if they were wrong, but we must remember that God is righteous and does nothing wrong. I do not think there is anything wrong with questioning God, if we are looking for answers. We step over the line when we accuse God of doing something wrong.

While we may acknowledge that God is not the cause of evil, He allows it to happen regardless of its source. I will admit there are times we may think God is the cause of evil, for example, He sent the flood that is recorded in the seventh chapter of Genesis. We must consider God's perspective and realize there is a difference between God's judgment and God causing evil in the world.

Our final pledge must be to trust God, because we know He is righteous. We may not understand His actions or His choices to allow certain things to happen, but we can know with certainty that He is righteous. It gives me great comfort to know that if something is allowed into my life, it has first passed through the fingers of my righteous God.

God is also *"compassionate."* In other places, the Bible tells us that God is love (see 1 John 4:8), and we know that because of God's love for the world, He sent His one and only Son (see John 3:16). To say that God is *"compassionate"* is to say that God acts out of His loving nature. It means He feels our pain (empathy), and His heart goes out to us (sympathy). This quality leads God to certain acts that demonstrate His love and tenderness.

It is because of God's compassion that He is not offended by my prayer for help when I have lost my car keys or my checkbook. Think about it for just a moment. Isn't it a bit presumptuous on our part to think that the God Who made the universe and Who is keeping everything functioning as it is supposed to, the God Who is working with missionaries in some of the dangerous parts of the world to make His name known, the God Who is involved in spiritual warfare on a level we cannot begin to imagine should bend His ear to our request to find keys that were lost only because we were careless? Does He really have time for that? YES! He does because He is compassionate. He is touched by my struggles and disappointments. When I have a bad day, He cares about it. Nothing is too small to share with your Heavenly Father. He is involved with every detail of our lives – the big and the small. This is why the Psalmist concluded, *"You have rescued my soul from death, my eyes from tears, my feet from stumbling."* If we will allow it, God will put us on a detour which saves us from stumbling and heart ache.

Verses nine through nineteen tell us how we should respond to a God Who is gracious and compassionate toward us. First, we are to *"walk before the LORD In the land of the living."* We know that God sees all things, so we should not think that walking before the Lord is anything special. This verse, however, means that we should walk in such a way as to live in His favor. It means that as we live day by day, we know that we are living in His presence, and we are not ashamed of anything we do, say, or think.

He said in verse thirteen that he would "*lift up the cup of salvation.*" This probably referred to the cup of salvation that was drunk at the Passover meal. The Psalmist is recognizing that salvation always belongs to the Lord, and he will always express gratitude to God for his deliverance. He further expresses his dependence upon God in future days. Not only will he lift up his cup in thanksgiving, but he will also call upon God in the future. He has looked upon God's faithfulness and commitment to him in the past, and he is confident that God will not abandon him in the future. It is our past experience with God that helps us to hold to Him during future uncertainty. Whenever you find yourself going through difficult times, it will help you to think back to past experiences where God has delivered you. This will bring comfort and faith as you face the unknown.

I believe that King George VI had God's past faithfulness in mind when he quoted from a poem in a speech during the early days of the Second World War:

And I said to the man who stood at the gate of the year:
"Give me a light that I may tread safely into the unknown."
And he replied: "Go out into the darkness and put your hand into the Hand
of God. That shall be to you better than light and safer than a known way."

Knowing that one's hand is held tightly by the Almighty God has brought comfort and encouragement to many a weary soul who might otherwise face the future with fear and dread.

He also announced he would "*pay [his] vows to the LORD.*" To what vows do you suppose he referred? The fact is we do not know. It is possible that as Hezekiah lay dying in his bed, he may have offered vows to God. Sometimes when people find themselves in a desperate place, they make vows to God as if they could bargain with God or manipulate His decisions. We must not take vows lightly. If we promise to God, or to anyone else for that matter, to do anything, we should do everything in our power to fulfill our vows. This means that when we take out a loan or make a financial commitment, we must fulfill our vow. Even if people go through the unfortunate experience of bankruptcy, it does not remove them from a moral obligation to pay their debtors. It may take a lot longer, but we bear a positive witness when we fulfill our obligations. When we make a commitment to God, we should fulfill it. I realize that unforeseen things happen that may affect our financial abilities; I have had that kind of experience in my life. In those cases, I have learned some difficult lessons about presuming upon tomorrow and being careful with my commitments, but at the same time, I will do everything in my power and God's provision to fulfill my commitment.

The vow could have referred to the basic commitments or obligations of the Jewish faith. We could translate that into our lives as followers of Jesus. We have commitments that we must keep as well. This involves financial commitments to give, but it also includes many other kinds of commitments God has asked us to make. For example, have you ever made a vow to take better care of your body? The Bible says that our bodies are the temple of the Holy Spirit (see 1 Corinthians 6:19-20), and we are told to glorify God in our body. Think about this for just a moment. If I make a vow and surrender my mind, will, body, emotions, and spirit to God as a follower of Jesus Christ, then it means that how I treat my body matters to God. My friend, Steve Reynolds, has written a book called *Bod 4 God*, and he emphasizes in his book that every decision to put something into our bodies (donuts, desserts, carrots, or green beans) is a spiritual decision. Wow, that kind of hurts, but I suppose it hurts because it is true. Maybe it is easier to talk about money instead of flab, but God is equally interested in both.

Verse fifteen is an interesting verse that at first glance seems to come out of left field. The Psalmist had faced some type of situation that was life-threatening, and he was thanking God for delivering him from it. Suddenly, he throws in this verse: "*Precious in the sight of the LORD is the death of His godly ones.*" Could it be that our response to the faithful, compassionate response of God is to gain His perspective regarding our death? God says that the death of a believer is "*precious*" to Him. He uses a word that describes the value of a rare jewel. God says that our death is a rare treasure to Him that He cherishes and values. Is that strange to you? We fight it, avoid it, and dread it, but God cherishes it. Really? I think that God sees our death as precious because He cherishes us. Death is the door through which we walk into eternity. We dread it because we love and value life, as we should, but God sees there is so much more beyond. Life should be valued and cherished, and we should be good stewards of it, realizing that our death is God's decision. At the same time, we should also see death as an incredible blessing.

I just spoke with someone in our church family who lost her mother-in-law today. This death is precious in the eyes of God. The sweet saint has stepped into eternity and is now dwelling with the One Who died for her and rose again from the dead so she too could have victory over the grave. Her death was precious because she is now whole. We need God's perspective on life *and* death.

The Psalmist concludes with a summary declaration: *"Praise the LORD!"* To all God is and all He has done, our proper response is heartfelt praise.

Further Thought…

- Have you ever thought of God as One Who stoops? What does that image bring to your mind?

- The Psalmist said, *"I shall call upon Him as long as I live."* Can you make that same commitment? How would your life be different if you always called upon the Lord?

- How have you seen God's grace and compassion in your life? Why not tell someone today of something God has done in your life to express His love for you?

- Are you walking before the Lord now? How might your life change as you acknowledge that every moment you live is on display for the One who loves you and died for you?

- Have you ever considered your death as being precious? Does that change your view of death?
- What changes can you make in your life so that every day is lived as a declaration of praise to God?

PSALM 118:1-9

The Goodness of God

Give thanks to the LORD, for He is good; for His lovingkindness is everlasting. 2 Oh let Israel say, "His lovingkindness is everlasting." 3 Oh let the house of Aaron say, "His lovingkindness is everlasting." 4 Oh let those who fear the LORD say, "His lovingkindness is everlasting." 5 From my distress I called upon the LORD; the LORD answered me and set me in a large place. 6 The LORD is for me; I will not fear; what can man do to me? 7 The LORD is for me among those who help me; therefore, I will look with satisfaction on those who hate me. 8 It is better to take refuge in the LORD than to trust in man. 9 It is better to take refuge in the LORD than to trust in princes.

My group stood in the balcony of the old cathedral while the other half stood toward the back of the main platform. As the choir at the front of the auditorium began the antiphonal praise, my group echoed their words of worship as this ancient building filled once again with song. It was my privilege to be a part of the Concert Choir of the University of Georgia when I was studying music for my undergraduate degree. I found that this group of musicians were not only talented, but also many of them were faithful followers of Christ. It was interesting that when I transferred from a Bible college to the University, I was warned that I was leaving heaven to go to hell. My friends were quite wrong. While on tour, my Christian friends and I would gather in hotel rooms to intercede for our classmates and to pray for revival in our land.

On this particular occasion, our director, Dr. Pierce Arant, divided us into two groups. He placed my group in the balcony of the church, and the people entering the auditorium for the concert had no idea we were even there. I'm sure they thought the University of Georgia Concert Choir was a little smaller than they had anticipated because there were at least twenty-five of us hidden away in the balcony. The concert started with a song of worship as the group on the main platform began to sing. The audience suddenly came to life during a pause as my group in the balcony began to sing in response to the first group's words of praise. Not only was it a powerful expression of worship, but it was also reminiscent of how Israel must have worshiped at times in Jerusalem.

Antiphonal worship was not unusual to Israel. The word "antiphon" comes from a Greek compound word meaning "opposite" and "voice." It was the idea of placing two groups of people on opposite sides of a room singing responses to one another. Psalm 118 begins with antiphonal phrases. You can almost imagine one group of singers standing on the wall surrounding the temple compound singing, "*Give thanks to the* LORD, *for He is good*," and then the group on the opposite side of the courtyard answers, "*for His lovingkindness is everlasting.*" Some think that this Psalm was sung by the Jews as they processed up the hill to the temple. The mass of people would have been divided into two groups who would alternate singing in antiphonal style.

The first phrase of the Psalm is a great reminder of God's character, and this trait particularly is something that is easy to forget when things seem to be going wrong. God really is "*good.*" This truth is refreshing to us because it is a reminder that when bad things happen, they first had to pass through the hands of a good God. We come to realize that when we go through the valley, it is only because God knows that the journey through difficulty will later enhance the peaks of blessing. God uses the bad times to prepare us to enjoy the good times. God enrolls us into the school of sorrow so that our character can be shaped and our spirits matured. Isn't it true that we grow more during times of trouble than we do during times of peace? We must always remember that by going through the school of sorrow, we can graduate to a life of joy. God really is good.

If I were arranging this Psalm for a group to sing, I would have the split choirs sing verses one through four, but then I would have a soloist step forward on verse five. While we have no way of knowing exactly how the Jewish choirs of old sang this song, you can definitely see a change in the fifth verse: "*From my distress I called upon the LORD; the LORD answered me and set me in a large place.*" The Psalmist encountered something distressful that lead him to cry out to God. It is also possible that he was reflecting upon the difficulty of the people of Israel, and how the Jews cried out to God during their struggle. Some have thought this Psalm was written after the Jews returned from exile and the second temple was dedicated. In that case, the "*distress*" would have been the captivity of the Jews.

The occasion does not really matter as we see that the Psalmist called out to the Lord *from* his distress. Have you ever been in a situation like that? There may have seemed to be no way out of your struggle, and from within the grip of your distressing circumstances, you cried out to the Lord. The word "*distress*" really means "*straight place*" and it carries with it the idea of a place of restraint. We might call it being between "a rock and a hard place." When you understand that imagery, the next phrase makes more sense: "*the LORD answered me and set me in a large place.*" The "*large place*" stands in contrast to the place of confinement or "*distress.*" It is a place of freedom and space; it is a picture of relief and hope.

Verse six seems to be a focal point of this section of the Psalm: "*The LORD is for me; I will not fear; what can man do to me?*" In the earlier verses, the Psalmist sang about the everlasting lovingkindness of God. We must remember that this was probably being written after the Jews were held captive by the Babylonians for over fifty years. This worshiper realized that even in the midst of distress, "*the LORD is for me.*" This is an awesome thought. God is for me! Repeat that last phrase slowly and think about every word: God...is...for...me! It is sort of a picture of God sitting on the bleachers during the game in which you are the starting pitcher. As you begin to contemplate your next pitch, there is a voice coming from the crowd that is distinct and true: "You can do it, my son. You're the best. I believe in you." You know without even looking that it is your Everlasting Friend. The God of the universe is for you and not against you. Sometimes we feel as if

God is doing things that will undermine our future, but we must remember that the Lord is for us.

I have stood beside many grieving families and stared into the face of incredible suffering. Sometimes it is difficult to find God in such tragedy or think of God as being good. Even though great calamity may cause us to question God and even push us to the brink of losing faith, we must always fall back into the arms of a God Who loves us. Whether we can see the goodness of a situation or not, we can trust God's Word when He says, *"And we know that God causes all things to work together for good to those who love God, to those who are called according to His purpose."* I have determined in my heart that I will always trust God and look for the good in every circumstance. If I cannot find good at the moment, I will choose to wait with expectant faith knowing that God will eventually bring good out of my circumstances. Every situation will eventually be for my good and God's glory.

Because God is on my side, I will not fear. Think for a moment about the consequences of fear. Fear can keep us from thinking clearly, acting rightly, and planning appropriately. Fear is a large obstacle that we must overcome, and it is one of Satan's most lethal tools. It hinders our spiritual growth, and it can lead us into numerous destructive habits. One big result of fear is doubt. When we experience fear, it is because we have abandoned faith. Fear and faith cannot coexist, so we must choose to abandon one or the other. God calls us to faith even when others are trying to pull us down.

The Psalmist presents a question to us that we really need to ponder: *"what can man do to me?"* From one view, a human being can do a lot to us, but in comparison to God's eternity, the things people do to hurt us are actually quite small. God wants us to adopt an eternal perspective. The fact is that as the rapture of the Church draws ever closer, persecution of Christians will grow greater. We will see Christians harmed just because of their faith, and one of those Christians may be you. As we consider eternity and the joy of God's blessings, we will be able to look at our momentary trials as insignificant. When persecution of followers of Christ grows in intensity,

God will speak to believers through this passage and challenge them to put this kind of persecution into the proper perspective.

Look for a moment at the last two verses of this section: *"It is better to take refuge in the LORD than to trust in man. It is better to take refuge in the LORD than to trust in princes."* The Psalmist is presenting to us two options. We can either put our trust in mankind, or we can put our trust in God. We can either find refuge in government, or we can find refuge in the Lord. We are told in this passage to always trust in the Lord. People will let you down. Even people with the greatest of intentions will let you down, but God is always faithful. The word *"refuge"* means "a place of shelter or protection from danger." This passage is saying that God is the ultimate Protector. It is not saying we should never trust people. I realize there are some who struggle with trusting others because of certain events in their past, but we need to learn to trust the people in our lives. However, God must be our ultimate source of safety.

What about trusting *"princes?"* I think the passage before us contains a warning. If we trust our government to be our protector and provider, we will eventually be sorely disappointed. Governments can be used by God, and there are passages in the Bible telling us to be good citizens. God, however, is the One who provides for us and protects us. All governments, good and bad, eventually disappoint. This passage reminded me of the words found in Psalm 20:7 *"Some trust in chariots and some in horses, but we trust in the name of the LORD our God."* One problem with government is that it is led by men and women who are fallible and easily swayed. God is infallible and always firm; we can always find refuge in Him.

Further Thought...

- Can you imagine the antiphonal choir singing of God's goodness? How have you personally experienced the goodness of God?

- Does reflecting upon God's goodness affect how you view the circumstances in your life? Have you ever questioned God's goodness? When you go through future trials, are you willing to declare that "God is good," and therefore trust Him regardless of the circumstances?

- Have you ever been between a "rock and a hard place?" Facing "*distress*" can be challenging to our faith. God says that we should cry out to Him, and He will set us in a "*large place.*" What does that "*large place*" represent to you?

- Have you ever felt all alone? What does it mean to you to think that "*God is for you?*" How does this knowledge affect your thoughts and future actions?

- What are the dangers of trusting only in government? What is the problem, sometimes, when we put our trust in people? Can you see other problems if you decided to trust no one? What do you think is the proper perspective on trusting in God?

PSALM 119:9-16
Loving the Word of God

How can a young man keep his way pure? By keeping it according to Your Word.
10 With all my heart I have sought You; do not let me wander from Your
commandments. 11 Your Word I have treasured in my heart, that I may not sin
against You. 12 Blessed are You, O LORD; teach me Your statutes. 13 With my
lips I have told of all the ordinances of Your mouth. 14 I have rejoiced in the way of
Your testimonies, as much as in all riches. 15 I will meditate on Your precepts and
regard Your ways. 16 I shall delight in Your statutes; I shall not forget Your Word.

What is something you really cherish? I don't mean someone you
cherish, because I am sure that list is quite long. I thought through my
possessions trying to determine whether or not I cherished something
I own. I do have an original edition of Charles Sheldon's book *In His
Steps*. That's pretty special. I'm not sure I can say that I cherish it,
however, because as I'm writing this, I can't remember where it is. It's
packed away somewhere, safe I hope.

I am reminded of a story I once heard. A man was talking to a
book collector. The collector loved rare books. He cherished the
yellowed pages and ancient smells. He practically worshipped the
raised lettering on the smooth, leather covers and often dreamed of the
countless hands that had touched his ancient tomes.

"I once found an old Bible in my grandfather's attic," the man told
the collector, just making idle conversation. "Somebody named
Guttenberg had printed it."

"Guttenberg!" the collector declared. "Where is it now?"

"Oh, I tossed it out. It was really old, not much use."

"Do you realize what you've done? That was one of the first Bibles
ever printed. One copy recently auctioned for two million dollars."

"Ah," the man reasoned, "not mine. Mine wouldn't have brought more than a buck or two. I couldn't even read the crazy thing. Some idiot named Martin Luther had scribbled all over it."

I have read true stories of people throwing out treasure without realizing what they had. One man threw away some treasure only to retrieve it later after discovering its worth. Yahoo News reported the story of an English man's discovery while walking his dog down the beach. The inquisitive canine began sniffing at a stone-like object, and the man picked it up. The smell was foul, so he quickly dropped it and walked away. Returning home with the object tugging on his mind, he began researching in an effort to determine exactly what the mysterious discovery may have been. He discovered, to his shock, that he had picked up some ambergris: whale vomit. Even more amazing was that whale vomit is quite valuable to perfume makers, so the man hurried back to the beach and retrieved the seven-pound object. I imagine he wore gloves the second time around. At the time the article was written, one French dealer had already offered him $50,000.00! The Yahoo News writer ended the article by saying, "If only cat hairballs had the same market value."

The writer of Psalm 119 knew that he had something of great value, and he was not willing to cast it aside. As a matter of fact, we have the same thing, but often times Christians do not seem to cherish it in quite the same way. Near the end of the chapter, the writer said, "*I shall delight in Your commandments, which I love.*" Do you really love the Word of God?

Psalm 119 is the longest chapter in the Bible, and it was written as an acrostic on the Hebrew alphabet. In our English translations, we cannot see the poetic nature of the acrostic, but most editors include the names of the ancient letter above each section of eight verses. There are twenty-two stanzas, consistent with the twenty-two letters of the alphabet, and the verses in each stanza all begin with the corresponding letter. The theme of the whole chapter is the Word of God.

We will look only at the second stanza of the chapter that begins in the original text with the second letter of the alphabet: beth (pronounced "bet"). The Psalmist begins with a question: "*How can a young man keep his way pure?*" This is an important question that most people have pondered. Whether we are male or female, we have often sought how to do what is right. If you are a parent, you have tried to discover ways to lead your children to do right. While the Hebrew word for "*pure*" means "not mixed," it always carries a moral concept.

How can we live our lives purely devoted to God always doing the right thing and not presenting a life that is clouded with immorality? He answers the question: "*By keeping it according to Your word.*" The theme of the chapter is quickly mentioned in the first verse of this second stanza. We will live a life untainted by sin if we adjust our lives to the teachings of the Bible.

It is interesting that as you read through this chapter, the Psalmist reveals through God's Spirit a variety of results that come from reading God's Word. Verse ten says, "*With all my heart I have sought You; do not let me wander from Your commandments.*" It almost seems that those two phrases are not the same thing, but God inspired the writer to write them in a parallel fashion. He indicates to us that if we will not wander from God's commandments, we will be seeking God. Do you equate obeying God with seeking God? There is more to obeying God than doing so just because it is the right thing to do. The real issue is that God wants us to seek Him. We seek Him, in part, by following His commandments.

The Psalmist confessed that he seeks God "*with all [his] heart.*" If the writer had said that he was seeking God with all of his mind, it would not have carried the same emphasis as it does when he stated, "*with all my heart.*" The search was not just a mental exercise; it was a heart-felt passion. This makes sense because Christianity is a relationship and not just a theological pursuit. A lot of people throughout history have understood theology who did not know God. For example, Jesus quoted the prophet Isaiah in making reference to the Pharisees, one of the most religious groups in Judaism: "*This people honors Me with their lips, but their heart is far away from Me*" (see Matthew 15:8). God wants a love relationship with you not just a head that is full of intellectual facts about God. We quickly see that we cannot passionately seek a relationship with God if we are not willing to obey His commands.

In a way, verse eleven is a reiteration of verse nine: "*Your Word I have treasured in my heart, that I may not sin against You.*" This verse is one I learned very early in my life, and I believe it carries a significant message for the Christian seeking to live a holy life. If you want to overcome sin, you will do so by loving the Word of God, studying it regularly, meditating on it consistently, memorizing it systematically, and obeying it constantly. We cannot love God's Word and disobey it at the same time. Will you go back and read that last sentence again? We also cannot say we love God's Word if we are doing nothing to learn it.

Jesus modeled the importance of using God's Word to overcome sin when He was tempted by Satan in the wilderness (see Matthew 4:1-11). Three times when Satan tempted Jesus to sin, Jesus quoted Scripture. Do you see the significance of this? If God quoted Scripture to defeat the evil one, how much more do we need to do so? I challenge you to find passages in the Bible that relate to areas you find to be spiritual weak spots or even strongholds for the enemy, and memorize those passages in order to be better equipped the next time you are tempted to sin.

When I was a teenager, I memorized the sixth chapter of Romans. It was an amazing and effective tool to help me overcome temptation. When I was tempted to sin, I began quoting: "*What shall we say then? Are we to continue in sin so that grace may increase? May it never be! How shall we…*" By the time I got to "*For the wages of sin is death, but the free gift of God is eternal life in Christ Jesus our Lord,*" the temptation to sin was defeated.

Do you gladly speak to others of God's Word? Notice the words of verse thirteen: "*With my lips I have told of all the ordinances of Your mouth.*" One way to cement the Word of God in your mind and in your heart is by talking to others about it. I remember reading a secular book about life management, and the author emphasized not only reading about the principles but also teaching them to others. He said that it is through teaching that we really become students. I think this is true. Not only does it place the truths firmly in our minds, but it also proclaims the truths to others. It is possible that people within your sphere of influence may not have God's Word on their minds, but as you mention it to them, they will be inspired to follow God's Truth.

Did you notice the Psalmist used the word "*all?*" How can you tell of "*all the ordinances of [God's] mouth*" if you do not know them? We must develop and follow Bible reading plans that involve not only casual reading but also detailed study. Reading large portions of Scripture is important, but there is also a time to dissect shorter passages and even individual words. God inspired the words and not just the concepts. Even the verb tenses were inspired and carry special meanings.

Look at verse fourteen: "*I have rejoiced in the way of Your testimonies, as much as in all riches.*" Can you honestly say that God's Word leads you to rejoice "*as much as in all riches?*" I was walking across the Wal-Mart parking lot a while back, and I looked down to discover a ten-dollar bill at my feet. I picked it up and looked around. There was no one nearby, and I had no way of knowing who had dropped the bill. I can't call ten dollars "*riches,*" but I got pretty excited about it. I probably should have given it to missions, but I think I bought gas for my car.

Thinking back on my enthusiasm, I have to ask myself, "Do you get that excited about reading God's Word?" Is reading God's Word better than finding a stray ten-dollar bill in the parking lot? Let's up the price a little. Suppose you were walking down a country road, and you found a three-carat diamond ring? Would you say that you rejoice in reading God's Word as much as you would at your amazing discovery of the ring?

One problem we have is that God's Word is so accessible to us. I have read stories of people, who did not have access to a Bible, risking their lives to read just a page. I am afraid we simply take having a Bible for granted.

Robert L. Sumner told an amazing story in his book, *The Wonders of the Word of* God. A Kansas City man was injured in an explosion, and his face was badly damaged. He lost his eyesight and both hands. He was a new Christian, and his greatest disappointment was that he could no longer read the Bible. He heard about a lady in England who read Braille with her lips, but when he tried it, he learned that the nerve endings in his lips had been so damaged that he could not feel the raised dots.

One day while trying again to read the Braille, he accidently touched the raised portion with his tongue and discovered he could make out the letters. He began reading the Bible by using his tongue. When Sumner wrote his book, this man had read through the entire Bible four times with his tongue. Wow! It kind of makes me wonder what my excuse is for not reading the Bible more.

In verse fifteen, the Psalmist said that he will meditate on God's Word. I am afraid that we have a misunderstanding of this very important spiritual discipline. The idea of meditation conjures up in our minds the idea of a bald man in a toga sitting in the lotus position, humming.

The Hebrew word that is translated *"meditate"* is the same word that describes the repeated sound made by a dove or what a cow does when it chews the cud. A cow will chew on some grass, swallow it, bring it back up, chew on it some more, swallow it again, bring it back up, chew on it some more…You get the idea. Meditating on Scripture is done in exactly the same way. We simply keep the passage of Scripture on our minds for long, extended periods so we can digest all of the spiritual nutrients possible that are contained in that particular passage. Meditating is called a discipline in part because it is not that easy. You must train your mind to focus on just that one thing. You

might need to get in an environment where there will be
tions. You will probably need to memorize the Scripture firs

When I meditate, I keep a pad handy. The pad actually serves in
two different ways. First, if distracting thoughts come to my mind, I
find that if I write them down on the pad, I can quit thinking about it
for a while because it is securely saved on my pad for later thought.
The second purpose is that if God speaks to me in a fresh way about
the passage upon which I am meditating, I can write down the
thoughts for later reflection.

As we apply the disciplines of Bible reading, study, memorization,
and meditation, we are working to remember God's Word and live it
out. The Psalmist ended with this declaration: *"I shall not forget Your
Word."* Are you willing to make that your prayer and your commitment
in response to this great Psalm?

Further Thought...

- What are some things you cherish? Can you say that you cherish
  God's Word?

- Have you found spiritual strength to overcome sin by quoting
  Scripture?

- What is a sin with which you have struggled in the past? Find a
  passage of Scripture related to that particular sin. Are you willing to
  commit that passage to memory so you will have greater, spiritual
  strength next time you are tempted?

- Have you discovered that you learn more about a topic when you
  talk about it? How can you talk about God's Word so that it sticks
  more firmly to your mind?

- What do you think about the man who reads the Bible with his
  tongue? How does that make you feel about the excuses you have
  made about not reading the Bible?

- Have you ever meditated on Scripture? Will you give it a try? What
  are some things you need to do so your meditation experience will

be a good one? What would be a good passage for you to meditate upon?

PSALM 139
Fearfully and Wonderfully Made

O LORD, You have searched me and known me. 2 You know when I sit down and when I rise up; You understand my thought from afar. 3 You scrutinize my path and my lying down, and are intimately acquainted with all my ways. 4 Even before there is a word on my tongue, behold, O LORD, You know it all... 13 For You formed my inward parts; You wove me in my mother's womb. 14 I will give thanks to You, for I am fearfully and wonderfully made; wonderful are Your works, and my soul knows it very well. 15 My frame was not hidden from You, when I was made in secret, and skillfully wrought in the depths of the earth; 16 Your eyes have seen my unformed substance; and in Your book were all written the days that were ordained for me, when as yet there was not one of them. 17 How precious also are Your thoughts to me, O God! How vast is the sum of them! 18 If I should count them, they would outnumber the sand. When I awake, I am still with You... 23 Search me, O God, and know my heart; try me and know my anxious thoughts; 24 and see if there be any hurtful way in me, and lead me in the everlasting way.

Holding my precious first-born, I marveled at her beauty and perfection. Ten fingers, ten toes, and a beautiful, round, hairy head – everything was in place and exquisitely designed. The birth had been difficult, but our beautiful, little girl had made it safely into the world. I had some time alone with our cherished blessing in the early minutes of her life, and I could not take my eyes off her perfect, tiny body. How had God done that? I was in awe at the whole process and grateful for the heavenly masterpiece.

It makes sense that God would know us inside and out; we are His masterpiece. King David began this wonderful song by expressing God's thorough knowledge of humanity: "*O LORD, You have searched me and known me.*" When he used the word "*searched,*" he did not mean studying something that was unknown or previously misunderstood, but rather David was describing a steady, unblinking gaze. It may have been something like my gaze at our new daughter, but in God's case, there was nothing baffling about what He saw.

As God's eyes take us in, He knows every little detail about our bodies and our lives. He knows our strengths, and He knows our weaknesses. He knows where we will excel, and He knows when we are going to need extra help. There is nothing in our lives that is hidden from our heavenly Father. How does that make you feel? At times, it is a little unsettling for me.

I remember getting a sling shot for my birthday when I was seven years old. My friend, Chris, and I walked down the street shooting at tree trunks and cans with my new toy. It was quite powerful, and I was amazed at the strength of that band of rubber. Chris had a wild idea to shoot at the front windshield of an antique car sitting in the driveway of the neighbor's house. Within seconds there was an ear-splitting crack as the ancient windshield crumbled, and two guilty boys ran off into the woods. What were we going to do? If my Dad found out about what we had done, he would have torn up my backside.

We put together a plan. We were going to save up our money and pay the man for his windshield. In the meantime, we vowed to tell no one. What I did not know was that we didn't need to tell anyone because the man saw us running into the woods. That night, he called my father, and my father confronted me. I told him that I didn't do it, which technically I didn't. My friend was the one shooting the sling shot, so that made me innocent. Right?

As time passed, my neighbor was getting quite agitated with my father. In the end, it was my brother who discovered our scheme when he decided to play a joke on me and Chris by answering the phone and pretending to be me. The first thing out of my buddy's mouth was, "How much money have you saved?" It didn't take long for my brother to figure out what was up, and he wasted no time in ratting me out. I had my father convinced that I was totally innocent, but the truth was, I was as guilty as I could be. True, I didn't shoot the sling shot, but I may as well have done it. I survived to write about it, but trust me, it was not pleasant.

While we may be able to deceive others, we cannot deceive God. He has looked deep into our minds and our hearts, and He knows us completely. Even when we do not know ourselves, God knows everything about our lives. King David acknowledged, *"You know when I sit down and when I rise up; You understand my thought from afar."* Not only does God know our inner thoughts, He even knows everything we do and when we do it. He understands us. That's amazing because sometimes, I do not understand myself.

It is important to grasp this truth because there are times when we wonder if God has forgotten about us. He even knows when we sit down with our head in our hands wondering how we're going to make it through another day. Not only does He know our actions, but He knows our motives. According to verse four, He even knows what we are going to say before we say it.

I've got a friend who habitually finishes my sentences, but God knows the whole sentence before I even utter a word. I wonder if having this knowledge could change what we say. If I am about to say something ugly, and God knows it before it comes out of my mouth, knowledge of this truth may help me to show restraint and self-control. Knowing that God anticipates my words may help me to speak only those things that honor the Lord. How does God know us so well? Obviously, He is God, so there is nothing that He does not know.

David pointed out another truth in verse thirteen: *"For You formed my inward parts; You wove me in my mother's womb."* God knows us because He made us. I think we understand something about the physical process of conception and the growth of a baby in the mother's womb, but this passage says that God *"formed"* us and *"wove"* us in the womb. These words bring two different images to mind. The first image is that of a potter sitting before his wheel fashioning a piece of pottery. As the wheel turns, he works with great care and attention to create the perfect masterpiece that will accomplish the purpose of the design.

The second image is that of a seamstress or a weaver working meticulously on a useful piece of clothing. It reminds me of the woman I saw a couple of weeks ago in Oaxaca, Mexico weaving a dress. I bought one of her finished products for my granddaughter that will be born in another month. The dress is beautiful with intricate designs of flowers around the neck. While there is a natural process of a baby's development, God is somehow fashioning the child in just the right way to accomplish His purpose. While this points to several things, it certainly underscores the worth of this unborn child.

As David reflected upon God's intimate knowledge of him, he overflows in praise and adoration of God's creative power: "*I will give thanks to You, for I am fearfully and wonderfully made; wonderful are Your works, and my soul knows it very well.*" Isn't that an interesting contrast? We are both *fearfully* and *wonderfully* made. In other words, when we consider the details of our bodies, the amazing structure of our DNA, and the intricacies of our bodies' systems, it is proper to respond in both fear and awe.

We respond with fear because we realize that our Creator is a powerful and awesome God. He is much bigger than us, and His creative genius should foster respect, and even a healthy fear, in us. The original Hebrew word literally means "producing awe or reverence." It is almost as if when we study the details of the human body, we have no alternative but to fall on our face in silent, awe-struck worship and acknowledge God's greatness.

The word that is translated as "*wonderfully*" came from a term that means "distinguished." This idea means that there is nothing else in all of creation like mankind. We are distinguished in many ways, but I suppose the greatest way is that God breathed into us His breath of life (see Genesis 2:7). He gave us the capacity to know Him and to live forever with Him in His heaven.

It is as if the Psalmist cannot cease overflowing with praise as he reflected upon God's creative brilliance seen in the human body: "*wonderful are Your works, and my soul knows it very well.*" God's works are full of wonder, and deep down, we know it. This passage makes me think about Romans 1:18-20 that points out the fact that God has made Himself plain to us through the creation that is around us. God declared that this creation, including the creation of mankind, is enough to cause people to seek after God, so much so that we are all without excuse.

Our soul knows that there is something amazing about the human body that screams aloud the concept of design. If there is a design, then there must be a designer.

Take just a moment to reflect upon your own body. Have you ever given any thought to the creation of a blood clot or to the amazing process of a paper cut healing nearly overnight? Have you ever studied with detail how cells reproduce or how DNA functions to create a unique pattern that distinguishes you from every other human being that ever lived? Approximately three billion distinct chemical letters make up your DNA code that define your uniqueness. Your DNA contains so much information that it would take twelve sets of *The Encyclopedia Britannica* to contain it all. Twelve sets offer a total of 384 volumes worth of detailed information that would fill up forty-eight feet of library shelves.

While our DNA contains a lot of information, God has shrunk it all down to where its actual size is only two millionths of a millimeter thick. I can't picture that. Molecular biologist Michael Denton said that a teaspoon of DNA could contain all the information needed to build the proteins for all the species of organisms that have ever lived on the earth, and "there would still be enough room left for all the information in every book ever written" (Evolution: A Theory in Crisis, p. 334). DNA did not randomly happen by accident. You were *"fearfully and wonderfully made."*

Look again at verse sixteen: *"Your eyes have seen my unformed substance; and in Your book were all written the days that were ordained for me, when as yet there was not one of them."* God affirmed that before you were born, He had a plan for your life. Your days were *"ordained,"* or "set apart." You are not an accident that came about through a cosmic collision and random natural processes. You were intentionally created for an eternal purpose. Your purpose begins with a personal relationship with your Creator, through Jesus Christ.

Our secular world would like for you to believe that humanity is an accident, and you have no real purpose. Satan would love for you to think that people have no worth. This, of course, is far from true; you are special to God. Before your birth, He had a plan for your life. Our challenge is to determine the path God would have us to take and the purpose He would have us to fulfill.

God's thoughts of you cannot be numbered: *"How precious also are Your thoughts to me, O God! How vast is the sum of them! If I should count them, they would outnumber the sand."* If you are married, think back to when you were dating and not yet able to spend all of the moments of your life with your beloved. I remember having to make myself leave Sandra on Sunday nights so I could drive back to Athens in order to attend class at the University the next day. It was like amputating my arm. I thought of her constantly.

Those thoughts cannot even begin to compare to God's thoughts of us. The sum of them is vast. Isn't it amazing to think that the God of the universe is thinking about you? He loves you. As a matter of fact, He is crazy about you. I love Max Lucado's reflection upon this idea: "If God had a refrigerator, your picture would be on it. If he had a wallet, your photo would be in it. He sends you flowers every spring and a sunrise every morning. Whenever you want to talk, he'll listen. He can live anywhere in the universe, and he chose your heart. And the Christmas gift he sent you in Bethlehem? Face it, friend. He's crazy about you" (*A Gentle Thunder*, 1995. p. 115).

The final two verses are the culmination of the Psalm: *"Search me, O God, and know my heart; try me and know my anxious thoughts; and see if there be any hurtful way in me, and lead me in the everlasting way."* Remember that God knows you better than you know yourself. After contemplating, the Psalmist acknowledged that the only way he would come to know himself would be if God gave to him a clear understanding of his own heart. He asked God to search him out or dissect his inner thoughts.

David was very aware of how easily he was deceived, so he wanted God to help him understand his thoughts and ways.

He asked God to lead him *"in the everlasting way."* This meant the path of life as contrasted with the wicked way that leads to destruction. If we trust our own wisdom to lead us down the right path in life, we will be in serious trouble. We need God to help us understand our true motives and the basis for our anxious thoughts. Who better to search our hearts than the One who created us? Since we are *"fearfully and wonderfully made,"* let's yield to the One who truly knows us so that our path will be right and lead us to joy.

Further Thought...

- Have you ever stopped to ponder the fact that God knows everything about you?

- How does it make you feel to know that God knows when you sit down and when you stand up?

- Stop for a moment and reflect upon the astonishing details of your body. Consider for a moment how perfectly everything has to work just so your body stays in balance. How were you *"fearfully and wonderfully made?"* Does it make you feel special or significant to think that God's power and design are seen so clearly in your body?

- Do you feel like there might be some areas deep in your mind and life that you keep hidden – even from yourself? What do you think might be some things God would show you if He searched you out?

- What would the *"everlasting way"* look like for you? Would it be much different than the path you are on right now?

- Why not pause and thank God for creating you? Ask Him to search you and to help you come to really know yourself. Take the last two verses and turn them into your personal prayer asking for God's intervention in your life.

PSALM 150
Discovering Praise

Praise the LORD! Praise God in His sanctuary; praise Him in His mighty expanse. 2 Praise Him for His mighty deeds; praise Him according to His excellent greatness. 3 Praise Him with trumpet sound; praise Him with harp and lyre. 4 Praise Him with timbrel and dancing; praise Him with stringed instruments and pipe. 5 Praise Him with loud cymbals; praise Him with resounding cymbals. 6 Let everything that has breath praise the LORD. Praise the LORD!

I sat on the front porch of Mrs. Nunally's duplex and felt sorry for this forlorn, elderly woman. Just ten minutes earlier, I had been a fourteen-year-old kid minding my own business while trying to get home in time for dinner, and just like that, my life was changed forever. When I raised my hand to say hello, as any good neighbor should do, this petite, gray-haired woman began talking to me as if I were sitting with her on her porch. I had never met the sweet lady. I decided I may as well join her for a moment because she seemed lonely. Little did I realize the valuable discovery I was about to make in the most unexpected and unlikely relationship that would continue to impact me throughout my life.

Mrs. Nunally had been born in 1888, and though she had been married at one time, her husband died many years earlier. She now appeared to be all alone in the world. During our conversation, I discovered she had not eaten since the day before because she was afraid to turn on her stove. I told her that my mother was preparing dinner, and I would bring a plate back to her. That night, I started a practice I would enjoy every night for the next several years. I brought two plates of food back to her house, and we sat together at her elegant, oak table for dinner. One problem was that her house was infested with roaches. She didn't think she had the money to hire someone to take care of the pests, so I eventually used some of my paper route money to buy bug spray. I think I depleted the black army of nasty insects from several billion to a few million. Maybe I'm exaggerating a bit, but she had a real problem.

Not only was Mrs. Nunally old, but her furniture was ancient. Her bed had come from her great, great grandfather's ship. He was a sea captain, and the antique bed, held together with pegs and strung with huge rope, had been in the captain's quarters on his ship in the mid 1700's. I stood at the foot of the bed wondering what ports of call this bed had encountered while sitting in the cabin of this ancient vessel. It was incredible.

Over the following months, I repaired door knobs, bought her groceries, fixed her bed, and just sat and listened. My dear friend was beginning to go a bit senile, and at night, she would revert back to the days of her childhood. She talked to me about her family, as if I knew them. If I didn't know who she was talking about, she would get upset. I had to get to know her family as much as possible by studying her family history kept in a large, black, leather Bible. Her uncle was a Confederate soldier in the Civil War, and another family member fought in World War I. Because I had to pretend like I was her family member living in the late 1800's, I sat in awe night after night as I experienced first-hand, sort of, what it was like to interact with a relative who had fought "the Yanks."

One day I went out back to find a rake and discovered an antique car in her old, dilapidated garage. It was a 1933 Rockne that had not been driven in years, and she eventually asked me if I would be interested in buying it. Because I had been delivering papers for a few years and been frugal, I had enough money to make the purchase, and my father pulled it home with his Gran Torino station wagon. I eventually got the thing to run, and years later, my wife and I drove away from our wedding ceremony in grand style.

Though Mrs. Nunally died when I was seventeen, I had the opportunity to experience the past in unusual and impactful ways. I discovered things about our history that I never would have known if I had not simply waved to an elderly woman sitting on a porch. Those years were a time of great discovery for me. I discovered some ancient relics, an antique car, and a precious woman who thought of herself as poor. The truth was she was not poor but actually quite wealthy with old stock certificates she had long forgotten.

Just before her death, Mrs. Nunally had an accident on the snow in her yard. While she was in the hospital, I discovered a distant relative, who came, after my phone call, to take Mrs. Nunally to a nursing home in Illinois and to retrieve all of her things.

Discovery is an inspiring thing that can bring wonder and awe. This amazing book of Psalms is a book about discovery. God has shared things with us to help us discover ourselves, but He has also helped us to discover things about Him. In response to everything we have studied, the final chapter calls us, yet again, to the discovery of praise. I call it a discovery because it is not easily found by Christians, or anyone else for that matter.

One thing that hinders the discovery of praise is self-centeredness, and self-centeredness is an epidemic among humanity. Even after we become Christians, we are still plagued with this malady. One indicator of this problem is the content of our prayer lives. Make note sometimes of the things you pray about. For many of us, prayer simply means asking God for things. If I had been a self-centered fourteen-year-old, I would not have discovered the treasure of an old friend. I wish I could say I always did the right thing while growing up, but I am grateful God helped me choose wisely that time. Praise is a critical element missing in our prayers and selflessness is the guiding light to discovering it.

The Psalmist begins this final chapter of the book with a call to praise: "*Praise the LORD! Praise God in His sanctuary; praise Him in His mighty expanse.*" Consider this: thirteen of the seventy-two words of this Psalm are the word "praise." Several different Hebrew words are translated as "praise," and this one is "*halal*" or "hallelujah." Isn't it interesting that the word "hallelujah" seems to be the same in many languages? It means to "boast in someone or something." When we praise God, we are boasting in Him. We are enunciating the things that make Him great and unique.

Many times we confuse praise with thanksgiving. Thanksgiving is giving God thanks for what He has done. Praise is declaring Who God is. This call to praise in the opening verse of the last Psalm is basically saying we should praise God at all times. We should praise God *"in His sanctuary,"* and we should praise Him *"in His mighty expanse."* The *"expanse"* refers to the atmosphere or all the space around the earth. I believe we can all agree that this concept covers anywhere we might be. Praise is not just limited to a Sunday morning experience bound within the close confines of a building of worship. You should praise God as you climb a mountain and when you arrive at the picturesque mountaintop. You can praise God while driving to work, sitting in a meeting, changing a diaper, preparing dinner, or mowing the lawn.

Verse two calls us to praise God *"for His mighty deeds"* and *"according to His excellent greatness."* Remember that praise is a focus upon God's character and not His actions, so the first phrase is pointing to the truth that God's *"mighty deeds"* reveal His awesome nature. It is important that we learn to observe the activity of God and connect it to the character of God.

Can you think of something you have seen God do that points to some aspect of His nature? Since praise is God-centered and not man-centered, our focus should not be upon ourselves when we worship. We can easily fall into the pattern of anticipating the benefits of God's activity, which comes from a man-centered focus, and not allow God's activity to reflect upon His nature. If we are really going to praise God, we are strictly focusing on Who He is, regardless of the blessings we receive.

Consider the salvation God offers to us through the death and resurrection of Jesus Christ. Through Christ's actions, His death on the cross, we learn that He is redemptive, sacrificial, and His love is unconditional. It would be easy for our focus to turn to our salvation, forgiveness, and the promise of heaven when we die. If you think about it, that type of thinking is self-centered. We do not become

Christians because of the fringe benefits. We respond to God's invitation for a relationship. It is not just about heaven and eternal blessings. Therefore, when we think about God's redemptive actions, our first thought must be upon the character and nature of a God Who would leave heaven, come to earth as a man, and die on a cruel cross for the sin of humanity.

The second section of this Psalm is a call to instrumental praise. The Psalmist calls for praise from using the trumpet, harp, lyre, timbrel, stringed instruments, pipe, and cymbals. Some of these instruments may be quite familiar to us. We have probably all seen a trumpet, and some of us have played one. It is one of the more popular band instruments, especially for boys. When I was growing up, I always wanted to play the drums, but my mother encouraged me toward the piano and brass instruments.

One time, my band director had me play one note on a bass drum during a concert. It was really kind of embarrassing. Before the song began, I left my place in the trombone section and walked around the symphonic band, taking my spot behind the bass drum. The one hit of the drum came on a strange syncopated beat that the normal bass drummer just could not seem to get right. My drum career was short lived, and it was not nearly as much fun as I had once anticipated.

While harps are not as popular, most of us have seen one before. Years ago, I gained a new appreciation for the harp. I had always connected it to sweet, gentle sounds made with delicate fingers until I attended a concert by Greg Buchanan, a Christian concert harpist. He was incredible, and I believe he could have made his harp moonwalk if he wanted to. It is a fascinating instrument and quite challenging to play.

The lyre is more unusual. We might think of it as a small, lap harp, though that description falls short of really describing it well. It does resemble a small harp, and it is made of seven strings. This was the instrument that David played when he went to sooth King Saul. The lyre was often used to accompany solo singing, and therefore sort of reminds me of an early guitar. A timbrel is an antiquated tambourine. This was a very popular instrument for Jewish people. Stringed *instruments* certainly include harps and lyres, but they also included instruments like the nebel azor (a ten-stringed instrument) and the lute, which would have been an ancestor to the guitar.

It is difficult to distinguish between two different types of cymbals, but there is no doubt that a variety of cymbals existed in antiquity. Some people consider the *"pipe"* to be an organ, but even the ancestor to an organ was not invented until around 230 B.C. The *"pipe"* would have been a long tube, or even more than one tube combined with others, through which a musician would blow to make various sounds. With all of these instruments mentioned, the Psalmist is calling us to take every instrument imaginable and play it to the glory of God.

This passage also mentions *"dancing."* He must not have been Baptist because I've always heard that Baptists do not believe in dancing. I say that tongue-in-cheek because I am Baptist. I have people ask me from time to time if Baptists can dance. To that, I always reply, "I don't know, but this one can't." No Baptist doctrine exists stating dancing is wrong, and I have no doubt that even theologians and church leaders from years ago in the Baptist church would have acknowledged that David danced in praise to God.

I feel confident that some Christians in the past placed a restriction on dancing because of what it had become in the secular world. So, what do we do with that? Should we not use dance in worship because the secular world has tainted it with sexual innuendos and vulgarity? Let's process that position for just a moment. I once worked in a large recording studio in Dallas, Texas, and sometimes late at night, we would record mariachi bands. As these Mexican musicians hauled in their instruments, the instruments would reek with the smells of alcohol from the bars in which the musicians had been playing. On one such occasion, a guy's organ smelled like someone had dumped a keg of beer on it. Since this organ was used in settings that were offensive, does that disqualify the instrument from worship? Of course not. Our enemy comes to kill, steal, and destroy the good things of God.

Dance is not necessarily good or evil. God created the Fine Arts, and the Church needs to embrace them for His Glory. We can use our bodies in expressions of worship that are tasteful and God-honoring. I think that sometimes we frown upon expressions of worship that are different than the expressions with which we are more familiar. If you grew up in a setting that did not use dance in worship, you may feel a little awkward with this practice. I became quite accustomed to worshipful dance when I used to sing the tenor part in a community passion play put on by a local Christian dance studio. It was incredibly beautiful and unimaginably worshipful. After watching ballet to Christian music, I decided that surely the angels must dance on toe in heaven. It was so engaging and led me right into God's throne room to give Him praise.

Was David wrong to dance before the Lord (see 2 Samuel 6)? Not at all. Would we be wrong to dance before the Lord? Of course not. The Bible gives directives for worship, and whatever is done, must be done in order and in a way that honors God. It must be done to bring glory to God.

God inspired the writer of this last chapter to call believers to let go of inhibitions and glorify God through music and dance. This calls for celebrative worship. Worship involves more than just celebration (contemplation, reflection, submission, repentance, etc.), but there is celebration. It is fitting to shout out our praise of the Almighty God. You may even want to move your body in expressions of worship. If I do, I'll probably do it alone, but since God is the audience anyway, I suppose that would be okay. Reach deep into your heart and into your talents. Whatever you find within your being, release in worship of the God Who is worthy of our praise.

Further Thought...

- After reading this chapter, how would you define praise?

- Do you see yourself as someone who needs to discover praise?

- Think for a moment about your prayer life. What percentage of your prayers is focused on asking God for things and what percentage is more directed toward praise?

- Do you have your favorite worship instruments? Does it make you feel a little awkward to include instruments in worship that are not on your "favorite" list? Take a moment and ask God to help you adopt a Psalm 150 understanding of how all instruments can be used in worship.

- Do you share my inhibitions in expressive worship through dance? Though I will not be putting on another pair of ballet shoes in this life (I did have to study ballet when I sang in the opera, but that's another story), God has helped me to see the value of dance in worship. Do you need to ask God to expand your understanding of the use of one's body in expressive worship?

- Have you ever considered the role of Fine Arts in worship? How could dance, painting, music, drama, the spoken word, and other forms of the Arts be used to bring glory to God?

WHAT'S NEXT?

Now what? Have you ever completed an objective and then wondered what you should do next? I remember walking away from the recital hall at the University of Georgia after singing in my last vocal jury of my college career. I had completed all of my classes, played in my piano jury, taken all of my finals, and then sang before a panel of professors for my grade in voice. I was done. I asked myself the question as I walked past the renowned bell tower, "What now?"

It was really kind of a crazy question because I knew I would eventually start seminary. I pastored a church, and I was married to my beautiful bride. I still had a sense of not knowing what to do next. I think it came because I had spent nearly five years pouring myself into a degree in music with a double concentration, and now I felt as if my goals had been accomplished, but my "goals" weren't really my life's objective. What I'm saying is that my goal of getting a bachelor's degree in music was not really why God put me on the planet. There was more – a lot more. I wanted to ring the historic bell anyway, but I think they removed the rope to keep people like me from making unnecessary racket. I pondered my life in the short jaunt to the car and planned the moves that eventually led me to the place I'm at now: sitting at my desk writing this closing chapter.

You have just completed a journey through the Psalms. I know you only read thirty of the 150 Psalms, but you still traveled through some of the ancient writings that have inspired Christians through the centuries, and hopefully you have been inspired as well. The question is, "Now what?" I want to encourage you to consider several things as you bring this study to a close.

First of all, consider reading it again. While the "it" could be this book, and reading *Songs from the Heart* again is not a bad idea, I am really talking about the Psalms. I could even be talking about the Bible in general. The Bible is not just ancient words on a page written by people who are now dead. Hebrews 4:12 tells us, *"For the Word of God is living and active and sharper than any two-edged sword, and piercing as far as the division of soul and spirit, of both joints and marrow, and able to judge the thoughts and intentions of the heart."* You might want to read this book and the Psalms passages again. Every time I read them, God speaks to me in fresh ways, and I am reminded that God's Word is *"living and active."* You can read the same passage of Scripture three days in a row and receive three different messages from God. I know there are some things that will remain consistent, but God has a way of speaking fresh thoughts into our minds that have perfect application in the moment.

You can read the book of Psalms with this book as a companion, and I believe God will speak new thoughts to your mind. You may want to re-read *Songs from the Heart* with a close friend or with members of your small group. God may have some new ideas for you to ponder. I think reading the Psalms in a systematic and regular way will encourage you spiritually and bring growth in your life. Did you know that if you read five Psalms a day, you can read the entire book of Psalms in a month? I have read five Psalms and one Proverb a day to complete both books together over a thirty-one-day period. One response you may have to this book is to simply read it again.

I hope another response is to deepen your intimacy with God. The book of Psalms is really a book about meeting with Him. The Christian life is not just an empty, ritualistic life filled with calendared events and lifestyle choices that are fixed and rehearsed. It is a vital experience with an amazing God. While reading through this longest book of the Bible, you have read the inspired words from men, and maybe women, who learned that what God wants more than anything else is a close, intimate relationship. God wants to be loved up close!

You could re-read the Psalms with an eye toward those passages that help you learn about what God is like. I once used a blue marker to make note of every passage that said something about God's character and nature. I later went back and read all of the "blue" passages so I could reflect upon God's nature.

You could take passages from the Psalms and pray them back to God. Praying the Psalms can really be life changing. Instead of just reading, *"The LORD is my Shepherd, I shall not want....,"* you can pray, "Jesus, You are my Lord and the personal Shepherd of my life. Because You are leading me, there is nothing in life that I lack. You are my Provider..."

Worship is another fitting response to the Psalms. I have a burden for the Church and our lack of authentic worship. I know that I cannot judge what is really going on inside a person, but I believe there is a worship deficit in the Church today. We have been deceived into thinking that worship is about us, when it really is about God. We have been numbed to the vibrancy that should be ours through a personal relationship with Christ. We have been lulled by an entertainment driven society that leads us to walk away from worship disappointed because it didn't "do anything for us."

I love the definition of worship I once heard from Dr. Bruce Leafblad: "Worship is communion with God in which believers by grace center their minds' attention and their hearts' affection on the Lord Himself, humbly glorifying God in response to His greatness and His worth." When you gathered with your local congregation last Sunday, did you feel as if your church was really engaged in worship? Did the service you attended bring more of a yawn instead of a shout? It is my prayer that there will be such a yearning among the body of Christ for authentic, life-changing worship that we will refuse to be content with spiritual mediocrity where worshipers are more focused on lunch menus than the Word of God. I long to be part of a church that cannot wait to gather Sunday after Sunday instead of one that practices a "time-share worship experience" where we all take turns attending service in order to fulfill our monthly obligation.

Worship is a discipline and worship is a choice. For me to meet with God on Sundays, I must prepare my body, my spirit, and my mind. Is it any wonder that the Jews sang the Psalms of Ascent as they headed toward the temple? Maybe we need to incorporate some things into our lives that will help us and our families to prepare for one of the most important hours of our week – the hour of worship. Choosing to worship means that I engage my mind as I enter the auditorium and encounter God through my worship experience. It means I sing songs to the Lord and tell Him how much I adore Him. It means I engage my body in celebration and my mind in contemplation as the life-giving experience of worship permeates my inner being. I think it is time for the Church to get excited about our salvation and to be broken over our sin. It is time to meet with God and experience His glory.

As believers gather to worship, there is a powerful evangelistic result for those who do not know Christ. People come to church because they are looking for God. When they encounter a people meeting with God, it is life-changing. They want a faith that is dynamic and real.

I wonder if when people go to your church or to mine, do they find God? Do they find a people who know what it is to meet with God and celebrate His worth? I do wonder when unbelievers attend a service that yields more watch-checking than heart-checking if there is any spiritual pull from the body of Christ to the Lord of the Church. I do not think so.

People all around you on Sunday will be impacted by your worship, and though people are not our focus, they will receive ministry by observation and association. Will you pledge now to make preparations to meet with God on Sunday? Your preparations will need to begin on Monday, not Sunday morning as you get out of bed. I suggest that you also begin preparing clothing for Sunday morning on Saturday night. I encourage people to play worship music at home on Sunday mornings and in their cars and homes throughout the week. Find some of the songs you typically sing in worship and incorporate them into your personal worship and everyday lives.

I must mention one final thing that has great importance. We must think about helping our children meet with God through the Psalms. This means that we guide them in reading this wonderful book of worship and intimacy with the Father. It means that we model for them what it is to be worshipers and Christians seeking a vibrant relationship with God. Your children and grandchildren are hungry to see an authentic faith. Will they see it in you? They need to see that we have a hunger for God and a desire to meet with Him in worship. They need to see us *"clapping our hands unto the Lord and shouting unto God with the voice of triumph."* It will change their lives.

Children attend your church who could be impacted by an adult friend who knows what it is like to meet with God. I am so grateful for a woman in my mother's church who reached into a young girl's life and showed her what it meant to know God. It changed my mom's life, and eventually changed my life, as well.

Whatever you do, don't just move on, unchanged by your experiences in the Psalms. Before you close this book, make a few notes of what's next for you. I have also included an appendix, following this chapter, that offers guidance on how to become a Christian. If you have never made the decision to enter into a personal relationship with Jesus, I encourage you to read over that material.

Thank you for reading *Songs from the Heart: Meeting with God in the Psalms.* I hope it has been a blessing to you and encouraged you in your spiritual journey. I would be grateful if you would take a moment to express your thoughts about this book on Amazon.com by writing a brief review. May God bless you as you seek to meet Him daily and find His song in your heart, and may your life be lived as if you are a song of worship to the Most High God.

Appendix

HOW TO BECOME A CHRISTIAN

The book of Psalms is often read as a source of comfort and encouragement. It is important that we all understand that comfort and encouragement begins with a relationship with Jesus Christ. This appendix is provided to help you enter into a personal relationship with the One Who loves you and died so you can obtain eternal comfort and lasting security. If asked, many people in the United States would claim to be Christians, but what does it really mean to be a Christian? How does one "cross over" to a life of faith?

We must first understand a few truths. One critical thing we need to know is that God made us for relationships, and the number one relationship He made us for is the relationship with Himself. While God wants a relationship with us, the fact is that deep down in our hearts, we long for a relationship with God. Sometimes we try to fill that longing with all manner of things such as careers, accomplishments, financial success, patriotism, sex, hedonism... The  list could go on and on. In all of our attempts to fill the void in our lives, we simply come up empty-handed, or maybe I should say "empty-hearted." Earlier in this book, I referred to Pascal's quote: "There is a God-shaped vacuum in the heart of every man." If we try to fill the void in our lives with anything other than God, the void will remain just that—a void. Our longing, or our hunger, is for God and God alone.

The Bible teaches that every human being is born separated from God because of sin. Romans 3:23 says, *"For all have sinned and fall short of the glory of God."* A few verses prior to this, the Bible says, *"There is none righteous, not even one"* (Romans 3:10). Our society has tried to hide the reality of sin, but the fact is sin is not only all around us, but it is also all in us.

Sin could be defined as missing the mark of God's perfection. It is doing, saying, or thinking anything contrary to the ways and will of God. We are all guilty. We can try to redefine the term or compare ourselves to people of lesser morals, but the bottom line is that every human being is born with a nature to do wrong, and we also occasionally, or not so occasionally, chose to sin. One problem we have is that while we are not righteous, God IS righteous and holy. He can have nothing to do with sin, even though He loves the sinner (see Romans 5:8). This creates a great divide between us and God. The

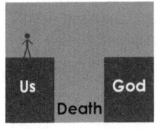

natural result of humanity apart from God is death. Romans 6:23 says, "*The wages of sin is death...*" This concept of death is more than just ceasing to have a heartbeat and a brain wave. This "death" means eternal separation from God.

People try to get to God through all manner of means. Most people think that if they are good enough, God will give them a pass into heaven. It is almost as if there is a large scale in heaven where all of our deeds are weighed. The good deeds are placed on the plate to the right and the bad deeds are placed on the left. If the good deeds outweigh the bad deeds, then we feel as if God is obligated to let us in to His heaven. The Bible says in Isaiah 64:6 "*all our righteous deeds are like a filthy garment,*" and Ephesians 2:8-9 clearly says we are not saved by doing good works: "*For by grace you have been saved through faith; and that not of yourselves, it is the gift of God; not as a result of works, so that no one may boast.*"

While God is compassionate, merciful, and gracious, He is also holy, righteous and just. If God simply gave us a pass and let us into His heaven, He would not be righteous and just. If He just sent us all to hell with no hope for eternal life, He would not be gracious. God's answer, and our solution, is Jesus Christ. God sent His Son to die for the sins of the world. John 3:16 says, "*For God so loved the world, that He gave His only begotten Son, that whoever believes in Him shall not perish, but have eternal life.*" Jesus paid for our sins with His own life and then rose again from the dead declaring He is indeed God (see Romans 1:4).

God has given to us an option: either we pay for our sins through our own eternal death and separation from God, or we allow Christ's death to pay for our sins as we trust Him as our Savior. In essence, Jesus became our bridge to the Father. Through Jesus Christ, and only through Jesus Christ, we can enter into a relationship with our Creator.

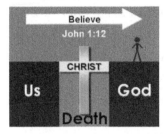 Jesus said, "*I am the way, and the truth, and the life; no one comes to the Father but through Me.*" Acts 4:12 says of Jesus, "*And there is salvation in no one else; for there is no other name under heaven that has been given among men by which we must be saved.*"

We enter into a relationship with God through repentance of our sin and faith in Jesus Christ. Repentance means turning around. Whereas, once we were following our own way and our own desires, to repent means we turn and follow God's way and seek to fulfill His desires. Placing our faith in Jesus means more than just intellectually accepting the facts about Christ's identity and work. The Bible says in James 2:19: "*You believe that there is one God. Good! Even the demons believe that—and shudder*" (NIV). True faith comes as we surrender our lives to Jesus Christ allowing Him to be the King of our heart and the Leader of our life. Romans 10:9-10 says, "*If you confess with your mouth Jesus as Lord, and believe in your heart that God raised Him from the dead, you will be saved; for with the heart a person believes, resulting in righteousness, and with the mouth he confesses, resulting in salvation.*"

Christianity is a choice to surrender to Jesus Christ as the Lord of your life. Surrender means totally giving your life into the hands of someone else. Imagine drowning in a lake, and a lifeguard swims out to rescue you. The only way you can be saved from sure death is to quit fighting and surrender to the saving grasp of the lifeguard. Becoming a Christian is not just praying a prayer. It is not just going to church. It is

260

not just trying to reform your life. Becoming a Christian is turning from sin and self and choosing to follow Jesus as your Sovereign King.

You can express this decision in a prayer as you cry out to God. If you have never done this and would like to, why not bow your head right now and tell Jesus that you acknowledge you are a sinner in need of forgiveness. Tell Him you believe that He died for you and rose again, and ask Him to forgive you for your sin and come into your life. Commit yourself to be a Christ-follower for the rest of your days. Thank Him for His grace, and pledge yourself to begin your new life today by seeking to grow as a new believer. I encourage you to do this right now. The Bible says in 2 Corinthians 6:2, *"Behold, now is the acceptable time; behold, now is the day of salvation."*

What's next? While going to church doesn't save you, it sure helps you grow as a Christian. You will build relationships with other Christians who are seeking to grow in Christ and serve God with their lives. You will be encouraged in your faith and will grow in your understanding of the Bible, God's Word. I encourage you to find a Bible-believing church to attend where the Bible is taught and good Christian friendships can be enjoyed.

Is there someone who would like to hear of your decision to become a Christian? Why not call them right now and let them know of your new faith? Do you have Christian friends whom you admire? Why not call them right now and ask if you can go to church with them on Sunday? If you do not have Christian friends with whom you can share your decision, simply tell someone close to you. If you already attend a Bible-believing, Bible-teaching church, give your pastor a call, and let him know of your decision to trust Christ as your Savior.

Welcome to the Family of God!

Special thanks to Heather Bible Chapel (http://heatherbiblechapel.org) for assistance with "The Bridge" graphics.

More Books from GreenTree Publishers

Immovable: Standing Firm in the Last Days
By Dr. Tim Riordan

Does Bible prophecy indicate that we are living in the last days? What should Christians do to be ready for the days ahead? Dr. Tim Riordan shares biblical truths on Bible prophecy and how the church can stand firm in the last days. This book also offers a small group discussion guide. Release updates will be posted on Dr. Tim Riordan's website at www.timriordan.me. *Immovable: Standing Firm in the Last Days* is available from Amazon and other retail outlets in both paperback and digital formats.

The Published Pastor – Book 1
Expanding Your Ministry Through Writing and Publishing
By Dr. Tim Riordan

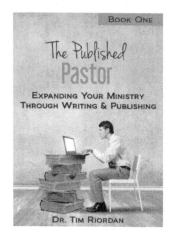

Have you ever considered writing or publishing a book? If you are a pastor, would you like to expand your ministry by turning your next sermon series into a book your congregation can pass on to others? The Published Pastor series is a collection of books that will encourage you to write and offer you the step-by-step help you may need to become a published author. This first book in the series will challenge you and help you to see that you can become a writer. Dr. Tim Riordan uses his experience in writing and publishing books to show you practical guidelines in taking your sermons from the pulpit to the publisher. Dr. Riordan has been a pastor for over 35 years and is the author of eight books. Dr. Riordan can be your mentor in helping you to accomplish your goal of writing and publishing your next book.

The Published Pastor – Book 2
How to Write and Publish Books
By Dr. Tim Riordan

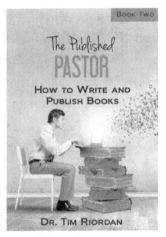

Are you ready to become a published author? Have you ever wondered how to publish a book? Would you like to learn how to write a book so your ministry can be expanded? *How to Write and Publish Books* is the second book in *The Published Pastor* series. It is offered to help pastors, Bible teachers, or anyone else who gathers material on a regular basis to turn their lessons or sermons into a published book. Join Dr. Tim Riordan as he shares from his experience and research on how to become a published author. He compares the differences between traditional publishing and self-publishing, and he offers a step-by-step approach to self-publishing your book.

The Long Way Home
By Judah Knight

Dive into an adventure of scuba diving, treasure hunting, danger and suspense in Judah Knight's exciting novel, The Long Way Home. When Meg was stranded in the Bahamas, her life was dramatically changed through an encounter with an old friend that turned into adventure, danger, discovery, and love. Enjoy Judah Knight's flinch-free fiction that is safe for the whole family. Available in paperback and e-book formats from Amazon.

Consider other books in the Davenport Series

VICTORIA TEAGUE

Reaching for Life
By Victoria Teague with Connie J. Singleton

Following an eleven-year cocaine addiction and a dangerous career as a dancer in Atlanta's sex industry, Victoria Teague experienced what can only be called a miraculous rescue. For ten years after she left the clubs, she sat respectably in the pews of her church with a grateful heart and a zip-locked mouth. She built an entirely new life on top of embarrassing secrets from her past, and only a precious, trusted few knew her spiritual rags-to-riches story. That is until one ordinary day when she was asked to do anything *but* the ordinary. On that day, she was called not only to share her secrets, but also to spotlight them. To use them as her "street cred" to minister to other women in the strip clubs who desperately need a lifeline like the one she was offered. To seek the lost and give them hope for a better life. Available in paperback and e-book formats from your favorite retailer.

Made in the USA
Coppell, TX
18 May 2020

25716586R00157